ZHIYE YUANXIAO DAOYOU FUWU SAIXIANG
HEXIN JINENG ZHINAN

职业院校导游服务赛项核心技能指南

主　编 ◎ 蒋庆荣
副主编 ◎ 刘夕宁　刘明

ZHIYE YUANXIAO DAOYOU FUWU SAIXIANG
HEXIN JINENG ZHINAN

华中科技大学出版社
http://press.hust.edu.cn
中国·武汉

内容简介

"职业教育看大赛",职业院校技能大赛是检验职业院校办学水平及人才培养质量的重要依据。导游服务赛项自开设以来,围绕导游服务技能和讲解核心能力,其知识技能要点集中体现在导游知识水平、导游词创作、讲解服务、才艺运用、英文导游等几个方面。本书针对以上几个导游服务核心技能点,选出近年来导游考证知识和技能大赛中具有代表性的题目,编制应考、应赛参考资料。通过以上技能训练,可以帮助学习者提高讲解能力、导游证书通过能力、导游工作持续学习能力。

图书在版编目(CIP)数据

职业院校导游服务赛项核心技能指南/蒋庆荣主编. -- 武汉:华中科技大学出版社,2025.1.
ISBN 978-7-5772-1495-5

Ⅰ. F590.63-62

中国国家版本馆CIP数据核字第2024R4Z334号

职业院校导游服务赛项核心技能指南
Zhiye Yuanxiao Daoyou Fuwu Saixiang Hexin Jineng Zhinan

蒋庆荣　主编

策划编辑:李家乐	
责任编辑:鲁梦璇	
封面设计:廖亚萍	
责任校对:刘　竣	
责任监印:周治超	
出版发行:华中科技大学出版社(中国·武汉)	电话:(027)81321913
武汉市东湖新技术开发区华工科技园	邮编:430223
录　　排:孙雅丽	
印　　刷:武汉市洪林印务有限公司	
开　　本:787mm×1092mm　1/16	
印　　张:18.75	
字　　数:403千字	
版　　次:2025年1月第1版第1次印刷	
定　　价:79.90元	

本书若有印装质量问题,请向出版社营销中心调换
全国免费服务热线:400-6679-118　竭诚为您服务
版权所有　侵权必究

PRCFACE 序

让每一位选手都能发挥最佳的水平

2013年6月初,首届全国职业院校技能大赛(高职组)导游服务赛项在浙江旅游职业学院隆重举行,全国近80所院校的137名选手参加了中英文两个组别的赛事,自此开启了导游服务赛项的历程。十二年来,大赛多次在浙江旅游职业学院、漳州职业技术学院、南京旅游职业学院、西宁城市职业技术学院和上海旅游高等专科学校举办,数百所院校的师生们参加了比赛。赛场上,师生们有欢笑、有泪水;有收获、有教训;有艰苦、有锤炼。通过大赛,我们培养了一批批的行业新秀,大赛促进了教育教学改革,大赛带来了业界与教育的交会碰撞,大赛也让社会各界更多地了解旅游业。可以说,导游服务赛项不仅仅只是一项赛事,更是检验旅游类专业办学质量的一面镜子,是学生走上职业生涯前的一次考试,是促进旅游职业教育"三教"改革的一种动力,其意义深远。

但是,我们不难发现,历届大赛获奖的院校和选手都相对集中在少数院校,一等奖获得者主要来自专门的旅游院校,这是由于各地办学的历史情况和现状不同,生源数量和质量也存在差异,指导教师的能力不同,同时一些院校备赛仓促、师资不足、资料不全、经验欠缺。换言之,参赛院校的起跑线不一样。作为在旅游职业教育战线耕耘了近30年的　名教育工作者,多么希望优秀选手都能够发挥出应有的水平,而不受其他因素的影响。

值得庆幸的是,华中科技大学出版社及时出版了《职业院校导游服务赛项核心技能指南》(简称《指南》),本书由珠海城市职业技术学院蒋庆荣教授主编。《指南》以2023年导游服务大赛内容为基础,结合珠海城市职业技术学院旅游管理学院备赛导游服务赛项的实践与探索,梳理了知识和技能的基本要求,邀请有关专家分别就导游词写作、导游口语运用、才艺表现等专题撰写了文章。

自设置导游服务赛项以来,各省、市、自治区都举办了省级的导游服务大赛，一些职业院校为了选拔参赛选手，还举办了校级的赛事，因此，每年参加各级导游服务赛事的学生数以千计。《指南》可以使师生了解大赛的基本情况，可以有效地指导师生准备赛事，可以全面地帮助不同地区、不同类型院校提升参赛的水平。

导游服务赛项已经走过了10余年，取得了巨大的成就，但是仍然需要不断改进、完善、提高，大赛如何真实反映旅游职业教育的水平，如何平等均衡地选拔选手，如何有效可信地测试选手……这些都需要进一步研究、探索与实践。

导游服务赛项仍在发展路上，我们要围绕"以赛促学、以赛促教、以赛促改、以赛促建"原则，坚持育训结合、德技并修，深化产教融合、课赛融通，着力推进三教改革，进一步促进旅游教育与旅游业的教育链、人才链、产业链、创新链有机衔接，形成旅游教育和旅游行业统筹融合、良性互动的发展格局，创新旅游人才培养模式，提高旅游人才培养质量，共同推进旅游经济强国建设。

2024年4月于杭州

CONTENTS 目 录

第一部分 赛项准备 /1
导游服务赛项的探索与实践 /2
导游词撰写及导游讲解的基本方法 /5
如何有效准备导游英语口语测试 /8
才艺运用环节的设计原则与注意事项 /11

第二部分 导游知识测试 /15
时政及文化旅游热点题库 /16
导游基础知识题库 /30
旅游法规题库 /62
导游业务题库 /95

第三部分 自选导游词创作 /137
司城旧址雄荆南　唐崖胜景遗沉浮 /138
阿者科 /139
上海四行仓库抗战纪念馆 /141

第四部分 现场导游词创作 /143
2023年全国职业院校技能竞赛导游服务赛项题库 /144

第五部分 英语口语测试 /209

第一部分 赛项准备

导游服务赛项的探索与实践

珠海城市职业技术学院是珠海市唯一一所市属公办高校，是广东省示范性高职院校、省内高水平高职院校。旅游管理学院建立于2011年，根据中国科教评价网（金平果排名）公布的高职专业历年评价数据，旅游管理专业连续四年被评为"五星级"专业，2022年专业排名全国第九，2023年全国排名第十一。

自2021年起，旅游管理专业连续三年获得职业院校导游服务赛项一等奖、二等奖、三等奖，获得广东省职业院校技能大赛导游服务赛项一等奖共8项（含2024年省赛）。培养全国优秀指导教师1人、导游服务赛项指导教师3人、省赛一等奖指导教师8人。作为一所地方性综合类职业院校，能够在一个专业赛项上连续四年获得较好成绩，通过竞赛全面激发教师学生的积极性，充分体现"职业教育看竞赛"的指导思想，现将实践和体会分享如下。

一、通畅竞赛选手校内选拔机制

导游服务赛项竞争激烈，以广东省为例，每年约有50所院校100余名选手参加导游服务赛项，比赛成绩在前10%的选手可以获得一等奖，前两名获奖选手才有机会代表广东省参加全国职业院校技能大赛，可谓是百里挑一。同时，因为导游的职业技能要求及竞赛规程的要求，该赛项对参赛选手的综合素质要求较高，选手想要走上导游服务赛项的舞台，其知识储备量、记忆力、外形条件、普通话水平、讲解技巧、英语水平、才艺基础、意志品质等方面必须均衡发展，可谓处处优秀。目前，学院旅游管理专业每届计划招生120人，符合报名条件的旅游大类专业学生每届计划招生320人，学生接受调剂而来的情况较多，专业基础其实并不理想。在此情况下，学院加大力度建设选手选拔机制，从新生入学教育入手，建立"四轮制"校内选拔制度。

"四轮制"即"自愿报名—校内初赛—重点选拔—省赛筛选"四个校内选拔环节，将学生自愿报名与授课教师推荐相结合，通过校内初赛选拔出4—6人，组成重点培养小组，让专家及教师对他们进行指导，最终选出2名学生参加省赛。未参加本年度省赛的选手，视情况培养其参加其他导游技能竞赛，也可以作为下一年种子选手进行培养。通过这种方式，"选手储备池"越蓄越满，解决了如何对优秀选手进行持续培养的难题。

二、探索专兼职教师团队分工协作专项指导模式

在竞赛指导教师队伍的培养及建设过程中,注重"全员参与、分工协作"的选手培养方式。根据本专业现有专任教师的不同特点,团队协同、按照周历值班,分别负责导游基础知识、导游词创作、导游词编写、英语对话等相关课程指导,同时聘请兼职老师,如邀请学校普通话测试站的老师辅导选手普通话,邀请学校外教辅导选手英语口音,邀请学校舞蹈老师辅导舞蹈等,推进选手全面发展。

三、创设多元实践场景训练

学院结合不同学生特点,进行个别内容设计,比如安排选手到本地景区进行实地讲解,组织开展"大手牵小手"活动,让选手为小学生组织授课,多方面、多途径锻炼选手能力。并且每周定期安排选手汇报学习情况,构建学院领导老师协同育人环境,让选手拥有极大的学习动力和成就感,通过参加各项实际讲解活动积累丰富的舞台经验。

四、注重细节全面助力选手成长

学院及指导老师针对每个选手的不同特点,从生活习惯、学习进度、餐食搭配,到身体状况、精神压力、气候变化等诸多方面,像父母对待孩子一样细致照顾和全面安排,尤其是在每年春节假期期间,食堂宿舍不方便,选手得到指导老师更加细致入微的关怀,衣服老师带回家洗,餐食老师一同购买,为选手能够坚持完成比赛的准备内容创造一切条件,同时,师生形成共同面对困难的强大勇气。

五、构建教师学生成长共同体

旅游管理学院建院以来就特别重视人文关怀,以"服务学习"理念开展学院建设,着力构建"SMILE"师生共同成长体,以"让师生笑得更灿烂"为目的,分别从服务精神(Service)、管理能力(Management)、创新思维(Innovation)、专注学习(Learning)、注重体验(Experience)五个维度引导学生德智体美劳全面发展。学院全体师生努力构建共同成长环境,教师带头参加本市的导游服务职业组赛项,连续获得本市第一名,2024年本市的导游服务比赛师生同台竞技,包揽了前三名,并荣获"市技能能手"。

总的来说,导游服务赛项内容多、技能全、重综合,赛项设计特色突出。近三年,旅游管理学院在办省赛、参加导游服务赛项的过程中,存在专业建设基础薄弱、专业学生基数较少、专业教师转型人数较多、文科专业投入有限等问题。在此背景下,旅

游管理学院积极探索和实践，总结了参加导游服务技能竞赛的相关经验，并对存在的问题进行思考，期盼给同类专业一定的借鉴意义，这是本书出版的重要目的，希望能够借此机会，抛砖引玉，与各类旅游类专业同仁共同探索以技能竞赛推动"岗课赛证训"融通发展的专业建设之路。

珠海城市职业技术学院旅游管理学院党总支书记、教授

2024年5月

导游词撰写及导游讲解的基本方法

在全国职业院校技能大赛评分标准中,导游词现场创作讲解占比35%,自选导游词讲解占比35%,两项加在一起总占比为70%,是能否获奖的关键因素。结合笔者30余年的导游工作经验,以及多年担任大赛评委的经验,针对导游词创作及讲解这两个赛项提出一些建议,供大家参考。

一、导游词创作及讲解

根据历年导游服务赛项规程,导游词创作及讲解环节一般有50个旅游文化元素、5个团型,详细内容于赛前一个月公布,供参赛选手赛前准备。在比赛中,选手现场抽选出一个旅游文化元素和一个团型,准备时长为30分钟,独立完成现场导游词创作(准备期间不允许查阅纸质资料,也不能借助电脑、手机等电子产品),要求在3分钟内用中文进行脱稿讲解。

根据竞赛规程中公布的"评分标准与分值段","导游词创作"满分20分,"导游词讲解"满分15分,不足2分30秒的扣2分。在导游词创作的评分标准中,首先要契合主题与团型(4分),同时注重选材合理、尊重史实和现实(2分),内容正确、科学、完整(2分),用词恰当、富有文采(2分),结构合理、详略得当(2分),具有文化内涵(3分),具有创新性(3分),具有时代特色(2分)。在导游词讲解中,仪态自然、富有亲和力(2分),语言(普通话)规范流畅(2分),讲解完整、清楚(2分),口齿清晰、流利(2分),肢体语言生动形象,符合导游规范(1分),讲解节奏控制合理、有层次感(2分),讲解生动有趣、富有感染力和渗透力(2分),导游讲解方法和技巧运用恰当(2分)。根据评分标准,大家可以看到,"导游词创作"占了20分,比讲解的分值更大。这就要求参赛选手和指导老师在赛前就要对导游词创作进行充分的准备。

首先,必须全面掌握所有的旅游文化元素,在赛前准备的一个月里,充分查阅资料,打好腹稿,甚至可以提前把50篇导游词全部写出来进行练习,因为现场30分钟的准备时间是不够学生临场创作一篇全新的导游词的。准备充分才能言之有物,对某一个元素掌握得不全面,比赛中就有可能会出现为了凑够时间而用注意事项、套话等"兜圈子"的情况,致使内容言之无物,大赛的评委和专家通常都具有很高的专业素养,这种行为无法被认可。

其次,必须跟团型紧密结合。在评分标准中,"契合主题与团型"占了4分。在历届大赛中,无论选手讲得如何出彩,只要导游词没有跟团型紧密结合,最好的成绩是进入第二梯队获二等奖。突出团型不是简单地把一篇导游词更改一下称呼。例如在一次大赛中,有一位选手抽到一个亲子团,在讲解过程中,他大约用了23个"大朋友们、小朋友们"的称呼,这种通过简单的称呼来突出团型的讲解很难在大赛中有亮眼的表现。

再次,注重时间的把控。比赛现场,工作人员会在导游词讲解到2分30秒时,对选手进行提醒,不足2分30秒的扣2分,3分钟到工作人员叫停,那么就会扣掉内容不完整的分数。2分在导游服务赛项赛场上非常宝贵,可以说,一旦出现时长不足或者超时的情况,一定会与优秀成绩失之交臂。因此,在导游词创作的过程中要注意字数和讲解时长,结尾处要有一些在带团过程中可以灵活运用的话语,一旦出现时长问题,选手在赛场上可以灵活处理。

最后,要保证讲解的清晰和流畅,一旦出现卡壳或者忘词的情况,便会与一等奖失之交臂。

简而言之,50个旅游文化元素加上5个团型,准备工作强度较大,但是付出都会有回报。

二、自选景点导游讲解

根据导游服务赛项规程,自选景点导游讲解由选手在赛前以某一旅游目的地(选材可为城市、乡村、景区、景点等)为讲解主题,准备一段4分钟的导游词和相应的PPT文档,用中文进行讲解。讲解到3分30秒时,工作人员会对选手进行提醒,不足3分30秒扣2分,4分钟到工作人员叫停。按照评分标准,导游职业仪态2分,主要考察选手的礼仪着装是否得体,是否符合职业情境或讲解主题;导游词组织及特色10分,其中包括:内容正确,结构合理、尊重史实和现实(3分),整体布局合理、严谨(3分),紧扣主题,特色鲜明,感染力强(3分),语言文字优美,富有文采(1分);导游讲解风范23分,其中包括:讲解语言流畅、规范,口齿清晰(1分),仪态自然,肢体语言恰当,符合导游规范(1分),讲解角度新颖(4分),主题特色鲜明(2分),讲解重点突出,层次清晰(2分),文化底蕴深厚,内涵丰富(3分),讲解节奏合理,节律感强(2分),语言组织运用艺术和能力较强(2分),导游讲解方法、技巧运用恰当(3分),富有感染力、亲和力、渗透力(3分)。可以说,这部分对选手的综合素质要求还是比较高的。

导游词撰写方面,一定要注意主题鲜明,角度新颖,文化底蕴深厚,内涵丰富。经过多年大赛,热门景点已经被选手们讲得差不多了,如果还是陈词滥调,讲的都是大家耳熟能详的内容,其实很难吸引评委和观众。以文促旅,以旅彰文,通过景区景点的介绍,讲好中国故事,传播中国文化,这才是当代导游的使命。作为高职院校的在校学生,导游词中是否能够体现当代大学生的使命担当,也是非常重要的一点。需要注意的是,使命担当不是喊口号,传播中国文化也不是简单地把新闻联播上的语句照搬,内涵需要挖掘,一定要有真情实感,首先要感动自己,然后才能感动观众和评委。

我在参加历届大赛中经常发现一个现象,有些导游词写得很有水准,但是选手却没能完全理解，没有真情实感，难以驾驭，所以给出如下指导：

第一，建议我们的指导老师，在撰写导游词的过程中要让学生自己参与其中，同时要像导演一样，善于给我们的选手"说戏"，让他们深度理解作品。

第二，注重与导游情境的结合。我们的大赛是导游服务赛项，而并非演讲大赛。导游和讲解员的方式是完全不同的两种表现形式。在比赛过程中，常常看到有许多选手的讲解虽然语言功底很深，但是缺乏现场讲解感，一开口就是播音腔，讲解得不自然，没有现场感。同时存在很多选手过度抒情的现象，情感过于充沛，这种情况只要对讲解风格进行微调，成绩就会截然不同。

第三，可以创新讲解形式。比如将贯口等其他才艺融入其中就是一个方向和很好的尝试。就像跳水比赛，难度系数3.0和2.0，最终的结果截然不同。平时带团是加法，大赛却是减法，大赛要求选手将所有的瑕疵掩盖起来，把自己的优点放大到极致。

第四，加强选手的现场应变能力。赛场就像战场，情况千变万化，在平时的训练中就应当注重训练选手的临场应变能力，不论出现任何情况，选手的反应都应该是符合导游的职业规范、职业礼仪与职业道德的，不论最终结果如何，选手都应当全力拼搏，这也是我们举办大赛的初衷，以赛促练，为导游行业选拔和输送优质人才。

最后，向每一位用心准备竞赛的选手和老师致敬。比赛成绩不是最终的目的，提高导游服务技能，诉说心中的热爱，用无数导游行业从业人员微薄的力量引领这个行业更好地发展，这才是我们每一个文旅人的使命！

青岛中之旅国际旅行社有限公司总经理、特级导游

2024年5月

如何有效准备导游英语口语测试

2023年导游证考试较往年呈现出新的特点，一些地区报考人数创新高，外语考生人数明显增多。其实，目前外语导游相对缺口还是比较大的，选择外语语种的考生占比增大，这表明我国导游国际化特征愈加鲜明，彰显外语导游的重要价值。

导游英语口语测试是导游服务赛项的重要模块之一。在导游服务赛项规程中，明确了该模块的测试方式为现场对话。测试内容主要为导游带团过程中的英语情境对话，涉及导游实际业务的诸多方面，着重考查参赛选手运用英语对游客进行导游服务的能力。按照惯例，该模块会在比赛前公开题库（80题），选手现场随机抽取一个题目，准备30秒后开始与裁判进行4分钟的情境对话。

从以往的比赛情况来看，在导游英语口语测试环节，选手们之间还是存在一定差距的，对于口语好又熟悉导游业务的选手来说，这是一次很好的拉分机会。下面笔者就对标备赛、赛教融合以及如何"讲好中国故事"等方面结合过往比赛选手的表现谈几点看法。

一、精研评分标准，设计话题情节

从高职学生外语学习现状来看，学生的英语基础与应用能力参差不齐。有的学生英语基础较好、词汇量丰富，善于口语表达；也有学生英语基础欠佳、词汇量积累不足，很难完成基本的口语对话。大赛官方每年发布的导游英语口语测试模块评分标准是裁判员打分的主要依据。其满分为10分，具体标准如下：

(1) 发音清晰，语调自然（2分）；
(2) 语句通顺，无明显语法错误，句意与语意完整（2分）；
(3) 交流顺畅，应对自如（1.5分）；
(4) 内容充实，能运用专业术语、词汇解决相关问题（3分）；
(5) 仪态大方，自然得体，肢体语言表达到位、符合职业设定（1.5分）。

上面的评分标准既是裁判员的打分依据，也是指导教师指导工作的重点方向。题库的80个情景对话，有的题目侧重于介绍内容，有的题目侧重于解决问题。通常来说，无论是从教学的角度还是从备赛的角度，交通、住宿、景点、美食、购物、应急等主题都是导游英语的基本话题，指导教师与选手应提前围绕这些主题，整理高频词汇、实用句型、习惯用法等，设计话题情节，并拓展其内容，有针对性地消除导游英语的疑难点，避免无话可说的尴尬。导游英语口语测试这一环节，注重考查选手运用英语服务游客的能力，题目设置的内容也是导游业务实操中经常遇到的场景再现。在备赛阶段，指导教师要善于结合话题巧妙地设计话题情节，通过师生之间、同学之间的模拟实战演练提高应变能力。

题库中有处理游客食物中毒的题目,旨在考查现实业务中导游的危机处理能力。这些题目要求选手遵循"以客为本,服务至诚"的服务理念来处理突发事件,对于参赛者来说,这不仅是一次展现其应变能力的机会,也是对其基本功和灵活应变能力的严峻考验。巧妙地设计话题情节包括:设计吸引人的开场白、丰富的内容以及合理的结束语等方面,且都需要与如何处理好危机相互结合,做到有始有终、表达完整。该题目属于危机情况处理,对选手提出了更高的要求,选手若能运用好专业术语和词汇合理处置危机,并且善于运用肢体语言在特定情景下进行交流,在评分标准中的(4)(5)两项将更容易获得裁判员的认可。

二、结合教学实践,着力学以致用

从以往的比赛来看,"全面、实用、简单"的口语表达是非常容易获得高分的,也正是"学以致用"的精髓所在。所谓"全面",就是要紧密围绕每个题目后面所列的业务或者介绍要点展开表达,不能有所缺失;所谓"实用",就是要力求围绕业务实际,要点清晰、重点突出,很自然地与裁判员形成良性互动;所谓"简单",就是要注重口语表达、句式简洁,避免使用过于花哨的长难句,这反而容易暴露自己的语法错误、基础薄弱等问题。

题库中有的题目主要涉及导游与前台沟通 Wi-Fi 使用方面的业务。该题目属于导游业务中十分常见的场景,旨在考查导游应用英语进行沟通与协调能力。从以往的选手表现来看,有的选手发音较为清晰,语调相对自然,开场阶段能够运用专业词汇进行沟通交流,且仪表仪态较好,肢体语言表达也相对到位。但是随着沟通的深入,涉及如何办理 Wi-Fi 业务、如何使用 Wi-Fi 等流程,选手理解则存在偏差,交流沟通开始出现不畅,表明在教学实践环节中,这部分学生很少真正处理过完整的业务流程,"学以致用"能力偏弱,对于导游实际业务理解可能是碎片化的,"只见树木,不见森林"。

三、讲好中国故事,展示文化精髓

中国独特的历史文化、风土人情吸引着外国友人的眼球。随着旅游业的快速复苏,入境游客的比例也呈现出上升的势头,越来越多的外国游客愿意来到中国旅游,体验东方文化的魅力。题库的80个情景对话,涉及机场迎接、欢迎词、酒店业务、景点介绍等导游业务场景,其实也是"讲好中国故事"的经典素材,通过挖掘情景对话中的中国元素,呈现我们中国文化的道德品质、传统文化,展现外语导游的职业素养,用精练的口语把所涉及的景区景点、历史文化、民间艺术充分表达出来,让更多外国人感受中国文化的博大精深。

题库中有的题目就是在去"锦绣中华"沿途进行相关介绍与讲解。沿途讲解是导游实际业务中的最常见工作场景,也是最能体现导游英语服务游客能力的展示舞台。这一题目主要考查选手的讲解能力以及与游客的沟通互动能力。该题目特点是以选手讲解为主,在讲解过程中,选手要善于运用相关的专业术语、词汇进行介绍,语速适当,语言应用仪态大方,自然得体。与此同时,选手应当积极掌握表达的主动权,善于引导话题的走向,在自己的预设场景中,选择熟悉的表达方式,努力挖掘导游业务知识与技能中所蕴含的思政元素,践行文化自信。

其实,前文所谈及的三个方面也有笔者想表达的内在逻辑。"精研评分标准,设计话题情节"强调如何对标和备赛;"结合教学实践,着力学以致用"强调活学活用,也是以赛促教的本质;"讲好中国故事,展示文化精髓"是我们课程思政的重要方面。作为老师,不但要"教书",更要"育人",育人的根本在于立德。《左传》中讲到"太上有立德,其次有立功,其次有立言",立德是教育的最高境界。我想,这也正是导游服务赛项设立导游英语口语测试模块的初衷。在这里,我有个建议,口语比较好且熟悉导游业务的同学可以尝试参加外语导游考试,通过备考拉动应赛,一举两得。

借本书出版之际,祝愿更多的参赛选手能够借助大赛的舞台尽情展示自我,放飞青春梦想,收获成长的喜悦。

大连外国语大学 教授、硕士生导师
2024 年 5 月

才艺运用环节的设计原则与注意事项

才艺运用环节在整个导游服务赛项中所占权重为10%,参赛选手需要"在4分钟30秒内完成带团过程中的导游情境描述及符合情境的才艺展示,才艺须符合导游职业特点,道具应便于随身携带。选手用中文对导游情境进行设计描述,描述时不可以有背景音乐与视频;才艺展示不少于2分钟30秒"。受本书编写组的委托,结合最近几年本人在导游服务赛项中的一点体会,下面谈一谈我对才艺运用环节的几点想法,仅代表一家之言,供大家参考指导。

一、解读文件,对标细则

建议指导老师和比赛选手一定要吃透比赛规则,反复研究大赛的一系列文件,特别是关于各环节的评分标准,做到每条必看,每字必读。不要"想当然",更不要"我认为"。首先吃透比赛的要求,其次按照评分标准创新、设计才艺运用环节,最后才是有步骤地让选手准备。在以往的比赛中可以看到,有些选手在时间的把控上明显不足,有的结尾太过仓促,有的情景设计薄弱,有的严重脱离导游工作实际,甚至有的与比赛精神相悖,这都是因为没有研读评分细则所导致的。

二、高度重视,注重细节

在以往的比赛中,有些选手才艺的确是精心准备,但在情景设计上显得很随性,甚至不重视。这显然把比赛的重心放在了才艺的表演上。其实我们的评分标准描述得很清楚,第一项就是"情境设置要符合导游工作实际,描述生动完整,与才艺展示结合紧密",分值还不少。同时,设定了专门的时间,请选手表述,足见"导游情景描述"的重要性,但一些选手表现平平。

建议选手和指导老师要高度重视"导游情景描述",做到"三适",即适时、适地、适人。巧妙将才艺表演与带团情景进行巧妙融合。选手在哪里带团,哪个景区带团,为什么要展示这个才艺,要突出怎样的主题,都应该在短短的1分30秒左右的时间里描述,要做到精心设计、巧妙编排、完美融合。

三、巧妙设计,服务导游

我们的比赛环节为"才艺运用环节",顾名思义,就是如何在带团中,将才艺与导游工作巧妙结合。不要为了才艺而才艺,为了表演而表演。单纯的才艺表演,脱离导游实际的才艺表演,即使再专业、再精彩,也未必能取得高分,因为我们的比赛不是"才艺表演"。

才艺运用环节的评分标准有如下说明:"妆容适宜,衣着得体,道具契合主题并适合导游具体工作场景要求。"故选手在选择才艺形式时,要注意两个服务:一要服务于旅游工作,二要服务于导游实际。我们鼓励广大导游,通过才艺的运用,让游客感知到旅游的美妙。所以,从导游大赛的角度来讲,才艺不是越专业越好,而是越能服务于导游工作越好。希望选手今后在才艺的选题、设计、表演上,要紧密结合旅游工作和导游工作的实际。

四、创设情境,首尾呼应

有些选手在结尾环节,戛然而止,略显尴尬。

在大赛的才艺运用环节,我们认为完整的表现应该分为三段:一是紧密联系实际的情景描述,二是贴近导游工作的才艺运用,三是主题升华的精彩结尾。当然结尾的处理有多种方式,比如与游客互动、与主题结合、与带团贴近,都是可以的,我们常说"凤头、猪肚、豹尾",应该有"画龙点睛"般的精彩结尾。

建议选手要注意比赛的完成性,要做到首尾呼应,不要虎头蛇尾。在结尾处,哪怕是几句话,也要精心设计一下,要时刻提醒自己,"我不仅是在比赛,而是在为游客表演才艺,是在用才艺讲述文旅故事"。

同时,建议大家要注意"串联词"的使用,无论是由情景描述到才艺表演的过渡,还是才艺表演到结尾的过渡,不要太生硬,要有起承转合,这样游客才会有强烈的代入感,才不会"出戏"。

五、精练节目、突出主题

展现选手的多才多艺是好事。在有限的时间内,一些选手想进行多元素、多节目、多主题的表达。

才艺是为导游工作服务的,在很短的时间内,我们能表述清楚一个主题、一个元素就很不错了,表达的元素越多,越有可能表达不清楚。"混搭风"搭配不好,就会是"四不像"。才艺运用应该恰到好处,不是弄巧成拙、画蛇添足。

还有一些选手没有主题,或者文不对题。才艺表演结束后,就是单纯的表演,想表达什么?想描述什么?不是很清楚。还有一些选手,情境设计描述的主题很好,但是在与才艺展示的主题"结合紧密"上有些牵强。

建议选手在才艺选择方面要扬长避短。选择的越多,想表现的越多,反而会让自己的缺点暴露得更多。我们不是专业的演员,才艺运用是为导游工作锦上添花的,并不是才艺越多越杂,会更显多才。大家可以按"宜新不宜多,宜精不宜杂"的原则选择才艺,突出主题,与时俱进,弘扬正能量。

六、开拓创新,加强互动

我们不是在舞台上表演才艺,而是在景区内展现魅力。评分标准中有这样一项描述,"表演自然流畅,感染力强,气氛好,符合旅游者审美标准",越是自然,越会有好的表现。

面对比赛,不要仅仅想着这里是赛场,要想象成在带团的路上。建议选手可以适当地加强一些互动。比如增加眼神上的互动,而不是自顾自地表演;比如语言上的互动,让游客融入你的表演中;比如表述上的互动,让游客感知到你表达的要素。此时此刻,你就是导游。

希望所有参赛选手,能够不忘初心,一直用得体的语言,讲述中国独一无二的气韵。比赛只是为了促进导游行业的教学和发展,赛场只是广大选手导游生涯的起点,我们希望在不久的将来,能在景区与你相逢,能在带团的路上与你相遇。

河北省旅游协会副会长、导游分会会长

2024年5月

第二部分　导游知识测试

　　本部分题目为2023年全国中等职业学校技能大赛导游服务赛项组委会公布的《导游知识测试题库》，资料源于全国职业院校技能大赛官网，参考答案为本书作者编写。

时政及文化旅游热点题库

一、判断题(正确请选 A,错误请选 B)

1.2022 世界旅游合作与发展大会于 9 月 1 日在北京国家会议中心召开。大会设置沙发论坛环节,围绕"携手推动世界旅游创新发展"这一议题进行了深入探讨。( )

参考答案:A

2.中国旅游日是每年的 9 月 27 日。( )

参考答案:B

3.2022 年 3 月 12 日,2022 河南智慧旅游大会开幕。此次大会,打造了国内首个规模最大、场景最丰富、持续时间最长的文旅元宇宙大会线上会议空间。( )

参考答案:A

4.2023 年 3 月,中国大寨村和荆竹村获颁联合国世界旅游组织"最佳旅游乡村"。( )

参考答案:A

5.2023 年,中西文化和旅游年开幕式在西班牙马德里举行。( )

参考答案:A

6.推进中小学生研学旅行应当坚持教育性、实践性、安全性和经济性四大原则。( )

参考答案:B

7.第 24 届冬季奥林匹克运动会,是由中国举办的国际性奥林匹克赛事,于 2022 年 2 月 4 日开幕,北京冬奥会、冬残奥会发布主题口号——"一起向未来"。( )

参考答案:A

8.2021 年 10 月,亚洲文化遗产保护对话会在北京召开,主题为"增进文明对话、共塑亚洲未来"。( )

参考答案:A

9.公元 1613 年 5 月 19 日徐霞客撰写《游天台山记》,成为《徐霞客游记》开篇之日。( )

参考答案:A

10.党的十八大以来,习近平总书记在不同场合反复强调,要牢固树立绿水青山就是金山银山的理念。( )

参考答案:A

11.文化和旅游部组织的2021年"订单式"人才援藏专家团队抵达拉萨开展工作,标志着2021年"订单式"文化和旅游人才援藏项目启动。(　　)

参考答案:A

12.电子导游证是导游执业证明,以电子数据形式保存于移动终端设备中。(　　)

参考答案:A

13.2022年5月19日是第12个中国旅游日,主题为:感悟中华文化,享受美好旅程。(　　)

参考答案:A

14.依据《国家旅游局关于旅游不文明行为记录管理暂行办法》,发生在境外的旅游不文明行为,可由事件发生地旅游主管部门通过外交机构、旅游驻外办事机构等途径进行调查核实。(　　)

参考答案:B

15.2021年5月21日晚,国家主席习近平应邀在北京以视频方式出席全球健康峰会,并发表题为《携手共建人类卫生健康共同体》的重要讲话。(　　)

参考答案:A

16.导游服务星级通过全国旅游监管服务信息系统自动生成,并根据导游执业情况每半年更新一次。(　　)

参考答案:B

17.外交部全球领事保护与服务应急呼叫中心热线电话是12308。(　　)

参考答案:A

18.2022年6月11日是我国第17个"文化和自然遗产日",主场城市活动在甘肃兰州举行,活动主题为"文物保护:时代共进 人民共享"。(　　)

参考答案:A

19.党的二十大报告中提出,坚持以文塑旅,以旅彰文,推进文化和旅游深度融合发展。(　　)

参考答案:A

20.2021年是西藏和平解放65周年,中共中央总书记、国家主席、中央军委主席习近平前往西藏,看望慰问西藏各族干部群众,给各族干部群众送去党中央的关怀。(　　)

参考答案:B

21.2022年"5•18国际博物馆日"活动聚焦的主题为"博物馆的未来:恢复与创新"。(　　)

参考答案:B

22.我国领队管理由资格准入制改为备案管理制,旅游主管部门不再对领队从

业进行行政审批。(　　)

参考答案：A

23.2022年11月29日,"中国传统制茶技艺及其相关习俗"在摩洛哥召开的联合国教科文组织保护非物质文化遗产政府间委员会上通过评审,列入联合国教科文组织人类非物质文化遗产代表作名录。(　　)

参考答案：A

24.《关于加强草原保护修复的若干意见》提出,推动草原地区绿色发展,充分发挥草原生态和文化功能,打造一批草原旅游景区、度假地和精品旅游线路,推动草原旅游和生态康养产业发展,引导支持草原地区低收入人口通过参与草原保护修复增加收入。(　　)

参考答案：A

25.2022年9月13日,第二届二十国文化部长会议召开。会议围绕"文化促进可持续生活"开展交流讨论。(　　)

参考答案：B

26.2022年11月20日,以"重构与振兴"为主题的2022中国旅游高峰论坛在张家界举行。(　　)

参考答案：A

27.根据中国海关总署规定,中国旅客进境携带在海外获取的个人自用进境物品,若不在"自用合理数量"范围内,海关将暂不予放行,并对物品进行暂存。(　　)

参考答案：A

28.2023年2月7日,习近平在学习贯彻党的二十大精神研讨班开班式上指出,中国式现代化深深根植于中华优秀传统文化,体现科学社会主义的先进本质。(　　)

参考答案：A

29.根据《中华人民共和国香港特别行政区维护国家安全法》,中央人民政府对香港特别行政区有关的国家安全事务负有根本责任。(　　)

参考答案：A

30.2021年11月11日,文化和旅游部发布《文化和旅游市场信用管理规定》,自2021年12月1日起施行。(　　)

参考答案：B

二、单项选择题(只有一个选项是正确的,多选、错选、不选均不得分)

1.联合国旅游组织正式通报,自2021年(　　)月25日起,中文正式成为联合国旅游组织官方语言。

A.1月　　　　　B.2月　　　　　C.3月　　　　　D.4月

参考答案：A

2.世界旅游日是由世界旅游组织确定的旅游工作者和旅游者的节日,定于每年的(　　)。

A.5月19日　　　B.5月29日　　　C.9月17日　　　D.9月27日

参考答案：D

3.我国首个以"公益+旅游"模式开发的无居民海岛是(　　)。

A.广东珠海三角岛　　　　　B.福建福清东壁岛

C.上海小洋山岛　　　　　　D.浙江舟山金塘岛

参考答案：A

4.11月26日,2022中国红色旅游博览会在(　　)开幕。

A.湖南韶山　　　B.湖南湘潭　　　C.陕西延安　　　D.贵州遵义

参考答案：A

5.中国旅游行业的核心价值观是(　　)。

A.热情友好、宾客至上　　　B.真诚公道、信誉第一

C.不卑不亢、一视同仁　　　D.游客为本、服务至诚

参考答案：D

6.景区门票价格调整要提前(　　)向社会公布。

A.3个月　　　　B.6个月　　　　C.9个月　　　　D.12个月

参考答案：B

7.2021年11月,文化和旅游部联合国家发展改革委推出"体验脱贫成就·助力乡村振兴"乡村旅游学习体验线路(　　)。

A.200条　　　　B.300条　　　　C.400条　　　　D.500条

参考答案：B

8.都江堰、灵渠、姜席堰和长渠于(　　)被国际灌排委员会确认为世界灌溉工程遗产。

A.2012年　　　B.2014年　　　C.2016年　　　D.2018年

参考答案：D

9.依据《导游管理办法》,导游通过与旅行社订立劳动合同取得导游证的,劳动合同的期限应当在(　　)以上。

A.1个月　　　　B.3个月　　　　C.6个月　　　　D.12个月

参考答案：A

10.依据《导游管理办法》,各级旅游主管部门应当积极组织开展导游培训,每年累计培训时间不得少于(　　)。

A.12小时　　　B.24小时　　　C.36小时　　　D.48小时

参考答案:B

11.在庆祝中国共产党成立100周年之际,中央宣传部新命名111个全国爱国主义教育示范基地。全国爱国主义教育示范基地总数达到(   )。

  A.385个   B.485个   C.585个   D.685个

  参考答案:C

12.2020年12月,全国人大常委会通过刑法修正案,( )未成年人犯故意杀人等罪,将不再是刑事"免责人群"。

  A.10至12周岁 B.12至14周岁 C.14至16周岁 D.16至18周岁

  参考答案:B

13.2021年7月25日,联合国教科文组织第44届世界遗产委员会会议审议通过,将"泉州:宋元中国的世界海洋商贸中心"成功列入《世界遗产名录》。泉州申遗成功成为中国第(   )世界遗产。

  A.54项   B.55项   C.56项   D.57项

  参考答案:C

14.世界上最古老的旅行社、拥有178年历史的英国托马斯·库克(Thomas Cook)集团于(   )宣告倒闭,预示着传统旅行社发展面临巨大的困境。

  A.1978年   B.1998年   C.2015年   D.2019年

  参考答案:D

15.根据2016年11月30日教育部等11个部门出台的《关于推进中小学生研学旅行的意见》,中小学生研学旅行的主导单位是(   )。

  A.旅游主管部门 B.旅行社   C.中小学校   D.研学基地和营地

  参考答案:C

16.下列国家级旅游度假区中,属于第一批公布的是(   )。

  A.海南省三亚市亚龙湾旅游度假区

  B.贵州省遵义市赤水河谷旅游度假区

  C.西藏自治区林芝市鲁朗小镇旅游度假区

  D.云南省阳宗海旅游度假区

  参考答案:D

17.从2023年4月开始,全党将自上而下开展学习贯彻习近平新时代中国特色社会主义思想主题教育,主题教育要牢牢把握(   )的总要求。

  A.学思想、强党性、重实践、建新功

  B.守初心、强党性、重实践、担使命

  C.学思想、担使命、强党性、重实践

  D.守初心、担使命、重实践、强党性

  参考答案:A

18.2022年文化和自然遗产日活动主题为( )。
A."文物赋彩全面小康"　　　　B."文物保护:时代共进、人民共享"
C."非遗保护,中国实践"　　　　D."多彩非遗,美好生活"
参考答案:B

19.2021年5月11日发布的第( )全国人口普查结果显示,全国人口共144349万人。
A.5次　　　　B.6次　　　　C.7次　　　　D.8次
参考答案:C

20.根据《中华人民共和国香港特别行政区维护国家安全法》,香港特别行政区设立维护国家安全委员会,由( )担任主席。
A.国家安全事务顾问　　　　B.行政长官
C.政务司长　　　　　　　　D.律政司长
参考答案:B

21.2021年2月25日,全国脱贫攻坚总结表彰大会在北京人民大会堂隆重举行。习近平总书记宣布,在中国共产党成立一百周年的重要时刻,我国脱贫攻坚战取得了( )。
A.阶段性胜利　　B.局部胜利　　C.完全胜利　　D.全面胜利
参考答案:D

22.国家级生态保护区建设应坚持保护优先,整体保护,见人见物见生活的理念,实现( )的目标。
A.遗产丰富、特色鲜明、民众受益、效益优先
B.遗产丰富、民众受益、保护优先、特色鲜明
C.遗产丰富、氛围浓厚、特色鲜明、民众受益
D.遗产丰富、生态优先、特色鲜明、民众受益
参考答案:C

23.我国1985年加入《世界遗产公约》以来,截至2022年底,已成功申报世界遗产( )项。
A.54　　　　B.55　　　　C.56　　　　D.57
参考答案:C

24."旅游不文明行为记录"信息保存期限为( ),实行动态管理。
A.半年至两年　　B.一至两年　　C.一至三年　　D.一至五年
参考答案:D

25.港珠澳大桥是世界上最长的跨海大桥,全长约( )。
A.25千米　　　B.35千米　　　C.45千米　　　D.55千米
参考答案:D

26.《在线旅游经营服务管理暂行规定》中所称的"在线旅游经营服务"是指通过互联网等信息网络为旅游者提供(　　)或者交通、住宿、餐饮、游览、娱乐等单项旅游经营活动。

　　A.半包价旅游服务　　　　　　　B.全包价旅游服务
　　C.个人旅游服务　　　　　　　　D.包价旅游服务
　　参考答案:D

27."锦绣中华——2021中国非物质文化遗产服饰秀"系列活动于2021年3月14日至15日在(　　)崖州古城举办。

　　A.海南三亚　　B.湖南长沙　　C.河南洛阳　　D.江苏苏州
　　参考答案:A

28.2022年11月29日,搭载神舟十五号载人飞船的长征二号F遥十五运载火箭,在(　　)点火发射,顺利将费俊龙、邓清明、张陆3名航天员送入太空。

　　A.太原卫星发射中心　　　　　　B.西昌卫星发射中心
　　C.文昌卫星发射中心　　　　　　D.酒泉卫星发射中心
　　参考答案:D

29.2017年12月,中国(　　)成功获选世界旅游联盟总部落户城市。

　　A.厦门　　　　B.杭州　　　　C.成都　　　　D.大连
　　参考答案:B

30.联合国世界旅游组织决定,2023年世界旅游日庆祝活动将在沙特阿拉伯举行,主题为:(　　)。

　　A.旅游促进绿色发展
　　B.重新思考旅游业
　　C.可持续旅游业如何促进发展
　　D.旅游促进发展,旅游促进扶贫,旅游促进和平
　　参考答案:A

31.教育部等11部门印发的《关于推进中小学生研学旅行的意见》,明确初中阶段以(　　)研学为主。

　　A.乡土乡情　　B.县情市情　　C.省情国情　　D.放眼世界
　　参考答案:B

32.2022年9月,全国多地举行了"祭孔大典",纪念孔子诞辰(　　)年。

　　A.2570　　　　B.2572　　　　C.2573　　　　D.2575
　　参考答案:C

33.媒体报道或社会公众举报的旅游不文明行为,由(　　)予以调查核实。

　　A.不文明行为发生地的公安部门
　　B.不文明行为发生地的旅游主管部门

C.当事人居住地的公安部门

D.当事人户籍所在地旅游主管部门

参考答案:B

34.文化和旅游部联合共青团中央推出"稻花香里说丰年"全国乡村旅游精品线路( )条,引导人民群众特别是青少年走进乡村、支持"三农"。

A.128　　　　B.180　　　　C.200　　　　D.120

参考答案:A

35.2023年11月17日,由文化和旅游部、福建省人民政府主办的第( )届"海上丝绸之路"(福州)国际旅游节在福州海峡国际会展中心开幕。

A.6　　　　B.7　　　　C.8　　　　D.9

参考答案:C

36.北京市政府天安门地区管委会发布《关于天安门广场实施预约参观措施的通告》,明确天安门广场2021年( )月15日起实施预约参观。

A.9　　　　B.10　　　　C.11　　　　D.12

参考答案:D

37.抗美援朝战争中,中国人民志愿军司令员兼政治委员是( )。

A.林彪　　　　B.朱德　　　　C.彭德怀　　　　D.叶剑英

参考答案:C

38.2021中国-东盟传统医药健康旅游国际论坛在世界长寿之乡——( )开幕。

A.广西巴马　　　B.福建泉州　　　C.江西萍乡　　　D.湖南吉首

参考答案:A

39.2022年11月4日,习近平在第五届中国国际博览会上发表主题为( )的致辞。

A."开放合作,命运与共"　　　　B."开放共创繁荣,创新引领未来"

C."让开放的春风温暖世界"　　　D."共创开放繁荣的美好未来"

参考答案:D

40.为打造文化特色鲜明的国家级旅游休闲街区,文化和旅游部牵头编制的《旅游休闲街区等级划分》(LB/T082—2021)行业标准于2021年( )起实施。

A.4月1日　　　B.5月1日　　　C.6月1日　　　D.7月1日

参考答案:A

三、多选题(至少有两个选项是正确的,多选、少选、错选、不选均不得分)

1.抗美援朝战争期间,中国人民志愿军涌现的特级英雄有( )。

A.杨根思　　　　B.黄继光　　　　C.邱少云
D.王海　　　　　E.罗盛教

参考答案：AB

2.讲好红色故事的三重维度是(　　)。
A.科学性　　　　B.生动性　　　　C.互动性
D.政治性　　　　E.趣味性

参考答案：ABD

3.我国2022年举办冬季奥运会的城市有(　　)。
A.哈尔滨　　　　B.北京　　　　　C.张家口
D.天津　　　　　E.石家庄

参考答案：BC

4.2023年2月7号,习近平在学习贯彻党的二十大精神研讨班开班式上指出,中国式现代化蕴含的独特世界观、(　　)等及其伟大实践,是对世界现代化理论和实践的重大创新。
A.价值观　　　　B.历史观　　　　C.文明观
D.民主观　　　　E.生态观

参考答案：ABCDE

5.按照《旅行社老年旅游服务规范》,以下说法正确的有(　　)。
A.人数超过50人需配随团医生
B.老年游客连续游览时间不宜超过3小时
C.连续乘坐汽车时间不超过3小时
D.老年团的领队要具备紧急救护技能
E.连续乘坐汽车时间不应超过2小时

参考答案：BDE

6.2018年中国的(　　)被国际灌排委员会确认为世界灌溉工程遗产。
A.都江堰　　　　B.灵渠　　　　　C.姜席堰
D.长渠　　　　　E.黄鞠灌溉工程

参考答案：ABCD

7.根据中华人民共和国旅游行业标准《滑雪旅游度假地等级划分》(LB/T083—2021)中的表述,滑雪旅游度假地需要具有良好的滑雪场地资源,满足滑雪场所开发条件,能够满足游客以滑雪运动为主,兼具(　　)等旅游需求的度假设施和服务功能集聚区。
A.山地运动　　　B.文化观光　　　C.户外运动
D.康养度假　　　E.休闲娱乐

参考答案：ACDE

8.依据《导游管理办法》,下列说法正确的有(　　)。

A.导游每年累计培训时间不得少于72小时

B.设立导游星级评价制度,共分为五级

C.导游星级评价不设立评定机构

D.导游从业可以不经旅行社委派

E.导游应向旅游者告知和解释文明行为规范、不文明行为可能产生的后果

参考答案:BCE

9.依据《国家旅游局关于旅游不文明行为记录管理暂行办法》,旅游者有下列行为(　　),将被纳入"旅游不文明行为记录"。

A.扰乱航空器、车船或者其他公共交通工具秩序

B.破坏公共环境卫生、公共设施

C.损毁、破坏旅游目的地文物古迹

D.参与赌博、色情、涉毒活动

E.破坏生态环境,违反野生动植物保护规定

参考答案:ABCDE

10.根据中华人民共和国旅游行业标准《研学旅行服务规范》(LB/T054—2016)中的表述,研学旅行产品可以按照资源类型进行分类,下面属于此类型有(　　)。

A.知识科普型　　B.体验考察型　　C.文化康乐型

D.商务研学型　　E.自然观赏型

参考答案:ABCE

11.《出境旅游领队服务规范》于2023年3月29日起实施,适用于出境旅游组团社提供的领队全程陪同服务,规定了出境旅游领队的职责,包括(　　)。

A.代表组团社监督地接社和地陪导游履行旅游合同

B.按照组团社的行程计划兑现接待服务承诺

C.维护组团社和旅游者合法权益

D.与地接社和地陪导游共同实施旅游接待计划

E.维护国家利益和民族尊严

参考答案:ABCDE

12.发生在境外的旅游不文明行为,可由(　　)通过外交机构、旅游驻外办事机构等途径进行调查核实。

A.国务院旅游主管部门

B.当事人户籍所在地旅游主管部门

C.当事人经常居住地旅游主管部门

D.当事人户籍所在地公安机关

E.当事人经常居住地外事部门

参考答案:ABC

13."旅游不文明行为记录"内容包括不文明当事人的(　　)等信息。

A.姓名和性别　　B.户籍省份　　C.不文明行为表现及影响

D.游客检讨书　　E.对不文明行为的记录期限

参考答案:ABCE

14.依据《导游管理办法》,导游应当自下列情形发生之日起10个工作日内,通过全国旅游监管服务信息系统提交相应材料,申请变更导游证信息(　　)。

A.姓名、身份证号、导游等级和语种等信息发生变化的

B.与旅行社订立的劳动合同解除、终止后,在3个月内与其他旅行社订立劳动合同的

C.在旅游行业组织取消注册后,3个月内在其他旅游行业组织注册的

D.经常执业地区发生变化的

E.经常居住地区发生变化的

参考答案:ABCD

15.依据《导游管理办法》,导游"经常执业地区"是指(　　)。

A.3个月内累计执业达到60日的省级行政区域

B.6个月内累计执业达到90日的省级行政区域

C.导游连续执业的市级行政区域

D.导游连续执业的省级行政区域

E.3个月内累计执业达到30日的省级行政区域

参考答案:DE

16.根据《国家级文化生态保护区管理办法》,申报国家级文化生态保护区的条件主要包括(　　)等。

A.传统文化历史积淀丰厚,具有鲜明地域或民族特色,文化生态保持良好

B.非物质文化遗产资源丰富,是当地生产生活的重要组成部分

C.非物质文化遗产传承有序,传承实践富有活力、氛围浓厚,当地民众广泛参与,认同感强

D.在省(区、市)内已实行文化生态区域性整体保护两年以上,成效明显

E.有文化生态保护区建设管理机构和工作人员

参考答案:ABCDE

17.2016年11月30日教育部等11个部门出台的《关于推进中小学生研学旅行的意见》,明确中小学校开展研学旅行应遵循的原则有(　　)。

A.教育性原则　　B.实践性原则　　C.安全性原则

D.公益性原则　　E.经济性原则

参考答案:ABCD

18.根据《民航旅客不文明行为记录管理办法》,下列( )等行为将受到处罚。

A.强行登机　　　　　　　　B.围堵值机柜台

C.机舱内打架斗殴　　　　　D.随意调换座位

E.妨碍民航工作人员履行职责

参考答案:ABCE

19.依据《旅游市场监督检查操作指南》,执法人员检查旅游团队时应重点检查以下内容( )。

A.带团导游的导游证、导游身份标识

B.受旅行社委派的相关材料

C.选择的车辆等履行辅助人是否符合要求

D.是否投保旅行社责任保险

E.检查行程是否与行程单相符

参考答案:ABCE

20.关于俄罗斯远东地区对部分国家发放免费电子签证的说法中,正确的是( )。

A.向包括中国在内的18个国家的公民发放免费电子签证

B.可持电子签证前往远东4个地区

C.可持电子签证前往远东5个地区

D.每人每次入境后最多可在俄境内逗留8天

E.电子签证自签发日起15天内有效

参考答案:ACD

21.以下哪些旅游区入选首批国家湿地旅游示范基地?( )

A.四川省邛海泸山景区　　　　B.黑龙江省扎龙生态旅游区

C.江西省东鄱阳湖湿地景区　　D.浙江省西溪湿地旅游区

E.上海潘安湖景区

参考答案:ABCD

22.2017年6月1日,中国海关总署《关于暂不予放行旅客行李物品暂存有关事项的公告》正式施行,明确规定以下几种行李情况,暂不放行( )。

A.旅客不能当场缴纳进境物品税款的

B.进出境的物品属于许可证件管理的范围,但旅客不能当场提交的

C.进出境的物品超出自用合理数量,按规定应当办理货物报关手续或其他海关手续,其尚未办理的

D.价值1000元的个人护肤品

E.对进出境物品的属性、内容存疑,需要由有关主管部门进行认定、鉴定、验核的

参考答案：ABCE

23.依据《国家旅游局办公室关于领队管理工作有关事宜的通知》，领队人员从业经历需要符合下列(　　)情形之一。

　　A.两年以上旅行社业务经营经历　　B.三年以上旅行社管理经历

　　C.两年以上导游从业经历　　D.两年以上旅行社管理经历

　　E.三年以上导游从业经历

参考答案：ACD

24.依据《国家旅游局办公室关于领队管理工作有关事宜的通知》，领队人员学历条件的认定需符合下列情形之一(　　)。

　　A.普通高校大专及以上的同等学历

　　B.成人高等学校招生统一考试大专及以上的同等学历

　　C.党校大专及以上的同等学历

　　D.高等教育自学考试专科以上学历

　　E.部队院校大专及以上的同等学历

参考答案：ABCDE

25.依据《国家旅游局办公室关于领队管理工作有关事宜的通知》，关于边境旅游领队、赴台旅游领队的条件，下列正确的是(　　)。

　　A.从事边境旅游领队业务的人员，应取得导游证，并与委派其从事领队业务的、取得边境旅游业务经营许可的旅行社订立劳动合同

　　B.赴台旅游领队暂不实施在线备案

　　C.边境旅游领队学历、语言、从业经历等条件执行全国统一规定

　　D.赴台旅游领队实施"全国旅游监管服务平台"在线备案

　　E.边境旅游领队学历、语言、从业经历等条件由边境地区省、自治区结合本地实际另行规定

参考答案：ABE

26.依据《国家旅游局办公室关于领队管理工作有关事宜的通知》，领队人员语言能力的认定需符合下列情形之一(　　)。

　　A.通过外语语种导游资格考试

　　B.取得国家级发证机构颁发的、出境旅游目的地国家(地区)对应语种语言水平测试的相应等级证书

　　C.全国大学英语3级以上

　　D.雅思5分以上

　　E.取得国际认证的、出境旅游目的地国家(地区)对应语种语言水平测试的相应等级证书

参考答案：ABDE

27.下列关于《旅游民宿基本要求与评价》(LB/T 065—2019)的表述,正确的有( )。
    A.是文旅部发布的强制性国家标准   B.于2019年7月3日起实施
    C.将旅游民宿分为3个等级   D.金宿级为高等级
    E.银宿级为普通等级
    参考答案:BC

28.2021年,二十国集团文化部长会议在意大利罗马召开。本次会议围绕( )等多个议题开展交流讨论。
    A.文化遗产保护
    B.通过文化手段应对气候危机
    C.通过教育和培训加强能力建设
    D.数字化转型与文化领域中的新技术应用
    E.文化和创意行业推动发展
    参考答案:ABCDE

29.中共中央、国务院于2021年10月印发了《黄河流域生态保护和高质量发展规划纲要》,提出要保护传承弘扬黄河文化,打造具有国际影响力的黄河文化和旅游带。该规划范围为黄河干支流流经的( )等9省区相关县级行政区,国土面积约130万平方千米。
    A.青海、甘肃、四川   B.宁夏、内蒙古、陕西
    C.山西、河南、山东   D.河南、安徽、江苏
    参考答案:ABC

30.全党必须坚持的"四个自信"是指( )。
    A.道路自信   B.理论自信   C.制度自信
    D.政策自信   E.文化自信
    参考答案:ABCE

导游基础知识题库

一、判断题(判断描述正确请选 A,判断描述错误请选 B)

1.中国地理纬度最南端的城市是三亚市。( )

参考答案:B

2.中国现存规模最大、保存最完整的古代城垣是南京古城城墙。( )

参考答案:B

3.天津杨柳青年画和苏州桃花坞年画并称为"南桃北柳"。( )

参考答案:A

4.北京境内有潮白河、北运河、永定河、拒马河和蓟运河五大水系。( )

参考答案:A

5.火山地貌与熔岩台地同属于熔岩地貌。( )

参考答案:A

6.北京、上海、成都是国家重点建设的中国航空三大门户复合枢纽。( )

参考答案:B

7.春秋时山西是五霸之一的晋国,后从晋国分出韩、赵、魏三国。( )

参考答案:A

8.中岳嵩山岩石演变完整,有着中国最古老的岩系——"登封杂岩"。( )

参考答案:A

9.四川黄龙景区的"钙华"地貌无论单体规模还是群体数量都位居世界之首。( )

参考答案:A

10.中国古典园林强调几何规整,沿中轴线对称。( )

参考答案:B

11.北京国子监是明清两代的最高学府。( )

参考答案:A

12.济南市市区的"七十二"名泉属于天然涌泉。( )

参考答案:A

13.中国的峨眉山、黄山、庐山、武夷山都有佛光出现的记载,以"峨眉佛光"最为著名。( )

参考答案:A

14.颐和园是中国现存规模最大、保存最完整的皇家园林。( )

参考答案:A

15."长江三鲜"指的是鲥鱼、鲈鱼和河豚。( )

参考答案:B

16."雪顿节"是藏族预祝丰收的节日。( )

参考答案:B

17.中国古典园林叠山的石料选择主要有黄石和太湖石两种。( )

参考答案:A

18.中国面积最大的省级行政区是新疆。( )

参考答案:A

19.云南白药为清代彝族人曲焕章所创。( )

参考答案:A

20.山西拥有众多河流,被誉为"华北水塔"。( )

参考答案:A

21.赫哲族是黑龙江省独有的少数民族,以捕鱼为生。( )

参考答案:A

22.世界上"侧现蜃景"景观最著名的是日内瓦湖。( )

参考答案:A

23.西汉王褒《僮约》所记载的"武阳买茶",证明四川是中国已知最早种植商品茶的地方。( )

参考答案:A

24.四川省的北川县是全国唯一的羌族自治县。( )

参考答案:A

25.全国唯一的畲族自治县在浙江省的景宁。( )

参考答案:A

26.五粮液因选用高粱、大米、糯米、玉米、小麦五种粮食为酿酒原料而得名。( )

参考答案:A

27.菜肴"佛跳墙"的命名来自菜肴形态。( )

参考答案:B

28.白兰地又称科涅克(Cognac),是以葡萄为原料经发酵、蒸馏而成的酒。( )

参考答案:B

29.内蒙古高原平均海拔3000米左右。( )

参考答案:B

30.藏传佛教活佛班禅的驻锡地是布达拉宫。( )

参考答案:B

31."越陈越香"被公认是普洱茶区别于其他茶类的最大特点。( )

参考答案:A

32.世界旅游组织是全球唯一的政府间国际旅游组织。( )

参考答案:A

33.天津小吃"津门三绝"指的是狗不理包子、十八街麻花和耳朵眼炸糕。( )

参考答案:A

34.基督教初传中国是唐代贞观年间,有着"景教"之称。( )

参考答案:A

35.唐三彩因常用黄、绿、褐三种色彩而得名,一般用作家具摆件。( )

参考答案:B

36."姓"的起源可以上溯到母系氏族社会,其主要作用在于"明贵贱"。( )

参考答案:B

37."大煮干丝"是扬州传统名菜,它选用扬州当地产的方豆腐干,将其切片、切丝后作为主料。( )

参考答案:A

38.青花瓷烧造成功,使中国绘画技巧与制瓷工艺的结合更趋成熟,中国瓷器由此进入了彩瓷时代。( )

参考答案:A

39.河北吴桥是"杂技摇篮"发祥地,享有"杂技之乡"的盛誉。( )

参考答案:A

40.金银线垫绣是蜀绣特技,作品以"百鸟朝凤""龙凤"为代表。( )

参考答案:B

41.山海关是华北与东北交通的咽喉要冲。( )

参考答案:A

42.双面绣《猫》是苏绣的代表作品。( )

参考答案:A

43.秦始皇陵兵马俑于1996年被列入世界文化遗产。( )

参考答案:B

44.旋子彩画的两端靠中部位使用了卷涡纹花瓣,这种卷涡纹花瓣被称为旋子,旋子彩画因此而得名。( )

参考答案:A

45.唐朝的大明宫被称为"中国宫殿建筑的巅峰之作"。( )

参考答案:A

46.北京颐和园修建于清乾隆十五年,初建成时称"清晖园"。( )

参考答案:B

47.分布在我国东北地区的俄罗斯族、鄂温克族等少数民族信仰东正教。(　　)

参考答案:A

48.文殊菩萨的坐骑是六牙白象,表示威灵,是文殊菩萨愿行广大功德圆满的象征。(　　)

参考答案:B

49.乐山大佛为弥勒佛坐像,通高71米,是我国现存最高的佛教造像。(　　)

参考答案:B

50.雍和宫内的五百罗汉山、檀木大佛和金丝楠木佛龛并称雍和宫三绝。(　　)

参考答案:A

51.耶路撒冷是犹太教、伊斯兰教和基督教三大宗教的发源地。(　　)

参考答案:A

52.伊斯兰教是通过海上丝绸之路(香料之路)和陆上丝绸之路两条路线传入中国。(　　)

参考答案:A

53.故宫建筑"左祖右社"。其中"左祖"是指祖庙,又称太庙,供奉着五色土,代表"普天之下,莫非王土"。(　　)

参考答案:B

54.北京中山公园社稷坛是明清两代皇帝祭祀土地神和谷物神的地方。(　　)

参考答案:A

55.《圣经》由《旧约全书》和《新约全书》组成。(　　)

参考答案:A

56.哈尔滨圣索菲亚教堂属于俄罗斯拜占庭式建筑,是哈尔滨现存最大的东正教堂。(　　)

参考答案:A

57.周口店"北京人"遗址在世界同一阶段的古人类遗址中,材料最丰富、最系统,是公认的人类发祥地之一。(　　)

参考答案:A

58.土家族的"西兰卡普"与"摆手舞"并称为土家族人民的艺术之花。(　　)

参考答案:A

59.江苏是中国地势最低的一个省区,绝大部分地区在海拔50米以下。(　　)

参考答案:A

60.回族人忌食猪肉,日常递送物品必须用右手。(　　)

参考答案:A

61.苗族喜吃糯米、羊肉,忌吃狗肉;苗族做的酸汤非常著名。(　　)

参考答案:B

62.维吾尔族一年一度最为隆重的节日是古尔邦节、肉孜节。( )

参考答案:A

63.故宫"前朝"即为帝王上朝行政、举行大典之处。( )

参考答案:A

64.明清皇帝祭天在南郊,时间是冬至日;祭地在北郊,时间是夏至日。( )

参考答案:A

65.赛龙舟是端午节中一项重要的活动,现已成为国际性的体育赛事。( )

参考答案:A

66.除了藏族,蒙古族也有敬献哈达的习惯。( )

参考答案:A

67.朝鲜族以米饭为主食,以汤、酱、咸菜和泡菜为副食。每餐必有汤,调味品最爱用辣椒和豆酱,咸菜是佐餐的主要菜肴。( )

参考答案:B

68.端午节插艾和菖蒲有一定防病作用,因此端午节也是自古相传的卫生节。( )

参考答案:A

69.故宫"左祖右社"是古代敬天祭祖观念的集中体现。( )

参考答案:B

70.月饼最初是用来祭月神的祭品,"月饼"一词,最早见于南宋吴自牧《梦粱录》中。( )

参考答案:A

71.浙江省的海宁皮革城享有"小商品海洋,购物者天堂"美誉。( )

参考答案:B

72.世界上最早、最完备的建筑学著作是北宋时期李诫撰写的《营造法式》。( )

参考答案:A

73.商朝的司(后)母戊大方鼎是迄今发现的世界上最大古代青铜器。( )

参考答案:A

74.秦汉时期,中国才形成了"南稻北粟"的农业格局。( )

参考答案:B

75.春秋战国时期巨大的社会变革成为诸子百家思想产生的重要社会原因。( )

参考答案:A

76.1905年,我国第一部电影《雷雨》问世。( )

参考答案:B

77.清代蒲松龄的《聊斋志异》是我国古代白话文小说的高峰。( )
参考答案:B

78.古代把每月的第一日叫"晦",把最后一日叫"朔"。( )
参考答案:B

79.西汉武帝时期始办国家级最高学府太学。( )
参考答案:A

80.唐代以后,中国儒学从重视"五经"转向重视"四书"。( )
参考答案:A

81.京剧脸谱当中,金脸和银脸表示神秘,代表神妖。( )
参考答案:A

82."窗含西岭千秋雪,门泊东吴万里船"描写的是杜甫在成都的居所所见到的场景。( )
参考答案:A

83.安徽分淮北平原、江淮丘陵、皖南山区三大自然区域。( )
参考答案:A

84.各种特殊的火山地形景观及地质构造,是阳明山的一大特色。( )
参考答案:A

85.大三巴牌坊是澳门的标志。( )
参考答案:A

86.闽南语起源于泉州,在外省传播闽南话最广的地区是中国台湾。( )
参考答案:A

87.日本传统文化以"三道"为代表,即茶道、花道和武士道。( )
参考答案:B

88.圣陶沙是马来西亚本岛以外的第一大岛。( )
参考答案:B

89.德国科隆大教堂是世界上最高的双塔教堂。( )
参考答案:A

90."谥号"是古代对死去的帝王、大臣、贵族按其生平事迹评定后,给予褒贬或同情的称号。( )
参考答案:A

91.西安半坡氏族是黄河流域母系氏族公社的一个典型。( )
参考答案:A

92.古代纪时辰用十二地支,把一天划分为十二个时辰与之对应。( )
参考答案:A

93.三省六部制是唐代开始实行的中央官制。(   )
参考答案:B

94.封建科举考试体系中,乡试又被称为"春闱"。(   )
参考答案:B

95.皇帝的母亲和姑母依次称为皇太后、大长公主。(   )
参考答案:A

96.古代纪月,仲春、季夏、仲秋、孟冬依次指二月、六月、八月、十月。(   )
参考答案:A

97.对联是从律诗的对偶句中演化而来,一般要押韵。(   )
参考答案:B

98.泰国的"泰"是"自由"的意思。(   )
参考答案:A

99.秦腔是中国戏曲四大声腔中最古老、最丰富、最庞大的声腔系统。(   )
参考答案:A

二、单选题(只有一个选项是正确的,多选、错选、不选均不得分)

1.头上都蓄有一蓬头发,这是(   )男子最高贵的地方,忌旁人用手触摸。
A.藏族　　　B.彝族　　　C.黎族　　　D.傣族
参考答案:B

2.意大利旅行家马可·波罗在游记中称为"世界莫能与比"的城市是(   )。
A.长安　　　B.洛阳　　　C.汴梁　　　D.元大都
参考答案:D

3."丹霞地貌"是在巨厚的(   )砂砾岩岩层上,由内外营力作用发育而成的方山、奇峰、赤壁、岩洞等特殊地貌。
A.紫红色　　B.黑红色　　C.褐红色　　D.红色
参考答案:D

4.四川丹巴"碉楼"建筑的主人是(   )。
A.白族　　　B.羌族　　　C.藏族　　　D.彝族
参考答案:C

5."画栋朝飞南浦云,珠帘暮卷西山雨"是作者描写在(   )所见的情景。
A.镇海楼　　B.晴川阁　　C.蓬莱阁　　D.滕王阁
参考答案:D

6.阿注婚是(   )摩梭人的习俗。
A.土家族　　B.黎族　　　C.纳西族　　D.白族
参考答案:C

7. "三大炮"是( )地区著名小吃。
A.天津　　　　B.四川　　　　C.江苏　　　　D.安徽
参考答案:B

8. "移舟泊烟渚,日暮客愁新。野旷天低树,江清月近人"出自唐代孟浩然的( )。
A.《过故人庄》　　　　　　B.《宿建德江》
C.《春晓》　　　　　　　　D.《望洞庭湖赠张丞相》
参考答案:B

9. 下列风景名湖中,属于咸水湖的是( )。
A.青海湖　　　B.鄱阳湖　　　C.洞庭湖　　　D.太湖
参考答案:A

10. "抛绣球、碰红蛋、踢毽子、抢花炮"是( )中举行的活动。
A.彝族火把节　　B.壮族歌圩节　　C.苗族芦笙节　　D.白族三月街
参考答案:B

11. 世界上最早的敞肩石拱桥——赵州桥修建于( )。
A.商朝　　　　B.秦朝　　　　C.汉朝　　　　D.隋朝
参考答案:D

12. 下列剪纸中,制作工艺独树一帜,不是"剪",而是"刻"的是( )。
A.山西剪纸　　B.陕西剪纸　　C.扬州剪纸　　D.蔚县剪纸
参考答案:D

13. 著名的"天青瓷"产于( )。
A.汝窑　　　　B.钧窑　　　　C.哥窑　　　　D.定窑
参考答案:A

14. "文景之治"中的"文""景"二字是指皇帝的( )。
A.尊号　　　　B.庙号　　　　C.谥号　　　　D.年号
参考答案:C

15. "一山飞峙大江边,跃上葱茏四百旋"是毛泽东登临( )后写下的诗篇。
A.衡山　　　　B.庐山　　　　C.黄鹤楼　　　D.黄山
参考答案:B

16. 中国四大名绣中,绣工多为男工的是( )。
A.苏绣　　　　B.湘绣　　　　C.粤绣　　　　D.蜀绣
参考答案:C

17. "中国古代道教建筑的露天博物馆"位于( )。
A.武当山　　　B.三清山　　　C.青城山　　　D.龙虎山
参考答案:B

18.中国最大的群岛是( )。
A.南沙群岛　　B.西沙群岛　　C.东沙群岛　　D.舟山群岛
参考答案:D

19.安济桥又名赵州桥,建于隋开皇至大业年间,是世界上现存最大的( )。
A.联拱桥　　B.梁式桥　　C.浮桥　　D.敞肩桥
参考答案:D

20.按园林的使用者身份分,北京恭王府属于( )。
A.皇家园林　　B.私家园林　　C.宗教园林　　D.公共园林
参考答案:B

21.按照蒙古族习俗,人们到蒙古包做客,忌讳其坐在蒙古包的( )。
A.西北角　　B.东北角　　C.东南角　　D.西南角
参考答案:A

22.把"玄武门"改为"神武门","玄武大帝"改为"真武大帝"是避( )皇帝之讳。
A.康熙　　B.雍正　　C.乾隆　　D.道光
参考答案:A

23.被誉为"千河之省"的省份为( )。
A.湖北省　　B.四川省　　C.贵州省　　D.西藏自治区
参考答案:B

24.长江流经我国( )省、自治区、直辖市。
A.9个　　B.10个　　C.11个　　D.12个
参考答案:C

25.下列园林中,( )既是苏州现存最大的古典园林,也是苏州园林的代表作。
A.网师园　　B.拙政园　　C.留园　　D.豫园
参考答案:B

26.佛教所供奉的"东方三圣"中的佛是( )。
A.释迦牟尼　　B.药师佛　　C.阿弥陀佛　　D.如来佛
参考答案:B

27.嘉量是中国古代的标准量器,全套量器从大到小依次为( )。
A.斛、斗、合、升、龠　　B.斛、升、斗、合、龠
C.斛、斗、升、合、龠　　D.斛、斗、升、龠、合
参考答案:C

28.江南园林之中,被陈从周先生誉为"国内孤例"的是( )。
A.拙政园　　B.豫园　　C.个园　　D.留园

参考答案:C

29.具有"紫口铁足"特点的瓷器是( )。
A.越窑青瓷　　B.耀州窑青瓷　　C.哥窑青瓷　　D.汝窑青瓷
参考答案:C

30.成语"画龙点睛"的故事与下列哪位画家有关?( )
A.陆探微　　B.张僧繇　　C.顾恺之　　D.黄公望
参考答案:B

31.下列名酒与香型匹配的是( )。
A.宜宾五粮液—酱香型　　B.山西汾酒—浓香型
C.桂林三花酒—米香型　　D.陕西西凤酒—清香型
参考答案:C

32.明代以后,陶瓷釉色以( )为大宗。
A.青釉　　B.白釉　　C.黄釉　　D.釉里红
参考答案:B

33.世界上最典型的石英砂岩峰林峡谷地貌是我国的( )景区。
A.张家界　　B.齐云山　　C.华山　　D.云南石林
参考答案:A

34.世界上最早的纸币"交子"出现在( )时期。
A.北宋　　B.南宋　　C.元朝　　D.明朝
参考答案:A

35.世界园林流派中,强调水法,十字林荫路交叉处设置中心水池的是( )。
A.欧洲园林　　B.西亚园林　　C.中国园林　　D.美洲园林
参考答案:B

36.首个总部落户中国的国际性旅游组织是( )。
A.世界旅游组织　　　　B.太平洋亚洲旅游协会
C.世界旅行社协会联合会　　D.世界旅游城市联合会
参考答案:D

37.以"入窑一色、出窑万彩"的"窑变"瓷器著称的瓷窑是( )。
A.官窑　　B.汝窑　　C.哥窑　　D.钧窑
参考答案:D

38.诗句"江作青罗带,山如碧玉簪"所赞美的景观是( )。
A.乌江山水　　B.长江三峡　　C.塞上江南　　D.漓江山水
参考答案:D

39.土家族的传统舞蹈( )与祭祀祖先、祈求丰收相联系。
A.打柴舞　　B.摆手舞　　C.八宝铜铃舞　　D.茅古斯

参考答案:B

40.下列乐器中,属于维吾尔族民间乐器的是( )。
A.伽耶琴　　　　B.达甫　　　　C.马头琴　　　　D.芦笙
参考答案:B

41.道教流派中,正一道的祖庭位于( )。
A.四川青城山　　B.陕西终南　　C.江西龙虎山　　D.江苏茅山
参考答案:C

42.下列风景名湖中,中国唯一一个湖泊类世界文化遗产是( )。
A.青海湖　　　　B.鄱阳湖　　　C.西湖　　　　　D.千岛湖
参考答案:C

43.我国从( )开始推出旅游主题年。
A.1992年　　　　B.1993年　　　C.1995年　　　　D.1997年
参考答案:A

44.我国古代第一座启闭式桥梁是( )。
A.泉州洛阳桥　　B.潮州湘子桥　C.苏州宝带桥　　D.北京卢沟桥
参考答案:B

45.我国封建社会的科举考试中,能参加会试考试的是( )。
A.秀才　　　　　B.举人　　　　C.贡士　　　　　D.进士
参考答案:B

46.利用太阳的投影和地球自转的原理,借指针所生阴影的位置来显示时间的古代宫殿建筑的室外陈设是( )。
A.嘉量　　　　　B.日晷　　　　C.华表　　　　　D.沙漏
参考答案:B

47.以仿阿拉伯式邦克楼"光塔"著称于世的清真寺是( )。
A.泉州清净寺　　B.广州怀圣寺　C.扬州仙鹤寺　　D.杭州真教寺
参考答案:B

48.魏武王曹操"东临碣石,以观沧海",所观沧海是今天的( )。
A.黄海　　　　　B.渤海　　　　C.洞庭湖　　　　D.太湖
参考答案:B

49.下列名山中,连云港市云台山的( )为江苏最高峰,海拔625米。
A.紫金山　　　　B.栖霞山　　　C.玉女峰　　　　D.花果山
参考答案:C

50.我国拥有世界遗产项目最多的城市是( )。
A.北京　　　　　B.上海　　　　C.天津　　　　　D.重庆
参考答案:A

51.有"北方雅典""欧洲最有气势的城市"之称的是(　　)。
A.伦敦　　　　B.巴黎　　　　C.爱丁堡　　　　D.柏林
参考答案:C

52.被称为"蕨类植物之冠"的是(　　)。
A.银杉　　　　B.水杉　　　　C.桫椤　　　　D.珙桐
参考答案:C

53.下列国家中,素有"玉石之国"美誉的国家是(　　)。
A.缅甸　　　　B.印度　　　　C.中国　　　　D.泰国
参考答案:C

54.在明代帝陵规制中具有承上启下作用的帝陵是(　　)。
A.明定陵　　　B.明长陵　　　C.明献陵　　　D.明显陵
参考答案:D

55.在桥梁建筑中采用了"垒址于渊、种蛎固基"方法的著名石桥是(　　)。
A.河北赵州桥　B.苏州宝带桥　C.泉州洛阳桥　D.程阳永济桥
参考答案:C

56.在世界遗产名录中,黄山归类为(　　)。
A.世界文化遗产　　　　　　B.世界自然遗产
C.世界自然与文化双重遗产　　D.文化景观遗产
参考答案:C

57.中国第一座道观是(　　)。
A.白云观　　　B.草楼观　　　C.永乐宫　　　D.文昌宫
参考答案:B

58.中国山地"五岳"中主峰海拔最高的是(　　)。
A.泰山　　　　B.衡山　　　　C.华山　　　　D.恒山
参考答案:C

59.中国乌龙茶的主产区是(　　)。
A.安徽祁门　　B.杭州梅家坞　C.台湾阿里山　D.福建安溪
参考答案:D

60.中国以梯田为主的世界遗产地只有一处,即哈尼梯田,它位于(　　)。
A.云南省　　　B.四川省　　　C.贵州省　　　D.西藏自治区
参考答案:A

61.左思所写的(　　)轰动一时,留下了"洛阳纸贵"的历史佳话。
A.《两都赋》　B.《二京赋》　C.《三都赋》　D.《上林赋》
参考答案:C

62.中国佛教最早的寺院是(　　)。

A.金山寺　　　　B.白马寺　　　　C.大慈恩寺　　　D.宝光寺
参考答案:B

63.(　　)创造了丰富多彩的文化艺术,他们常用歌舞表达自我情感,他们所独有的银饰工艺、蜡染、织锦、刺绣享誉国内外。
A.壮族　　　　　B.土家族　　　　C.苗族　　　　　D.黎族
参考答案:C

64.(　　)的婚礼仪式隆重,分别在女方家和男方家各举行一次,并在家庭中盛行"男主外、女主内"风俗。
A.朝鲜族　　　　B.土家族　　　　C.满族　　　　　D.回族
参考答案:A

65.(　　)青年婚前社交自由,晚上吹芦笙串姑娘,"串寨子""丢包"等都是选择对象和表达爱情的方式。
A.傣族　　　　　B.纳西族　　　　C.白族　　　　　D.彝族
参考答案:A

66.下列名茶中,采用全发酵法制成的茶叶是(　　)。
A.绿茶　　　　　B.红茶　　　　　C.乌龙茶　　　　D.白茶
参考答案:B

67.(　　)是寺庙佛座上方或宫殿宝座上的凹进部分,含五行以水克火,预防火灾之意。
A.平棋　　　　　B.平暗　　　　　C.藻井　　　　　D.天花板
参考答案:C

68.(　　)是瑶族最盛大的节日。
A.三月街　　　　B.盘王节　　　　C.绕三灵　　　　D.三月三
参考答案:B

69.唐朝由政府颁定的(　　),是世界上第一部由国家颁布的药典。
A.《千金方》　　B.《神农本草经》　C.《唐本草》　　D.《本草纲目》
参考答案:C

70.(　　)是壮族古代文化艺术的精华。
A.花山原始崖壁画　B.铜鼓　　　　　C.壮锦　　　　　D.壮歌
参考答案:A

71.(　　)位于陕西西安临潼,是中国古代最大,也是世界最大的帝王陵墓。
A.秦始皇陵　　　B.汉茂陵　　　　C.唐昭陵　　　　D.唐乾陵
参考答案:A

72.(　　)以960平方米元代道教壁画著称于世,有道教壁画艺术宝库之誉,与佛教艺术宝库敦煌石窟交相辉映。

A.北京白云观　　　B.成都青羊宫　　　C.芮城永乐宫　　　D.沈阳太清宫

参考答案:C

73."火腿炖甲鱼",口味鲜香、营养全面,是(　　)中的名菜。

A.徽菜　　　　B.闽菜　　　　C.浙菜　　　　D.湘菜

参考答案:A

74."净"俗称花脸,它有许多分支。下列脸谱中,不属于其分支的是(　　)。

A.武二花　　　B.文花脸　　　C.大花脸　　　D.二花脸

参考答案:B

75.《九歌》《天问》《九章》的作者是(　　)。

A.墨子　　　　B.屈原　　　　C.宋玉　　　　D.李白

参考答案:B

76.我国成功发射的世界首颗量子科学实验卫星叫(　　)。

A."墨子号"　　B."玉兔号"　　C."嫦娥号"　　D."天宫号"

参考答案:A

77.《洛阳伽蓝记》描写的是(　　)时期洛阳佛教兴盛的景象。

A.三国　　　　B.东晋　　　　C.北魏　　　　D.隋朝

参考答案:C

78.《周易》中的八卦象征着八种基本自然现象,其中乾、坤、坎、离卦象征的是(　　)。

A.天、地、雷、风　　B.天、地、山、水　　C.天、地、山、风　　D.天、地、水、火

参考答案:D

79.北京牛街清真寺是北京地区规模最大、历史最久远的清真大寺,也是中国北方最古老清真寺之一,明代奉敕赐名(　　)。

A.清净寺　　　B.礼拜寺　　　C.真教寺　　　D.清修寺

参考答案:B

80.北京天坛由四组建筑组成,其中用于祭天的建筑是(　　)。

A.圜丘坛　　　B.祈年殿　　　C.皇穹宇　　　D.斋宫

参考答案:A

81.中国自行设计、建造的第一座大型水电站是(　　)。

A.新安江水电站　　B.葛洲坝水电站　　C.刘家峡水电站　　D.三峡水电站

参考答案:A

82.我国面积最大的湿地类型国家级自然保护区是(　　)。

A.可可西里自然保护区　　　　B.青海省三江源国家级自然保护区

C.柴达木梭梭林自然保护区　　D.隆宝自然保护区

参考答案:B

83.被誉为"人造宝石"的瓷器是( )。
A.景德镇颜色釉瓷　　　　　　　　B.景德镇粉彩瓷
C.景德镇青花玲珑瓷　　　　　　　D.景德镇薄胎瓷
参考答案:A

84.避讳始于周朝,盛于( )。
A.战国　　　　B.秦汉　　　　C.隋唐　　　　D.清代
参考答案:C

85.藏族农业区的传统节日中,除过藏历年外最热闹的是( )。
A.望果节　　　B.雪顿节　　　C.采花节　　　D.沐浴节
参考答案:A

86.朝鲜族最有名的乐器是( )。
A.独它尔　　　B.马头琴　　　C.伽倻琴　　　D.巴拉曼
参考答案:C

87.中国古代使用时间最长、精确度最高的历法是( )。
A.《授时历》　B.《黄帝历》　C.《太初历》　D.《大明历》
参考答案:A

88.穿斗式建筑的优点是( )。
A.减少室内对视线的阻碍　　　　　B.用料较少
C.使室内空间更具连续性　　　　　D.减少了隐性围合空间
参考答案:B

89.七曜中的( )又称为"明星""太白",亮度最强。
A.水星　　　　B.金星　　　　C.火星　　　　D.土星
参考答案:B

90.大量运用龙凤图案,间补以花卉图案,主要线条及龙、珠宝都用沥粉贴金的彩画是( )。
A.和玺彩画　　B.旋子彩画　　C.苏式彩画　　D.和子彩画
参考答案:A

91.东大寺是日本佛教( )总寺院,距今约有一千二百余年的历史。
A.禅宗　　　　B.天台宗　　　C.法相宗　　　D.华严宗
参考答案:D

92.东南亚地区最大的清真寺是( )。
A.泰国卧佛寺　　　　　　　　　　B.马来西亚国家清真寺
C.印度尼西亚三宝庙　　　　　　　D.泰国郑王庙
参考答案:B

93.下列名窑中,被世人称为"似玉、非玉、而胜玉"的是( )。

A.哥窑　　　　B.官窑　　　　C.汝窑　　　　D.定窑

参考答案：C

94.俄罗斯最流行的宗教是(　　)。

A.东正教　　　B.伊斯兰教　　C.萨满教　　　D.天主教

参考答案：A

95.新疆维吾尔自治区总面积占全国陆地面积的(　　),是全国面积最大的省级行政单位。

A.1/10　　　　B.1/8　　　　C.1/7　　　　D.1/6

参考答案：D

96.封建社会对帝、后在生前或死后奉上的尊崇称号为(　　)。

A.谥号　　　　B.庙号　　　　C.尊号　　　　D.陵号

参考答案：C

97.奉先寺中的卢舍那大佛是中国石窟史上空前绝后的佛像杰作,是(　　)艺术的代表作。

A.敦煌石窟　　B.云冈石窟　　C.龙门石窟　　D.麦积山石窟

参考答案：C

98.佛教未来世佛、现在世佛、过去世佛依次为(　　)。

A.释迦牟尼佛、弥勒佛、燃灯佛　　B.弥勒佛、燃灯佛、释迦牟尼佛
C.弥勒佛、释迦牟尼佛、燃灯佛　　D.燃灯佛、弥勒佛、释迦牟尼佛

参考答案：C

99.佛教四大名山中,(　　)是我国唯一兼有汉地佛教和藏传佛教道场的佛教圣地。

A.五台山　　　B.普陀山　　　C.峨眉山　　　D.九华山

参考答案：A

100.佛教四大天王中,身穿甲胄,手持琵琶的是(　　)。

A 东方持国天王　B.南方增长天王　C.西方广目天王　D.北方多闻天王

参考答案：A

101.新中国成立后建成的第一条铁路是(　　)。

A.成渝铁路　　B.成昆铁路　　C.宝成铁路　　D.京张铁路

参考答案：A

102.甘肃"酒泉"的地名据说来源于(　　)为激励士兵抗击匈奴,将汉武帝赏赐的酒倒在泉水里与士兵同饮的典故。

A.卫青　　　　B.李广　　　　C.霍去病　　　D.赵充国

参考答案：C

103.个园中的(　　)在扬州古代园林中别具特色,在国内也属罕见。

A.水景 B.山水景色 C.四季假山 D.城市山林

参考答案:C

104.各民族都有禁忌,其中( )妇女有文身习俗,但忌男人参与或偷看。

A.苗族 B.壮族 C.满族 D.黎族

参考答案:D

105.中国陆地最低点是位于( ),低于海平面154.31米,是中国陆地最低点。

A.艾丁湖 B.鄱阳湖 C.阳澄湖 D.洞庭湖

参考答案:A

106.根据钻石洁净度,I级钻石指的是( )。

A.内部无瑕级 B.极微瑕级 C.微瑕级 D.含瑕级

参考答案:D

107.中国历史上第一个帝王年号是( )时期的"建元"。

A.汉惠帝 B.汉文帝 C.汉景帝 D.汉武帝

参考答案:D

108.公元前16世纪的商代,中国已经成功烧制了( )。

A.原始青瓷 B.原始白瓷 C.原始黑瓷 D.原始彩瓷

参考答案:A

109.1957年10月建成的( )是中华人民共和国第一个天然石油基地。

A.大庆油田 B.胜利油田 C.渤海油田 D.玉门油田

参考答案:D

110.清代后期将故宫( )作为殿试的场所。

A.太和殿 B.中和殿 C.保和殿 D.交泰殿

参考答案:C

111.关于哈雷彗星的最早记录出现在( )。

A.《春秋》 B.《诗经》 C.《甘石星经》 D.《论语》

参考答案:A

112.古人使用十二地支计时,将一天分为12个时辰,其中子时是指( )。

A.23点—1点 B.11点—13点 C.17点—19点 D.21点—23点

参考答案:A

113.关羽被道教尊为关圣帝君。中国规模最大、保存最完整的关帝庙坐落在( )。

A.河南洛阳 B.湖北当阳 C.山西运城 D.陕西西安

参考答案:C

114.国酒茅台是( )酒的代表。

A.酱香型　　　　B.浓香型　　　　C.清香型　　　　D.米香型

参考答案:A

115.过年时常以年糕、糕点作祭品的是(　　)人。

A.中国台湾　　　B.日本　　　　　C.韩国　　　　　D.朝鲜

参考答案:A

116.下列名茶中,被称为"金镶玉"的是(　　)。

A.黄山毛峰　　　B.西湖龙井　　　C.君山银针　　　D.峨眉竹叶青

参考答案:C

117.黄公望的(　　)是中国十大传世名画之一。

A.《洛神赋图》　B.《送子天王图》　C.《清明上河图》　D.《富春山居图》

参考答案:D

118.汉代书法家中以隶书为代表的书法家是(　　)。

A.蔡邕　　　　　B.杜度　　　　　C.崔瑗　　　　　D.张芝

参考答案:A

119.汉人的信仰观念以(　　)为核心。

A.原始图腾　　　B.万物有灵　　　C.敬天祭祖　　　D.风水走向

参考答案:C

120."智者乐水,仁者乐山""三人行必有我师"出自语录体散文集(　　)。

A.《道德经》　　B.《论语》　　　C.《逍遥游》　　D.《庄子》

参考答案:B

121.回族有严格的饮食禁忌。不吃(　　)肉,不食用自死的禽畜和畜血。

A.牛　　　　　　B.羊　　　　　　C.驴　　　　　　D.驼

参考答案:C

122.绘画名品《清明上河图》的作者是(　　)。

A.阎立本　　　　B.张择端　　　　C.赵孟頫　　　　D.齐白石

参考答案:B

123.火把节是(　　)、傈僳、纳西、哈尼等民族传统节日。

A.壮族、朝鲜族　B.藏族、黎族　　C.苗族、土家族　D.彝族、白族

参考答案:D

124.济南趵突泉中的"云雾润蒸华不住,波涛声震大明湖"这副楹联属于(　　)。

A.节令联　　　　B.喜庆联　　　　C.杂感联　　　　D.名胜联

参考答案:D

125.清乾隆年间"四大徽班进京"对京剧的形成影响深远,四大徽班中最早进京演出并大获成功的是(　　)。

A.和春班　　　　B.四喜班　　　　C.三庆班　　　　D.春台班

参考答案：C

126.北魏时期,贾思勰撰写的( )被誉为"中国古代农业百科全书",也是中国早期农书中保存最完整的一部。

A.《氾胜之书》　B.《齐民要术》　C.《农桑辑要》　D.《农书》

参考答案：B

127.唐时,陆羽创作《茶经》,是世界上第一部关于茶叶的专著,陆羽因此被茶界奉为( )。

A.茶王　　　　　B.茶仙　　　　　C.茶圣　　　　　D.茶神

参考答案：C

128.楷书产生于( )。

A.春秋战国时期　B.秦代　　　　　C.汉末　　　　　D.隋唐时期

参考答案：C

129.被鲁迅誉为"史家之绝唱,无韵之离骚"的历史著作是( )。

A.《春秋》　　　B.《史记》　　　C.《三国志》　　D.《资治通鉴》

参考答案：B

130.孔子学说及儒家思想的核心是( )。

A.仁学　　　　　B.礼治　　　　　C.民本　　　　　D.性善

参考答案：A

131.向日葵是( )的国花。

A.美国　　　　　B.英国　　　　　C.法国　　　　　D.俄罗斯

参考答案：D

132.1954年12月,康藏公路与( )公路同时全线通车,有力促进了西藏经济建设,有利于维护国家统一和巩固国防。

A.青藏　　　　　B.新藏　　　　　C.滇藏　　　　　D.京藏

参考答案：A

三、多选题（至少有两个选项是正确的,多选、少选、错选、不选均不得分）

1.拱式桥是我国古代桥梁的重要类型,下列属于拱式桥的有( )。

A.苏州宝带桥　　B.河北赵州桥　　C.泉州洛阳桥

D.泉州安平桥　　E.北京卢沟桥

参考答案：ABE

2.中国武术宝库中著名的三大重要流派是( )。
A.少林派　　　B.武当派　　　C.青城派
D.峨眉派　　　E.崆峒派
参考答案:ABD

3.下列剧目属黄梅戏代表作的是( )。
A.《打猪草》　　B.《天仙配》　　C.《梁山伯与祝英台》
D.《女驸马》　　E.《红楼梦》
参考答案:ABD

4.京剧表演中扮演女性角色的"旦"除"正旦"外,还有( )。
A.花旦　　　B.武旦　　　C.彩旦
D.小旦　　　E.老旦
参考答案:ABCE

5.京杭大运河沟通( )等河流,是世界上最长的一条人工运河。
A.海河　　　B.黄河　　　C.淮河
D.长江　　　E.珠江
参考答案:ABCD

6.我国"四大菜系"是指( )。
A.粤菜　　　B.川菜　　　C.鲁菜
D.湘菜　　　E.淮扬菜
参考答案:ABCE

7.酒按原料分类可以分为( )。
A.白酒　　　B.啤酒　　　C.黄酒
D.米酒　　　E.果酒
参考答案:ACE

8.中国京剧四大名旦指的是( )。
A.荀慧生　　　B.梅兰芳　　　C.尚小云
D.程砚秋　　　E.谭鑫培
参考答案:ABCD

9.下列属梅兰芳代表作的是( )。
A.《贵妃醉酒》　　B.《霸王别姬》　　C.《红娘》
D.《昭君出塞》　　E.《锁麟囊》
参考答案:AB

10.下列属于北京小吃的是( )。
A.猫耳朵　　　B.驴打滚　　　C.艾窝窝
D.狗不理　　　E.豆汁

参考答案:BCE

11. 以下名酒产于四川省的有( )。
A.剑南春　　B.五粮液　　C.郎酒
D.水井坊　　E.泸州老窖

参考答案:ABCDE

12. 下列属于我国世界文化与自然双重遗产的是( )。
A.长城　　B.泰山　　C.武陵源
D.黄山　　E.武夷山

参考答案:BDE

13. 下列属于浓香型白酒的是( )。
A.郎酒　　B.泸州老窖特曲　　C.剑南春
D.洋河大曲　　E.古井贡酒

参考答案:BCDE

14. 茶叶提神主要是茶叶中( )的作用。
A.氨基酸　　B.维生素　　C.矿物质
D.咖啡因　　E.黄烷醇类化合物

参考答案:DE

15. 在煮酒论英雄的故事中,曹操所谓的英雄是( )。
A.曹操　　B.刘备　　C.袁绍
D.孙权　　E.刘表

参考答案:AB

16. "元曲四大家"包括( )。
A.马致远　　B.关汉卿　　C.白朴
D.汤显祖　　E.郑光祖

参考答案:ABCE

17. 下列属于"元四家"的画家有( )。
A.黄公望　　B.王蒙　　C.倪瓒
D.吴镇　　E.汪士慎

参考答案:ABCD

18. 欣赏中国书法的美应把握( )。
A.线条美　　B.结体美　　C.章法美
D.色彩美　　E.神韵美

参考答案:ABCE

19. 下列属于天津著名小吃的是( )。
A.狗不理　　B.酥麻花　　C.糯米烧卖

D.南翔馒头　　　E.黄桥烧饼

参考答案：AB

20.下列民间传统节日中,源自道教纪念日的有(　　)。

A.春节　　　　B.中元节　　　　C.中秋节

D.重阳节　　　E.腊八节

参考答案：ABCD

21.下列属于禅宗高僧的有(　　)。

A.玄奘　　　　B.道宣　　　　C.达摩

D.慧能　　　　E.神秀

参考答案：CDE

22.下列反映了中国绘画特点的表述是(　　)。

A."以咫尺之幅,写千里之遥"　　B."不似之似为真似"

C."无色如有色"　　　　　　　　D."有色如无色"

E."近看鬼打架,远看一张画"

参考答案：ABCD

23.下列属于江苏画派著名画家傅抱石代表作的有(　　)。

A.《井冈山黄洋界》　　　　　　B.《烟雨莽苍苍》

C.《千峰送雨图》　　　　　　　D.《转战南北》

E.《雨景图》

参考答案：ABC

24.曹禺是中国现代杰出的戏剧家,其代表作有(　　)。

A.《雷雨》　　　B.《日出》　　　C.《原野》

D.《北京人》　　E.《名优之死》

参考答案：ABCD

25.两宋理学代表人物有(　　)。

A.周敦颐　　　B.程颢　　　C.张载

D.朱熹　　　　E.王阳明

参考答案：ABCD

26.下列对中国话剧做出重大贡献的人物有(　　)。

A.曹禺　　　　B.田汉　　　C.欧阳予倩

D.袁雪芬　　　E.洪深

参考答案：ABCE

27.黑龙江省地貌特征是(　　)。

A.五山　　　　B.一水　　　C.一草

D.三分田　　　E.二地

参考答案:ABCD

28.下列关于园林植物象征意义的表述,正确的是( )。
A.竹子象征人品清逸和气节高尚　B.松柏象征坚强和长寿
C.梅花象征洁净无瑕　　　　　　D.兰花象征幽居隐士
E.玉兰、牡丹象征荣华富贵

参考答案:ABDE

29.中国古代皇帝祭拜的对象有不同的等级,其中最受重视的是( )。
A.天地　　　B.社稷　　　C.祖先
D.高山　　　E.大海

参考答案:ABC

30.下列关于社稷崇拜的说法中,正确的是( )。
A.社指土地神,稷指谷物神。
B.社稷成为国家的象征。
C.社稷坛用五色土组成祭坛,象征"普天之下,莫非王土"。
D.社稷坛中立"社主石",象征"江山永固,社稷长存"。
E.社稷崇拜源自对祖先的崇拜。

参考答案:ABCD

31.下列传说与母系社会有关系的是( )。
A.商代始祖"契",传说是其母误吞"玄鸟"蛋受孕所生
B.周代始祖"弃",传说是其母在野外踏足巨人脚印而生
C.传说中盘古狗身人面、女娲蛇身人面
D.我国最早的姓多带女旁,如姜、姬、偃、嬴等
E.中国古代有"三皇五帝"等神话人物

参考答案:ABD

32.下列画家中,属于吴门画派的是( )。
A.文徵明　　B.沈周　　　C.仇英
D.唐寅　　　E.石涛

参考答案:ABCD

33.以下事件在西周时期发生的是( )。
A."成汤灭夏"　B."文王之治"　C."牧野之战"
D."国人暴动"　E."共和行政"

参考答案:DE

34.下列关于台北故宫博物院的表述,正确的是( )。
A.位于台北市士林区外双溪,1965年建成
B.仿照北京故宫博物院形式

C.采用中国宫廷式设计

D.大楼前有蒋介石雕像

E.建筑由中央博物院与北平故宫博物院组成

参考答案:ABCE

35.京杭大运河经历了三次较大的兴修,其中元朝定都北京后修建的是(　　)。

A.邗沟　　　　B.江南运河　　　C.洛州河

D.会通河　　　E.通惠河

参考答案:CDE

36.下列作品为道教学者葛洪所著的有(　　)。

A.《肘后备急方》　B.《抱朴子·内篇》　C.《肘后一百方》

D.《千金方》　　　E.《黄帝内经》

参考答案:AB

37.禅宗丛林制度的创始人是(　　)。

A.达摩　　　　B.惠能　　　　C.神秀

D.马祖　　　　E.百丈

参考答案:DE

38.隋唐佛教流派众多,其中较具代表性的是(　　)。

A.天台宗　　　B.华严宗　　　C.净土宗

D.律宗　　　　E.禅宗

参考答案:CE

39.下列思想家中属于儒家代表人物的是(　　)。

A.孔子　　　　B.孟子　　　　C.老子

D.庄子　　　　E.荀子

参考答案:ABE

40.下列关于京剧的说法中,正确的是(　　)。

A."四大徽班进京"之后,京剧艺术形式基本成熟

B.京剧主要唱腔是"西皮"与"二黄"两类

C.京剧主要表演手法是唱、念、做、打

D.京剧主要角色有生、旦、净、丑

E.清末民初,杭州京剧界形成与北方传统京剧不同的风格,称为海派京剧

参考答案:ABCD

41.唐朝名医孙思邈,集毕生精力著成了(　　)。

A.《湿热条辨》　　　B.《唐本草》　　　C.《千金要方》

D.《唐·新修本草》　　E.《千金翼方》

参考答案:CE

42.中医辨证的总纲是"八纲辨证",包括( )。
A.阴阳   B.盈亏   C.表里
D.寒热   E.虚实
参考答案:ACDE

43.下列属于汉隶代表作的是( )。
A.《石门颂》   B.《孔宙碑》   C.《衡方碑》
D.《曹全碑》   E.《张迁碑》
参考答案:ABCDE

44.中医学的基本特点主要体现在( )等方面。
A.辨病治疗   B.整体观念   C.辨证论治
D.同病异治   E.对症治疗
参考答案:BC

45.中医"以表知里"的诊法包括( )等方法。
A.望   B.闻   C.问
D.切   E.按
参考答案:ABCD

46.中国陶瓷发展特点为( )。
A.南方以龙泉青瓷为代表   B.北方以景德镇青白瓷为代表
C.南方以越窑青瓷为代表   D.北方以邢窑白瓷代表
E.形成"南青北白"的瓷业格局
参考答案:CDE

47.下列属于宋代五大名窑的是( )。
A.南北官窑   B.南方越窑   C.南方哥窑
D.北方汝窑   E.定窑、钧窑
参考答案:ACDE

48.下列属于宋代六大窑系的是( )。
A.北方龙泉青瓷窑系   B.景德镇青白瓷窑系
C.南方定窑、钧窑系   D.耀州窑系
E.磁州窑系
参考答案:BDE

49.下列关于丽江古城的说法中,正确的有( )。
A.丽江古城是世界文化遗产
B.丽江古城没有城墙
C.丽江古城的建筑体现纳西族的艺术风格
D.丽江古城是我国保存最完整的明初县治砖城

E.丽江古城是中国茶文化的发源地

参考答案:ABC

50.关于中国陶瓷与其他艺术门类的关系,表述正确的是( )。

A.青花矾红彩始于清初,常见彩绘图案为海水行龙或海兽。

B.文学名著中的故事情节用于装饰陶瓷

C.款式多样、釉色隽美的陶瓷茶具满足了茶文化口味

D.有多种陶瓷乐器,如陶铃、陶鼓、陶铙、瓷瓯、陶腰鼓、瓷箫等

E.细腻的陶瓷釉色与优美的诗词相互融合

参考答案:BCDE

51.中国陶瓷对世界产生影响的名品是( )。

A.云南彩陶　　　B.景德镇青花瓷　　C.龙泉青瓷

D.宜兴紫砂陶　　E.德化的"中国白"瓷

参考答案:BCDE

52.下列关于青花瓷器的表述,正确的是( )。

A.产生于元代

B.瓷器画面呈现蓝色花纹

C.不含铅、镉等有毒元素,于人体健康无害

D.使中国瓷器从此进入了彩瓷时代

E.清代是青花瓷器发展最为重要的时期

参考答案:ABCD

53.下面对清代青花瓷器的表述,正确的是( )。

A.主要成就在民窑青花,以康熙民窑青花最为突出

B.发色鲜丽明爽

C.分水技法(即渲染)成熟

D.画面层次丰富、具有较强的节奏感和立体感

E.风格厚重稳健

参考答案:ABCD

54.在清代康雍乾年间,特别出名的颜色釉瓷器有( )。

A.铜红釉　　　B.三阳开泰釉　　C.窑变花釉

D.茶叶末结晶釉　　E.甜白釉

参考答案:BCD

55.下列属于中国瓷器主要产地的有( )。

A.湖南醴陵　　　B.江苏宜兴　　C.浙江龙泉

D.山东淄博　　　E.河北唐山

参考答案:ACDE

56.中国风筝制作技艺中的"四艺"是指( )。
A.扎 B.架 C.糊
D.绘 E.放

参考答案:ACDE

57.礼花在广东潮州一带又被称作为( )。
A.喜花 B.果花 C.喜笺
D.圈盆花 E.糕饼花

参考答案:BE

58.下列旅游景点中,位于加拿大温哥华的有( )。
A.狮门大桥 B.卡萨罗马城堡 C.尼亚加拉瀑布
D.斯坦利公园 E.惠斯勒滑雪场

参考答案:ADE

59.宋代官窑有( )等几种。
A.北宋官窑 B.民间官窑 C.南宋修内司官窑
D.郊坛下官窑 E.南北官窑

参考答案:ACD

60.中国唐代以黄、绿、( )等多种颜色为主要釉色的陶制品,俗称"唐三彩"。
A.蓝 B.褐 C.紫
D.红 E.黑

参考答案:ABC

61.建窑瓷器中最有名的是建盏,其名贵品种的工艺釉包括( )。
A.梨皮 B.兔毫 C.油滴
D.曜变 E.粒子

参考答案:BCD

62.中国剪纸一般用于( )。
A.张贴 B.摆衬 C.辟邪
D.刺绣底样 E.印染

参考答案:ABDE

63.下列河流中,被国际地理学界称为"世界三大强涌潮河流"的是( )。
A.恒河 B.钱塘江 C.塞纳河
D.亚马逊河 E.尼罗河

参考答案:ABD

64.下列作品中,为蜀绣代表作的有( )。
A.《猫》 B.《百鸟朝凤》 C.《熊猫》
D.《芙蓉鲤鱼》 E.《水草鲤鱼》

参考答案:CDE

65.辽宁省南临( )。
A.黄海　　　　B.渤海　　　　C.东海
D.南海　　　　E.西海

参考答案:AB

66.吉林省最具吸引力的旅游资源是( )。
A.生态旅游　　B.民俗旅游　　C.冰雪旅游
D.边境旅游　　E.海岸旅游

参考答案:ABCD

67.下列关于辽宁省特色产业的说法中,正确的是( )。
A.辽宁省是我国重要的老工业基地之一
B.辽宁省是全国工业行业最全的省份之一
C.辽宁省装备制造业比较发达
D.辽宁省缺乏原材料工业
E.辽宁省的石油化工业在全国占有重要位置

参考答案:ABCE

68.下列中国的世界遗产中,属于文化景观类别的是( )。
A.江西庐山　　B.山西五台山　　C.杭州西湖
D.新疆天山　　E.云南红河哈尼梯田

参考答案:ABCE

69.下列风物特产中,属于"荷兰四宝"的有( )。
A.风车　　　　B.郁金香　　　　C.啤酒
D.木鞋　　　　E.奶酪

参考答案:ABDE

70.下列景点中位于澳大利亚悉尼的是( )。
A.黄金海岸　　B.大堡礁　　　　C.海港大桥
D.皇家展览馆　E.悉尼歌剧院

参考答案:CE

71.南非是世界上唯一一个有三个首都的国家,这三个首都分别是( )。
A.茨瓦内　　　B.约翰内斯堡　　C.金伯利
D.布隆方丹　　E.开普敦

参考答案:ADE

72.下列景点中,位于意大利罗马的有( )。
A.圣马可广场　　B.斗兽场　　　C.花之圣母大教堂
D.许愿池(特莱维喷泉)　　　　E.比萨斜塔

参考答案:BD

73.意大利人最喜爱的三种颜色是( )。
A.绿色 B.紫色 C.黄色
D.蓝色 E.白色
参考答案:ACD

74."科隆三宝"指的是( )。
A.定制包 B.教堂 C.香水
D.狂欢节 E.汽车
参考答案:BCD

75.下列艺术作品中,珍藏于法国巴黎卢浮宫的是( )。
A.《蒙娜丽莎》 B.雕像《爱神维纳斯》
C.《胜利女神》 D.《最后的晚餐》
E.雕像《自由女神》
参考答案:ABC

76.被誉为马来西亚"三大珍宝"的是( )。
A.兰花 B.珍珠 C.巨猿
D.香料 E.蝴蝶
参考答案:ACE

77.下列城市中,属于印度著名"旅游金三角"的是( )。
A.新德里 B.孟买 C.斋浦尔
D.加尔各答 E.阿格拉
参考答案:ACE

78.下列寺院中,被称为泰国三大国宝的是( )。
A.大皇宫 B.玉佛寺 C.卧佛寺
D.金佛寺 E.郑王庙
参考答案:BCD

79.新加坡是购物天堂,其特色商品有( )。
A.鳄鱼皮制品 B.胡姬花饰品 C.螺细漆器制品
D.美珍香猪肉脯 E.肉骨茶
参考答案:ABDE

80.下列景区位于韩国首尔的是( )。
A.昌德宫 B.水原华城 C.宗庙神殿
D.梵鱼寺 E.朝鲜王朝的皇家陵墓
参考答案:ACE

81.下列曾被誉为"亚洲四小龙"的是( )。

A.韩国　　　　　B.中国香港　　　C.马来西亚

D.中国台湾　　　E.新加坡

参考答案:ABDE

82.下列著名菜品中,属于孔府菜的代表名菜是(　　)。

A.诗礼银杏　　　B.八仙过海　　　C.御笔猴头

D.怡红祝寿　　　E.老蚌怀珠

参考答案:ABC

83.下列关于啤酒的说法中,正确的是(　　)。

A.被称为"液体面包"　　　　　　B.按色泽可分为黄啤酒和黑啤酒

C.中国最著名的啤酒是青岛啤酒　　D.具有营养丰富、高热量、低酒度的特点

E.越陈越香,久藏不坏

参考答案:ABCD

84.中国"八大菜系"是在"四大菜系"的基础上增加了(　　)而形成的。

A.徽菜　　　B.湘菜　　　C.豫菜

D.闽菜　　　E.浙菜

参考答案:ABDE

85.中国"十大菜系"是在"八大菜系"的基础上增加了(　　)而形成的。

A.徽菜　　　B.湘菜　　　C.京菜

D.沪菜　　　E.浙菜

参考答案:CD

86."十二大菜系"是在"十大菜系"的基础上增加了(　　)而形成的。

A.豫菜　　　B.湘菜　　　C.京菜

D.沪菜　　　E.秦菜

参考答案:AE

87.下列菜品中,属于鲁菜代表名菜的是(　　)

A.响油鳝糊　　　B.油爆双脆　　　C.清蒸加吉鱼

D.海米珍珠笋　　E.九转大肠

参考答案:BCDE

88.花岗岩山地的石块与众不同,其景观美感特征由五种内在原因与外在条件相互作用而形成,即岩性坚硬,节理丰富,(　　)。

A.地壳抬升　　　B.流水切割　　　C.球状风化

D.岩体出露　　　E.岩体形成

参考答案:ABC

89.我国典型的花岗岩地貌名山有(　　)。

A.太行山　　　B.九华山　　　C.天柱山

D.三清山　　　　　E.井冈山

参考答案：BCDE

90.中国的火山活动可分为东西部两个活动带,其中最壮观、最著名的是（　　）。

A.五大连池火山群　　　　B.长白山火山群
C.腾冲火山群　　　　　　D.大同火山群
E.新疆火山群

参考答案：ABC

91.岩溶地貌又称喀斯特地貌,包括（　　）等主要类型。

A.石芽、石林　　B.溶蚀洼地　　C.峰丛、峰林、孤峰
D.漏斗、落水洞　E.赤壁丹崖

参考答案：ABCD

92.中国是世界上发现天坑最多的国家,下列表述正确的是（　　）。

A.重庆市奉节县的小寨天坑是目前已知的世界上最大的天坑
B.广西乐业是中国天坑分布最多、最集中的地区
C.广西桂林是中国天坑类型最多的地方
D.四川九寨天是中国天坑最美的地方
E.贵州六盘水有中国最险的天坑

参考答案：AB

93."鬼城"大致有两种类型,即（　　）。

A.干枯沙漠　　B.雅丹地貌　　C.风蚀城堡
D.连片黄沙　　E.风蚀砂石

参考答案：BC

94.我国钱塘江大潮壮观景象形成的人文原因包括（　　）。

A.八月十八出现是吉祥日
B.护堤工程
C.杭州的美誉对观潮游客吸引力的叠加
D.悠久的观潮文化对现代人的影响
E.历代著名诗人留下的观潮佳作

参考答案：BCD

95.地表水景自然色彩的成因包括（　　）。

A.地球万有引力的作用　　　　B.水体对阳光光波的物理性质
C.所在地理环境、水生植物的颜色　D.所含的泥沙、矿物结晶体的颜色
E.水体在自然界中不断运动

参考答案：BCD

96.下列中国列入《世界遗产名录》的项目名单中,属于自然遗产的有(　　)。

A.中国丹霞地貌　　　　　　　　B.云南红河哈尼梯田

C.云南澄江动物化石群　　　　　D.四川大熊猫栖息地

E.中国南方喀斯特

参考答案:ACDE

97.下列属于世界文化遗产的是(　　)。

A.四川九寨沟风景名胜区　　　　B.元上都遗址

C.云南三江并流保护区　　　　　D.青城山-都江堰

E.重庆大足石刻

参考答案:BDE

旅游法规题库

一、判断题(判断描述正确请选A,判断描述错误请选B)

1. 法制是一种治国的原则和方法。(　　)

参考答案:B

2. 全面推进依法治国,总目标是建设中国特色社会主义法治体系,建设社会主义法治国家。(　　)

参考答案:A

3. 党的二十大报告提出,坚持和发展中国特色社会主义,总任务是实现社会主义现代化和中华民族伟大复兴,在全面建成小康社会的基础上,分两步走在下个世纪中叶建成富强民主文明和谐美丽的社会主义现代化强国。(　　)

参考答案:B

4. 导游对旅游者承担侵权责任的方式主要有停止侵害、赔偿损失、赔礼道歉、支付违约金等。(　　)

参考答案:B

5. 党的领导是中国特色社会主义最本质的特征,是社会主义法治最根本的保证。(　　)

参考答案:A

6. 2020年6月29日,教育部办公厅发出通知,要求高校深入开展党史、新中国史、改革开放史、社会主义发展史学习教育活动。在高校师生、全体党员中开展党史学习与教育活动具有重大现实和深远的历史意义。(　　)

参考答案:A

7. 我们要坚持一个中国原则和"九二共识",实现祖国完全统一。(　　)

参考答案:A

8. 甲旅行社委托乙旅行社代理销售其旅游产品,乙旅行社在代理权终止后仍然以甲旅行社名义与旅游者小赵订立旅游合同,小赵有理由相信乙旅行社有代理权,那么该代理行为有效。(　　)

参考答案:A

9. 旅行社在组团时应当为参加团队旅游的旅游者投保人身意外伤害保险。(　　)

参考答案:B

10. 《中华人民共和国非物质文化遗产法》第4条规定,保护非物质文化遗产,应当注重其真实性、排他性、濒危性,有利于增强中华民族的文化认同,有利于维护国家统一和民族团结,有利于促进社会和谐和可持续发展。( )

  参考答案:B

11.国家重点保护的野生植物分为一级保护野生植物和二级保护野生植物。( )

  参考答案:A

12.某旅行社和旅游者小赵在签订旅游合同时,既约定违约金条款,又约定定金条款,那么如果旅行社违约,小赵可以要求旅行社支付违约金,同时双倍返还定金。( )

  参考答案:B

13.世界遗产是指被联合国教科文组织和世界遗产委员会确认的人类罕见的、目前无法替代的财富,是全人类公认的具有突出意义和普遍价值的文物古迹及自然景观。( )

  参考答案:A

14.2021年1月1日,《求是》杂志发表习近平2017年1月18日在联合国日内瓦总部的演讲《共同构建人类命运共同体》,其中指出,人类文明多样性是世界的基本特征,也是人类进步的源泉。( )

  参考答案:A

15.导游小张在带团前往韩国旅游过程中,发现游客老赵擅自脱离团队。对此,旅行社应当及时向公安机关、外事部门或旅游主管部门报告。( )

  参考答案:B

16.某旅行社导游小张在带团乘坐火车时,由于火车脱轨导致部分旅游者受伤,那么对于旅游者的人身损害,由铁路运输企业承担赔偿责任,旅行社承担补充赔偿责任。( )

  参考答案:B

17.处理个人信息应当遵循合法、正当、合理原则,不得过度使用。( )

  参考答案:B

18.珍贵文物中的孤品和易损品,禁止出境展览。( )

  参考答案:B

19.定金具有旅行担保功能,但不具有违约救济功能。( )

  参考答案:B

20.当旅行社违反和旅游者的包价旅游合同约定后,旅游者应当采取适当措施防止损失扩大;没有采取适当措施致使损失扩大的,不得就扩大的损失要求赔偿。( )

  参考答案:A

21.导游小张带团乘某航空公司航班飞往内地某城市途中,由于遭遇强对流天气导致飞机失控坠落,此时航空公司对每名旅游者的人身赔偿责任限额为人民币20万元。(　　)

　　参考答案:B

22.娱乐场所不得设在建筑物地下一层以下。(　　)

　　参考答案:A

23.党的十九大报告提出,我国社会主要矛盾是人民日益增长的物质文化需要和不平衡不充分发展之间的矛盾。(　　)

　　参考答案:B

24.民法是调整平等主体的自然人、法人和非法人组织之间的人身关系和财产关系。(　　)

　　参考答案:A

25.对于质量长期保持良好的食品,食品安全监督管理部门可以对其实施免检。(　　)

　　参考答案:B

26.全面推进依法治国涉及很多方面,牵引各方的总抓手就是建设中国特色社会主义法治体系。(　　)

　　参考答案:A

27.《中华人民共和国旅游法》规定,重点文物保护单位和珍贵文物收藏单位应当逐步免费开放。(　　)

　　参考答案:B

28.中华人民共和国国徽中间是五星照耀下的天安门,周围是谷穗和齿轮。(　　)

　　参考答案:A

29.自治区主席、自治州州长、自治县县长由实行区域自治的民族的公民担任,他们可以对上级的决议、决定、命令和指标变通执行或者停止执行。(　　)

　　参考答案:B

30.旅游突发事件是指突然发生、造成或者可能造成旅游者人身伤亡、财产损失,需要采取应急处置措施予以应对的自然灾害、事故灾难、公共卫生事件和社会安全事件。(　　)

　　参考答案:A

31.旅游者老孙携妻子和15周岁的儿子小孙参加团队旅游,在团队就餐期间,小孙故意移走旅游者小李的凳子,导致小李摔伤,此时应当由小孙承担对小李的侵权责任。(　　)

　　参考答案:B

32.《导游管理办法》第7条规定,导游证采用电子证件形式,由省级行政主管部门制定格式标准,由各级旅游主管部门通过全国旅游监管服务信息系统实施管理。( )

参考答案:B

33.物权是权利人依法对特定的物享有直接支配和排他的权利。( )

参考答案:A

34.某旅行社组团30人前往内地某城市旅游,其中有3名旅游者认为旅行社提供的团队餐与旅游合同约定不符,并以此为由向旅行社所在地旅游主管部门投诉该旅行社,这种投诉称为共同投诉。( )

参考答案:B

35.某旅行社未与旅游者协商,直接指定某玉器购物点,并非法获利1万元。针对这种违法行为,旅游主管部门可以对该旅行社并处2万元罚款。( )

参考答案:B

36.到2022年,实现全国文化和旅游消费场所除现金支付外,都能支持银行卡和移动支付,互联网售票和4G/5G网络覆盖率超过90%。( )

参考答案:A

37.建筑物、构筑物或者其他设施倒塌造成路过旅游者人身伤害的,由建设单位与施工单位承担连带责任。( )

参考答案:A

38.旅行社对交通、住宿等供应商未尽谨慎选择义务的,则应当承担相应的补充责任。( )

参考答案:A

39.不断壮大企业主导乡村旅游经营,吸纳当地村民参与经营或管理的"公司+农户"模式。( )

参考答案:A

40.中国共产党第二十次全国代表大会的主题是:高举中国特色社会主义伟大旗帜,全面贯彻新时代中国特色社会主义思想,弘扬伟人建党精神,自信自强、守正创新,踔厉奋发、勇毅前行,为全面建设社会主义现代化国家、全面推进中华民族伟大复兴而团结奋斗。( )

参考答案:A

41.某旅行社经营国内、入境、出境与边境旅游业务,同时在省外设立了两家分公司,经营国内与入境旅游业务,则该旅行社应当为这两家分公司增存旅游服务质量保证金70万元。( )

参考答案:B

42.16周岁以上不满18周岁的旅游者,以自己的劳动收入为主要生活来源的,视

为完全民事行为能力人。( )

参考答案：A

43.甲旅行社将旅游业务委托给乙旅行社的,应当向乙旅行社支付不低于接待和服务成本的费用。( )

参考答案：A

44.旅行社经与旅游者协商一致或者在旅行社要求下,且不影响其他旅游者行程安排,可以安排另行付费旅游项目。( )

参考答案：B

45.旅馆对旅客遗留的物品,经招领1个月无人认领的,要登记造册,送当地公安机关按拾遗物品处理。( )

参考答案：B

46.导游小李在带团服务过程中,向旅游者兜售登山雨衣。对此,由省级旅游主管部门对其所在的旅行社给予警告直至责令停业整顿。( )

参考答案：A

47.某旅游电商平台明知或者应知旅游供应商会利用平台侵害旅游者合法权益,未采取必要措施的,依法与旅游供应商承担连带法律责任。( )

参考答案：A

48.《中华人民共和国旅游法》第40条规定,导游为旅游者提供服务可以在条件允许情况下私自承揽导游和领队业务。( )

参考答案：B

49.在线旅游经营者运用大数据分析等技术手段,基于旅游者消费记录、旅游偏好等设置特殊交易条件的,属于正常经营行为。( )

参考答案：B

50.当旅游者起诉旅行社时,对其提出的诉讼请求,可以要求随团导游提供相应的证据。( )

参考答案：B

51.接到消费者赔偿要求的食品生产经营者,应当实行首付责任制,先行赔付,不得推诿。( )

参考答案：A

52.旅游者的不文明行为受到行政处罚或者法院判决承担责任的,"旅游不文明行为记录"信息保存期限为1-3年。( )

参考答案：B

53.侵权人因同一行为应当承担侵权责任和行政责任、刑事责任,侵权人的财产不足以支付的,先承担刑事责任。( )

参考答案：B

54.建筑物、构筑物或者其他设施及其搁置物、悬挂物发生脱落、坠落造成他人损害,所有人、管理人或者使用人如果不能证明自己没有过错,就应当承担侵权责任。( )

参考答案:A

55.我国国家级非物质文化遗产代表性项目名录由文化和旅游部建立。( )

参考答案:B

56.宾馆虽尽到安全保障义务,但游客仍然因第三人造成人身损害,则宾馆应当承担侵权责任。( )

参考答案:B

57.旅游主管部门是组织编制旅游发展规划的主体。( )

参考答案:B

58.景区提高门票价格应当提前3个月公布。( )

参考答案:B

59.景区在旅游者数量可能达到最大承载量时,超过最大承载量接待旅游者的,由景区主管部门责令改正,情节严重的,责令停业整顿1个月至6个月。( )

参考答案:A

60.申请和设立国家级文化生态保护区应本着少而精的原则。( )

参考答案:A

61.基于重大误解实施的民事法律行为,行为人应当请求人民法院予以撤销。( )

参考答案:B

62.与旅游服务合同相关的当事人之间确立合同关系、明确权利义务,首先适用《中华人民共和国民法典》合同编的规定,《中华人民共和国民法典》合同编没有规定的,适用《中华人民共和国旅游法》规定。( )

参考答案:B

63. 在线旅游经营者,是指从事在线旅游经营服务的自然人、法人和非法人组织,包括在线旅游平台经营者、平台内经营者以及通过自建网站、其他网络服务提供旅游服务的经营者。( )

参考答案:A

64.《最高人民法院关于民事诉讼证据的若干规定》第12条规定,以动产作为证据的,应当将原物提交人民法院。原物不宜搬移或者不宜保存的,当事人可以提供复制品、影像资料或者其他替代品。( )

参考答案:A

65.旅行社自交纳或者补足质量保证金之日起三年内未因侵害旅游者合法权益受到行政机关罚款以上处罚的,旅游行政管理部门可以将旅行社质量保证金的交存

数额降低50%。(　　)

参考答案:B

66.国家级文化生态保护区是指以保护非物质文化遗产为核心,对历史文化积淀丰厚、存续状态良好,具有重要价值和鲜明特色的文化形态进行整体性保护,并经文化和旅游部同意设立的特定区域。(　　)

参考答案:A

67.县级以上人民政府应当依法将旅游应急管理纳入政府应急管理体系,制定应急预案,建立旅游突发事件应对机制。(　　)

参考答案:A

68.旅游经营者组织、接待老年人、未成年人、残疾人等旅游者,应采取相应的安全保障措施。(　　)

参考答案:A

69.博物馆举办陈列展览,不得使用复制品、仿制品。(　　)

参考答案:B

70.旅游者王某未经导游许可,故意脱离旅游团,在自行游览过程中,不慎摔伤,王某请求旅行社赔偿损失,人民法院不予支持。(　　)

参考答案:A

71.从事食品生产、食品销售、餐饮服务以及食用农产品销售,应当依法取得许可。(　　)

参考答案:B

72.消费者因商品缺陷造成人、财产损害的,可以向销售者要求赔偿,也可以向生产者要求赔偿。(　　)

参考答案:A

二、单选题(只有一个选项是正确的,多选、错选、不选均不得分)

1.中国特色社会主义事业总体布局是(　　),战略布局是(　　)。
A."四个全面""五位一体"　　　B."五位一体""四个推进"
C."五位一体""四个全面"　　　D."四个推进""五位一体"

参考答案:C

2.2021年6月25日,习近平在主持中共中央政治局第三十一次集体学习时指出,(　　)是我们党艰辛而辉煌奋斗历程的见证,是最宝贵的精神财富。
A.红色资源　　B.红色血脉　　C.红色景点　　D.红色精神

参考答案:A

3.2020年11月24日,习近平在全国劳动模范和先进工作者表彰大会上的讲话中强调,劳模精神、劳动精神、工匠精神是以(　　)为核心的民族精神和以改革创新为核心的时代精神的生动体现,是鼓舞全党全国各族人民风雨无阻、勇敢前进的强大精神动力。

A.艰苦奋斗　　　B.百折不挠　　　C.民族振兴　　　D.爱国主义

参考答案:D

4.导游小张所带的旅游团队遭遇山洪,为保护旅游者人身和财产安全,经旅行社同意租用直升机将旅游者撤离到安全区域,为此支出的费用应当由(　　)承担。

A.旅行社承担　　　　　　　　B.旅游者承担
C.旅行社或旅游者承担　　　　D.旅行社和旅游者分担

参考答案:D

5.文化景观,是(　　)才正式确立的一种文化遗产类型,是指自然与人类的共同作品。

A.1990年　　　B.1992年　　　C.1993年　　　D.1994年

参考答案:D

6.下列合同属于无效合同的是(　　)。

A.因重大误解订立的合同

B.显失公平的合同

C.一方以乘人之危,使对方在违背真实意思的情况下订立的合同

D.一方以欺诈、胁迫的手段订立合同,损害国家利益

参考答案:D

7.风景名胜区是指具有(　　)价值,自然景观、人文景观比较集中,环境优美,可供人们游览或者进行科学、文化活动的区域。

A.观赏、文化或者历史　　　　B.观赏、文化或者科学
C.文化、艺术或者历史　　　　D.历史、文化或者科学

参考答案:B

8.旅游者小李在旅游行程结束后,向旅行社就包价旅游合同的某条款提出异议,双方各执已见,发生争议。该条款是旅行社的格式条款,那么关于该条款解释规则说法正确的是(　　)。

A.应当按照通常理解予以解释　　B.应当作出不利于旅行社的解释
C.应当采用相关非格式条款　　　D.应当作出不利于小李的解释

参考答案:A

9.中国共产党第十九次全国代表大会通过的党章修正案把(　　)确立为我们党的行动指南?

A.人类命运共同体

B.祖国统一

C.习近平新时代中国特色社会主义思想

D.科学发展观

参考答案:C

10.实现( )是近代以来中华民族最伟大的梦想。
A.生态文明建设　　　　　　　B.中华民族伟大复兴
C.社会和谐　　　　　　　　　D.祖国统一
参考答案:B

11.在国内航空运输中,对每名旅客随身携带的物品,承运人的赔偿责任限额是( )。
A.1000元　　　B.2000元　　　C.3000元　　　D.5000元
参考答案:C

12.旅游者扰乱所乘坐的高铁正常运行秩序的,处警告或者( )以下罚款。
A.100元　　　B.200元　　　C.300元　　　D.500元
参考答案:B

13.导游小张在酒店参与旅游者组织的赌博活动,经查赌资较大的,对小张处5日以下拘留或者( )以下罚款。
A.100元　　　B.200元　　　C.300元　　　D.500元
参考答案:D

14.根据《中华人民共和国出境入境管理法》第75条规定,中国公民出境后非法前往其他国家或者地区被遣返的,出入境边防检查机关应当收缴其出境入境证件,出境入境证件签发机关自其被遣返之日起( )不予签发出境入境证件。
A.6个月至1年以内　　　　　　B.1年至3年以内
C.6个月至3年以内　　　　　　D.6个月至2年以内
参考答案:C

15.在自然保护区中,可进入参观考察、旅游的区域是( )。
A.核心区　　　B.缓冲区　　　C.保护区　　　D.实验区
参考答案:D

16.某旅行社导游小张未经旅游者同意,擅自将团队带入行程单以外的某购物店购买商品,那么旅游者有权在( )要求旅行社为其办理退货并先行垫付退货货款。
A.购买商品后30日内　　　　　B.购买商品后30个工作日内
C.旅游行程结束后30日内　　　D.旅游行程结束后30个工作日内
参考答案:C

17.某旅行社的导游小张在带领旅游者游玩古镇讲解时,由于未尽到安全提示义务,导致旅游者小赵被门槛绊倒受伤,那么小赵( )。
A.只能要求旅行社承担违约责任
B.只能要求旅行社承担侵权责任

C.可以要求旅行社承担违约责任或者侵权责任

D.可以要求小张承担违约责任或者侵权责任

参考答案:C

18.在全面建成小康社会的基础上,再奋斗15年,基本实现( )。

  A.四个现代化   B.社会主义现代化

  C.富强民主新社会   D.世界强国目标

参考答案:B

19.《中华人民共和国消费者权益保护法》第7至15条规定了消费者的( )权利。

  A.9项   B.10项   C.11项   D.12项

参考答案:A

20.党的二十大报告提出,全面建成社会主义现代化强国,总的战略安排是分两步走:从二〇二〇年到( )年基本实现社会主义现代化;从( )年到21世纪中叶把我国建成富强民主文明和谐美丽的社会主义现代化强国。

  A.二〇二五 二〇二五   B.二〇三〇 二〇三〇

  C.二〇二五 二〇三〇   D.二〇三五 二〇三五

参考答案:D

21.旅行社投保旅行社责任保险,由旅行社与保险公司协商确定责任赔偿限额,但每人人身伤亡责任限额不得低于( )。

  A.10万元   B.15万元   C.20万元   D.30万元

参考答案:C

22.不可移动文物根据( ),可以分为全国重点、省级、市县级文物保护单位。

  A.历史、艺术和科学价值   B.历史、艺术和文化价值

  C.观赏、文化和科学价值   D.观赏、文化和历史价值

参考答案:A

23.要以培养担当民族复兴大任的时代新人为着眼点,把( )融入社会发展各方面,转化为人们的情感认同和行为习惯。

  A.社会主义核心价值观   B.做"四有新人"

  C.马克思主义思想   D.红色文化

参考答案:A

24."旅游不文明行为记录"信息保存期限最多为( )。

  A.1年   B.2年   C.3年   D.5年

参考答案:D

25.2005年8月15日,在( ),习近平同志创造性地提出"绿水青山就是金山银山"的重要理念。

A.浙江安吉余村　　　　　　B.湖南湘西十八洞村
C.安徽金寨大湾村　　　　　D.广东茂名柏桥村
参考答案:A

26.《中华人民共和国国歌法》规定,在公共场合,故意篡改国歌歌词、曲谱,以歪曲、贬损方式奏唱国歌,或者以其他方式侮辱国歌的,由公安机关处以警告或者(　　)以下拘留;构成犯罪的,依法追究刑事责任。
A.三日　　　B.五日　　　C.十五日　　　D.三十日
参考答案:C

27.根据可能对旅游者造成的危害程度、紧急程度和发展态势,风险提示级别分为四级,其中(　　)为特别严重级别。
A.一级　　　B.二级　　　C.三级　　　D.四级
参考答案:A

28.总书记赋予强军目标新的内涵,即实现强军目标,要把人民军队全面建成(　　)。
A.听党指挥能打胜仗的军队　　B.现代化军队
C.世界一流军队　　　　　　　D.战无不胜的军队
参考答案:C

29.必须继续坚持(　　)方针,推动两岸关系和平发展,推进祖国和平统一进程。
A."不承诺放弃使用武力"　　　B."一个中国"
C."九二共识"　　　　　　　　D."和平统一、一国两制"
参考答案:D

30.国家对食品生产经营实行许可制度,食品生产经营许可的有效期为(　　)。
A.1年　　　B.2年　　　C.3年　　　D.5年
参考答案:D

31.某旅行社在出发前7日向旅游者提出因团队人数未达到约定人数,需要解除合同,该团队是境内旅游团,那么旅行社应当支付旅游费用总额的(　　)作为违约金。
A.5%　　　B.10%　　　C.15%　　　D.20%
参考答案:B

32.二十大报告强调,"坚定不移全面(　　),深入推进新时代党的建设新的伟大工程"。
A.加强政治建设　　B.从严治党　　C.反腐倡廉　　D.管党治党
参考答案:B

33.某旅行社在提供组团旅游服务时有欺诈旅游者的行为,那么该旅行社应当按照旅游者的要求增加赔偿其受到的损失,增加赔偿的金额为旅游者支付旅游服务费用的(　　)。

A.1倍　　　　B.2倍　　　　C.3倍　　　　D.4倍

参考答案:C

34.设立国家级风景名胜区,由(　　)批准公布。

A.国务院环境保护主管部门　　　　B.国务院旅游主管部门

C.国务院建设主管部门　　　　　　D.国务院

参考答案:D

35.对于国家重点保护野生动物名录,由国务院野生动物保护主管部门组织科学评估后制定,并每(　　)根据评估情况确定对名录进行调整。

A.1年　　　　B.2年　　　　C.3年　　　　D.5年

参考答案:D

36.普通护照可以由公安部出入境管理机构或者公安部委托的(　　)签发。

A.县级以上公安机关出入境管理机构

B.市级以上公安机关出入境管理机构

C.县级或市级以上公安机关出入境管理机构

D.省级公安机关出入境管理机构

参考答案:A

37.在交通不便的地区,不能按期签发护照的,经护照签发机关负责人批准,签发时间可以延长至(　　)。

A.7日　　　　B.10日　　　　C.20日　　　　D.30日

参考答案:D

38.依据《中华人民共和国民法典》的规定,(　　)以上的未成年人为限制民事行为人。

A.8周岁　　　　B.10周岁　　　　C.16周岁　　　　D.18周岁

参考答案:A

39.旅游经营者给予或者收受贿赂的,由(　　)依照有关法律、法规的规定处罚。

A.旅游主管部门　　　　　　B.工商行政管理部门

C.税务主管部门　　　　　　D.质量监督管理部门

参考答案:B

40.由于履行辅助人的原因造成旅游者人身损害、财产损失的,旅游者(　　)。

A.只能要求组团社承担赔偿责任

B.只能要求履行辅助人承担赔偿责任

C.只能要求组团社、履行辅助人其中一方承担赔偿责任

D.可以要求组团社承担赔偿责任,也可以要求履行辅助人承担赔偿责任

参考答案:D

41.党的二十大报告指出加快建设( ),扎实推动乡村产业、人才、文化、生态、组织振兴。

A.文化强国　　　B.人才强国　　　C.农业强国　　　D.教育强国

参考答案:C

42.导游小张在带团过程中擅自决定在行程单上减少一处游览景点,该景点门票价格为80元,旅游费用总额2000元,那么旅行社应当向旅游者赔偿( )。

A.80元　　　　B.100元　　　　C.160元　　　　D.200元

参考答案:C

43.小赵因临时接受出差任务,将与某旅行社签订的休闲农庄一日游旅游合同中自身的权利义务转让给其父亲老赵,旅行社未提出异议,则老赵在旅游行程中增加的费用由( )承担。

A.小赵　　　　B.老赵　　　　C.小赵或老赵　　　　D.小赵和老赵

参考答案:D

44.甲旅行社未经旅游者同意,擅自将旅游者与乙旅行社的旅游者合并在一起拼团,并由乙旅行社组团,那么甲旅行社应当向旅游者支付旅游费用总额( )的违约金。

A.5%　　　　B.10%　　　　C.20%　　　　D.25%

参考答案:D

45.到( ),"互联网+旅游"融合更加深化,以互联网为代表的信息技术成为旅游业发展的重要动力。

A.2030年　　　B.2022年　　　C.2025年　　　D.2035年

参考答案:C

46.下列关于规范导游专座的说法正确的是( )。

A.导游专座应当设置在旅游大巴驾驶员后第一排乘客座椅靠通道侧位置

B.已设置折叠座椅的旅游大巴可以在合理范围内继续供导游使用

C.导游应自觉系好安全带,不得站立讲解

D.旅游大巴在旅游服务过程中,应当配备印有"导游专座"字样的座套

参考答案:D

47.某旅行社组团到马尔代夫旅游,但是最终未达到约定出团人数,此时可以解除旅游合同,但是至少应当提前( )通知旅游者。

A.7天　　　　B.10天　　　　C.15天　　　　D.30天

参考答案:D

48.根据《最高人民法院关于民事诉讼证据的若干规定》,下列关于电子数据和

视听资料的说法,正确的选项是( )。

A.电子数据的制作者制作的与原件一致的副本不能视为电子数据的原件

B.当事人以视听资料作为证据的,必须提供存储该视听资料的原始载体

C.当事人以电子数据作为证据的,必须提供原件

D.网页、博客、微博客等网络平台发布的信息可以认定为电子证据

参考答案:D

49.景区、住宿经营者将其部分经营项目或者场地交由他人从事住宿、餐饮、购物、游览、娱乐、旅游交通等经营的,应当对实际经营者的经营行为给旅游者造成的损害承担( )。

A.违约责任 B.侵权责任 C.补充责任 D.连带责任

参考答案:D

50.旅行社提供旅游服务有欺诈行为的,应当按照旅游者的要求增加赔偿其受到的损失,增加赔偿的金额最低为( )。

A.100元 B.200元 C.500元 D.1000元

参考答案:C

51.根据《旅游安全管理办法》规定,旅游突发事件发生在境外的,旅游团队的领队应当立即向( )、中国驻当地使领馆或者政府派出机构,以及旅行社负责人报告。

A.当地警方 B.人民政府

C.旅游行政管理部门 D.国务院旅游行政管理部门

参考答案:A

52.具有出境旅游经营资格的旅行社,每设立一个经营国内、入境与出境旅游业务的分公司,则应当向其旅游服务质量保证金账户增存( )。

A.20万元 B.30万元 C.35万元 D.40万元

参考答案:C

53.歌舞娱乐场所的包厢、包间内不得设置( ),并应当安装展现室内整体环境的( )门窗。包厢、包间的门不得有( )装置。

A.内锁、透明、通道 B.隔断、透明、内锁

C.通道、封闭、控制 D.隔断、封闭、内锁

参考答案:B

54.旅游者小赵在客机飞行过程中与小王发生争执,进而扭打在一起,扰乱了空中交通秩序,情节较重,那么由公安部门对小赵和小王处以( )拘留。

A.10日以下 B.15日以下

C.5日以上10日以下 D.10日以上15日以下

参考答案:C

55.按照突发事件发生的紧急承担、发展态势和可能造成的危害程度分为一级、二级、三级和四级,分别用( )标示。
　　A.红色、橙色、黄色、蓝色　　　　　B.红色、橙色、蓝色、黄色
　　C.橙色、红色、黄色、蓝色　　　　　D.红色、黄色、橙色、蓝色
　　参考答案:A

56."十四五"时期健全现代文化产业体系应坚持把( )放在首位。
　　A.文化效益　　　B.经济效益　　　C.社会效益　　　D.市场效益
　　参考答案:C

57.在旅游职业道德中,( )是集体主义原则在导游工作中的具体体现。
　　A.克勤克俭、游客至上　　　　　B.遵纪守法、敬业爱岗
　　C.团结协作、顾全大局　　　　　D.耐心细致、文明礼貌
　　参考答案:C

58.根据《旅游安全管理办法》规定,( )应当承担旅游安全的主体责任,加强安全管理,建立、健全安全管理制度,关注安全风险预警和提示,妥善应对旅游突发事件。
　　A.旅游行政管理部门　　　　　B.人民政府
　　C.旅游经营者　　　　　　　　D.国务院授权有关部门
　　参考答案:C

59.受到吊销旅行社业务经营许可证处罚的旅行社有关管理人员,自处罚之日起( )内不得从事旅行社业务。
　　A.1年　　　　B.2年　　　　C.3年　　　　D.5年
　　参考答案:C

60.2023年是习近平总书记提出"构建人类命运共同体"理念的( )周年。
　　A.8　　　　B.10　　　　C.12　　　　D.15
　　参考答案:B

61.《关于以标准化促进餐饮节约反对餐饮浪费的意见》指出,研制外卖餐饮( )加工和配送标准,鼓励网络餐饮数字化、标准化建设。
　　A.节约　　　B.绿色　　　C.环保　　　D.科学
　　参考答案:B

62.旅游者小赵在团队自由活动期间,前往某海鲜餐饮店就餐发生食物中毒,那么小赵除要求赔偿损失外,还可以向该餐厅要求支付( )的赔偿金。
　　A.价款1倍或损失3倍　　　　　B.价款3倍或损失10倍
　　C.损失1倍或价款3倍　　　　　D.损失3倍或价款10倍
　　参考答案:D

63.隐私是自然人的私人生活安宁和不愿为他人知晓的私密空间、私密活动和( )。

　　A.私密照片　　B.私密财产　　C.私密习惯　　D.私密信息

　　参考答案:D

64.依据《在线旅游经营服务管理暂行规定》,平台内经营者与旅游者发生旅游纠纷的,平台经营者应当积极协助旅游者维护合法权益。鼓励( )先行赔付。

　　A.平台内经营者　　　　　　　B.平台经营者
　　C.平台内经营者和平台经营者　　D.平台内经营者或平台经营者

　　参考答案:B

65.根据《旅行社责任保险管理办法》规定,保险责任中对导游或者领队人员的责任仅限于( )所应当承担的赔偿责任。

　　A.人身伤亡　　B.财产损失　　C.精神伤害　　D.心理伤害

　　参考答案:A

66.旅游者钱某一家3人在就餐后发生呕吐、腹泻,经查是由于酒店餐厅提供的食品变质所致,该餐厅是酒店承包给某餐饮公司经营,那么下列关于酒店的法律责任说法正确的是( )。

　　A.酒店不承担法律责任　　　　B.酒店对钱某一家承担主要责任
　　C.酒店对钱某一家承担补充责任　　D.酒店对钱某一家承担连带责任

　　参考答案:D

67.包价旅游合同是指旅行社预先安排行程,提供或者通过履行辅助人提供交通、住宿、餐饮、游览、导游或者领队等( )以上旅游服务,旅游者以总价支付旅游费用的合同。

　　A.1项　　B.2项　　C.3项　　D.4项

　　参考答案:B

68.( )主要签发给中华人民共和国驻外使馆、领馆或者联合国、联合国专门机构以及其他政府间国际组织中工作的中国政府派出的职员及其随行配偶、未成年子女等。

　　A.普通护照　　B.公务护照　　C.外交护照　　D.其他护照

　　参考答案:C

69.按照我国民航规定,旅客行李在航空运输中遗失,最迟不得超过从行李应当交付收件人之日起( )天以内提出索赔要求。

　　A.7　　B.21　　C.28　　D.35

　　参考答案:B

70.下半旗时,应当先将国旗升至杆顶,然后降至旗顶与旗杆之间的距离为旗杆全长的( )处。

A.二分之一　　　B.三分之一　　　C.四分之一　　　D.五分之一

参考答案：B

71.因保护他人民事权益使自己受到损害的,由侵权人承担民事责任,受益人(　　)。

A.可以给予适当补偿　　　　　B.应当给予适当补偿
C.可以给予全部补偿　　　　　D.应当给予全部补偿

参考答案：A

72.造成或者可能造成人员死亡(含失踪)30人以上或者重伤(　　)以上,构成特别重大旅游突发事件。

A.10人　　　B.30人　　　C.50人　　　D.100人

参考答案：D

73.要充分发挥(　　)等旅游服务热线和旅游投诉举报网络平台作用,鼓励社会各界积极提供各类违法违规行为线索。

A.12301　　　B.12110　　　C.12114　　　D.95580

参考答案：A

74.涉及遗产继承、接受赠予等胎儿利益保护的,胎儿(　　)。

A.具有民事权利能力　　　　　B.具有部分民事权利
C.视为具有民事权利能力　　　D.无民事行为能力

参考答案：C

75.第十二届全国人民代表大会常务委员会第十一次会议决定,我国国家"宪法日"为(　　)。

A.6月30日　　　B.10月30日　　　C.12月4日　　　D.12月30日

参考答案：C

76.根据我国宪法关于公民基本权利的规定,下列说法正确的是(　　)。

A.我国公民在年老、疾病或者遭受自然灾害时有获得物质帮助的权利
B.我国公民被剥夺政治权利的,其出版自由也被剥夺
C.我国公民有信仰宗教与公开传教的自由
D.我国公民有任意休息的权利

参考答案：B

77.为了公共利益的需要,依照法律规定的权限和程序征收、征用不动产或者动产的,应当给予公平、合理的(　　)。

A.赔偿　　　B.补偿　　　C.赔偿或补偿　　　D.赔偿和补偿

参考答案：B

78.根据《中华人民共和国旅游法》规定,(　　)建立旅游目的地安全风险提示制度。

A.国家 B.旅游主管部门

C.行政管理部门 D.国务院旅游主管部门

参考答案:A

79.当事人因重大误解而订立的合同属于( )。

A.无效合同 B.可变更可撤销合同

C.未生效合同 D.效力待定的合同

参考答案:B

80.根据《中华人民共和国民法典》规定,以下不属于违约责任承担方式的是( )。

A.继续履行 B.采取补救措施 C.支付违约金 D.赔偿精神损失

参考答案:D

81.经营境内旅游业务、入境旅游业务和出境旅游业务的旅行社应当在指定的银行存入旅游服务质量保证金( )。

A.20万元 B.120万元 C.140万元 D.160万元

参考答案:C

82.旅行社责任保险的保险期间是( )。

A.6个月 B.1年 C.2年 D.3年

参考答案:B

83.饭店在接待境外旅客住宿时,应当在( )内向当地公安机关报送住宿登记表。

A.12小时 B.24小时 C.36小时 D.48小时

参考答案:B

84.没有法定的或者约定的义务,为避免他人利益受损失而进行管理的人,有权请求受益人偿还由此支出的( )费用。

A.合理 B.合法 C.必要 D.适当

参考答案:C

85.乘客在航空器起飞、着陆、滑行以及飞行颠簸过程中擅自离开座位或开启行李架,可能面临( )元的罚款。

A.200—500 B.300—600 C.500—5000 D.500—10000

参考答案:D

86.下列关于国家机构的职权说法正确的是( )。

A.全国人大有权选举产生全国人大常委会委员长、副委员长、国家主席、副主席、国务院总理、副总理

B.国家主席有权决定战争和和平问题

C.国务院有权批准省、自治区、直辖市的建置和区域划分

D.国务院有权依照法律决定省、自治区、直辖市范围内部分地区进入紧急状态

参考答案:D

87.《中华人民共和国旅游法》第105条第2款规定,景区在旅游者数量可能达到( )时,未依照本法规定公告或者未向当地人民政府报告,未及时采取疏导、分流等措施,或者超过最大承载量接待旅游者的,由景区主管部门责令改正,情节严重的,责令停业整顿一个月至六个月。

   A.最大承载量   B.一定人数   C.核定人数   D.最大接待量

参考答案:A

88.旅行社应当与其聘用的导游( )。

   A.依法订立劳动合同,按规定支付劳动报酬和缴纳社保费,并为其投保人身意外险

   B.依法订立劳动合同,支付劳动报酬,缴纳社会保险费用

   C.依法签订用工合同,支付不低于当地最低工资标准的报酬,缴纳社会保险费用

   D.依法签订劳动合同,支付劳动报酬,并为其投保人身意外险

参考答案:B

89.履行费用的负担不明确,同时不能达成补充协议的,则( )。

   A.由享有权利一方负担

   B.由履行义务一方负担

   C.由享有权利一方或履行义务一方负担

   D.由享有权利一方和履行义务一方共同负担

参考答案:B

90.申请经营国内旅游业务和入境旅游业务的,受理申请的旅游主管部门应当自受理申请之日起( )内做出许可或者不予许可的决定。

   A.7个工作日   B.10个工作日   C.20个工作日   D.30个工作日

参考答案:C

91.造成或者可能造成人员死亡(含失踪)3人以下或者重伤10人以下的情形属于( )。

   A.特别重大旅游突发事件   B.重大旅游突发事件

   C.较大旅游突发事件   D.一般旅游突发事件

参考答案:D

92.因自愿实施紧急救助行为造成受助人损害的,救助人( )。

   A.不承担民事责任   B.应当承担全部民事责任

   C.应当承担部分民事责任   D.可以免除民事责任

参考答案:A

93.根据《最高人民法院关于审理旅游纠纷案件适用法律若干问题的规定》,下列关于旅游者的权利表述正确的是( )。

A.旅游者可以随意转让合同

B.旅游行程开始后旅游者单方解除合同,则无权请求旅游经营者退还尚未实际发生的费用

C.旅游者有权要求退回因拒绝旅游经营者安排的购物活动被增收的费用

D.旅游者可以要求旅游经营者同时承担违约责任和侵权责任

参考答案:C

94.下列不属于合同基本条款的是( )。

A.标的　　　　B.质量　　　　C.价款　　　　D.保密条款

参考答案:D

95.在国内航空运输中,承运人对每名旅客的人身赔偿责任限额为( )。

A.20万元　　　B.30万元　　　C.40万元　　　D.50万元

参考答案:C

三、多选题（至少有两个选项是正确的,多选、少选、错选、不选均不得分）

1.某旅行社导游小王在带团到国内某地转机前往旅游目的地时,机场发布消息称因交通管制延迟该航班起飞时间,从而造成旅游者滞留,那么下列说法错误的是( )。

A.空中交通管制属于不可抗力

B.空中交通管制属于意外事件

C.旅游者因滞留增加的食宿费用,由旅行社与旅游者分担

D.旅游者因滞留增加的返程费用,由旅行社或旅游者承担

E.旅游者因滞留增加的返程费用,由旅行社与旅游者分担

参考答案:BCD

2.在旅行社提供的格式合同中,下列哪些格式条款是无效的?( )

A.免除旅行社责任

B.加重旅游者责任

C.因过失造成旅游者财产损失的,旅行社可以免责

D.因故意造成旅游者财产损失的,旅行社可以免责

E.排除旅游者主要权利

参考答案:ABDE

3.下列选项中,关于升挂国旗的说法中,以下正确的是( )。

A.中央人民政府驻香港特别行政区有关机构、中央人民政府驻澳门特别行政区有关机构应当在工作日升挂国旗

B.图书馆、博物馆、文化馆、美术馆、科技馆、纪念馆、展览馆、体育馆、青少年宫等公共文化体育设施应当每日升挂、悬挂国旗

C.国庆节、国际劳动节、元旦、春节和国家宪法日等重要节日、纪念日,各级国家机关、各人民团体以及大型广场、公园等公共活动场所应当升挂国旗

D.民族自治地方在民族自治地方成立纪念日和主要传统民族节日应当升挂国旗

E.国家倡导公民和组织在任何场合使用国旗及其图案,表达爱国情感

参考答案:ABCD

4."旅游不文明行为记录"信息内容包括(　　)。

A.不文明行为当事人的姓名、性别、籍贯

B.不文明行为当事人的工作单位

C.不文明行为的具体表现

D.不文明行为所造成的影响和后果

E.不文明行为的记录期限

参考答案:CDE

5.导游人员调整或者变更接待计划的条件包括(　　)。

A.在引导旅游者旅行、游览过程中

B.遇到可能危及旅游者财产安全的紧急情形

C.征得多数旅游者的同意

D.征得旅行社同意

E.立即报告旅行社

参考答案:ACE

6.《中华人民共和国香港特别行政区维护国家安全法》第10条规定,香港特别行政区应当通过(　　)等开展国家安全教育,提高香港特别行政区居民的国家安全意识和守法意识。

A.学校　　　　B.国际组织　　　C.媒体

D.网络　　　　E.社会团体

参考答案:ACDE

7.下列选项中,关于奏唱国歌的场合,正确的包括(　　)

A.全国人民代表大会开闭幕　　　B.宪法宣誓仪式

C.私人丧事活动　　　　　　　　D.重大外交活动

E.重大体育赛事

参考答案:ABDE

8.《中华人民共和国旅游法》第80条规定,旅游经营者应当以明示的方式事先向旅游者作出说明或者警示的事项有(　　)

A.正确使用相关设施、设备的方法

B.必要的安全防范和应急措施

C.未向旅游者开放的经营、服务场所和设施、设备

D.不适宜参加相关活动的群体

E.可能危及旅游者人身、财产安全的其他情形

参考答案:ABCDE

9.导游小张在带团游览一处地势险峻的景点时,众人争相拍照,小张未提示相关安全注意事项。该团旅游者李某拍照时不慎将自拍杆碰到孙某导致其摔伤,下面说法正确的是( )。

A.旅行社对孙某损害结果不承担赔偿责任

B.李某应当对孙某承担赔偿责任

C.旅行社应当对孙某承担补充赔偿责任

D.小张应当对孙某承担侵权责任

E.李某应当对孙某承担补充赔偿责任

参考答案:BC

10.人民行使国家权力的机关是( )。

A.中国人民政治协商会议　　　　B.地方各级人民政治协商会议

C.全国人民代表大会　　　　　　D.中央及地方各级人民政府

E.地方各级人民代表大会

参考答案:CE

11.下列选项中,关于悬挂和使用国徽的说法中,正确的包括( )

A.北京天安门城楼、人民大会堂应当悬挂国徽

B.国家驻外使馆、领馆和其他外交代表机构应当在其网站首页显著位置使用国徽图案

C.公民不可以佩戴国徽徽章

D.国家出版的法律、法规正式版本的封面

E.国徽及其图案不得用于商标、授予专利权的外观设计、商业广告

参考答案:ABDE

12.《中华人民共和国英雄烈士保护法》第25条规定,对侵害英雄烈士的( )的行为,英雄烈士的近亲属可以依法向人民法院提起诉讼。

A.姓名　　　　B.籍贯　　　　C.肖像

D.名誉　　　　E.荣誉

参考答案:ACDE

13.《中华人民共和国宪法》规定的公民的基本义务包括( )。

A.劳动　　　　B.受教育　　　　C.抚育子女、赡养父母

D.旅游　　　　　E.创新创业

参考答案:ABC

14.《中华人民共和国宪法》规定的公民的基本权利包括(　　)。

A.劳动　　　　　B.受教育

C.平等权　　　　D.政治权利和自由权

E.创新创业

参考答案:ABCD

15.导游和领队在带团过程中应当注重证据的保留,根据《民事诉讼法》规定,证据的类型包括(　　)。

A.当事人的陈述　B.律师代理意见　C.书证

D.视听资料　　　E.电子数据

参考答案:ACDE

16.参加导游资格考试成绩合格,(　　)的人员可以申请取得导游证。

A.与旅行社订立劳动合同　　　B.与旅行社订立劳务合同

C.在导游服务公司注册　　　　D.在导游协会注册

E.在旅游协会的导游分会注册

参考答案:ADE

17.根据《宗教事务条例》,宗教事务管理坚持(　　)的原则。

A.保护合法　　　B.制止非法　　　C.打击违法

D.抵御渗透　　　E.遏制极端

参考答案:ABDE

18.根据《旅游安全管理办法》规定,旅游经营者的安全义务有(　　)。

A.安全防范、管理和保障义务

B.建立旅游目的地安全风险提示制度的义务

C.安全救助、处置和报告义务

D.安全说明或警示义务

E.统计分析本行政区域内发生旅游安全事故情况的义务

参考答案:ACD

19.旅游投诉的地域管辖标准包括(　　)。

A.旅游合同签订地　　　　　B.旅游合同履行地

C.投诉者所在地　　　　　　D.被投诉者所在地

E.损害行为发生地

参考答案:ADE

20.旅游服务质量保证金的使用情形包括(　　)。

A.用于旅游者权益损害的赔偿

B.垫付旅游者人身安全遇到危险时紧急救助的费用

C.发生不可抗力造成旅游者滞留的食宿费用

D.旅行社因解散、破产或其他原因造成旅游者预交旅游费用损失的

E.人民法院判决、裁定认定旅行社损害旅游者权益但旅行社拒绝或无力赔偿的

参考答案:ABDE

21.《国务院安全生产委员会成员单位安全生产工作职责分工》中落实了国务院旅游主管部门的安全生产工作职责分工,主要包括( )。

A.负责旅游安全监督管理工作

B.会同国家有关部门对旅游安全实行综合治理

C.负责全国旅游安全管理的宣传、教育、培训工作

D.负责旅游行业安全生产统计分析

参考答案:ABCD

22.下列关于设立博物馆必须具备的条件的说法,正确的包括( )。

A.固定的馆址　　　　　　B.足够多的藏品

C.大量的专业技术人员　　D.必要的办馆资金

E.确保观众人身安全的设施、制度及应急预案

参考答案:ADE

23.依据《风景名胜区条例》规定,在风景名胜区内禁止的活动包括( )。

A.破坏景观、植被和地形地貌的活动

B.修建储存爆炸性、易燃性、放射性、毒害性、腐蚀性物品的设施

C.在景物或者设施上刻画、涂污

D.举办大型游乐活动

E.乱扔垃圾

参考答案:ABCE

24.在订立包价旅游合同时,旅行社应当向旅游者告知的事项包括( )。

A.包价旅游合同的成本和费用构成

B.旅游活动中的安全注意事项

C.旅行社依法可以减免责任的信息

D.旅游者应当注意的旅游目的地相关法律、法规和风俗习惯、宗教禁忌

E.旅游者不适合参加旅游活动的情形

参考答案:BCDE

25.国家级文化生态保护区建设应坚持( )的理念。

A.保护优先　　B.合理开发　　C.整体保护

D.民众受益　　E.见人见物见生活

参考答案:ACE

26.《中华人民共和国宪法》规定的劳动保障制度包括(　　)。

A.国家规定职工的工作时间和休假制度

B.坚持按劳分配为主体,多种分配方式并存的分配制度

C.国家规定企事业职工的退休制度

D.国家培养为社会主义服务的各种专业人才

E.国家通过各种途径,创造劳动就业条件,加强劳动保护,提高劳动报酬和福利待遇

参考答案:ABE

27.国家对消费者权益的保护主要通过以下途径(　　)。

A.立法保护　　B.行政保护　　C.司法保护

D.舆论保护　　E.组织保护

参考答案:ABC

28.《中华人民共和国突发事件应对法》第3条第2款规定,按照社会危害程度、影响范围等因素将自然灾害、事故灾难、公共卫生事件分为(　　)四级。

A.重大　　B.特别重大　　C.较大　　D.一般

参考答案:ABCD

29.旅行社责任保险的保险范围具体包括(　　)。

A.因旅行社疏忽或过失应当承担赔偿责任的

B.因旅行社故意或重大过失应当承担赔偿责任的

C.因发生意外事故旅行社应当承担赔偿责任的

D.因发生不可抗力旅行社应当承担赔偿责任的

E.国务院旅游主管部门规定的其他情形

参考答案:ACE

30.导游小张在带团前往欧洲旅游时,旅游团集体遭到抢劫。此时小张应当向(　　)报告。

A.旅游主管部门　　B.公安机关　　C.相关驻外机构

D.当地警方　　E.中国驻该国使领馆

参考答案:ACDE

31.非公有制经济包括(　　)。

A.个体经济　　B.集体经济　　C.私营经济

D.外资经济　　E.股份制经济

参考答案:ACD

32.出入国(边)境应当遵守相关法律规定,中国公民不准出境的情形包括(　　)。

A.未持有效出境入境证件或者拒绝、逃避接受边防检查的

B.被判处刑罚尚未执行完毕或者属于刑事案件被告人、犯罪嫌疑人的

C.有未了结的民事案件,人民法院决定不准出境的

D.可能危害国家安全和利益,国务院有关主管部门决定不准出境的

E.不能保障在国外所需费用的

参考答案:ABCD

33.导游小张在带团过程中,擅自变更行程单中的接待计划,那么下列关于对小张的行政处罚正确的是( )。

  A.对小张责令改正   B.没收小张违法所得

  C.暂扣小张导游证1至3个月   D.暂扣小张导游证3至6个月

  E.情节严重的,吊销小张导游证

参考答案:ADE

34.民事法律行为的生效要件包括( )。

  A.行为人具有完全民事行为能力   B.行为人具有相应的民事行为能力

  C.意思表示真实   D.不违反法律、行政法规的强制性规定

  E.不违背公序良俗

参考答案:BCDE

35.债权人可以将合同的权利全部或者部分转让给第三人,但是也有除外情形,这些除外情形包括( )。

  A.根据合同性质不得转让   B.根据合同形式不得转让

  C.根据合同履行时间不得转让   D.按照当事人约定不得转让

  E.依照法律规定不得转让

参考答案:ADE

36.甲旅行社将旅游业务委托给乙旅行社的法定要求包括( )。

  A.接受委托的乙旅行社具有相应的资质

  B.甲旅行社征得旅游者的同意

  C.甲旅行社书面告知旅游者

  D.甲旅行社与乙旅行社签订委托合同

  E.乙旅行社与旅游者签订包价旅游合同

参考答案:ABD

37.小张使用假导游证在某景区门口收客带团,对此,下列关于旅游主管部门对小张实施的行政处罚说法正确的有( )。

  A.责令改正   B.没收违法所得

  C.处1000元以上1万元以下罚款   D.处1000元以上3万元以下罚款

  E.情节严重的,暂扣或吊销导游证

参考答案:ABC

38.以习近平新时代中国特色社会主义思想为指导,按照( )的发展理念,着力解决影响广大游客旅游体验的重点问题和主要矛盾,推动旅游业高质量发展。

A.创新　　　　B.协调　　　　C.绿色

D.开放　　　　E.共享

参考答案:ABCDE

39.保健食品的标签、说明书应当载明的信息包括( )。

A.适宜人群　　　　　　　　B.不适宜人群

C.声明"本品可以代替药物"　　D.功效成分或者标志性成分

E.功效成分或者标志性成分含量

参考答案:ABDE

40.导游小张为旅游者代管的行李遭到毁损、灭失,此时旅行社应当承担赔偿责任,但是也有一些除外情形,这些除外情形包括( )。

A.损失是由于旅游者未听从小张事先提示将现金、贵重物品随时携带而造成的

B.损失是由于不可抗力、意外事件造成的

C.损失是由于旅游者的过错造成的

D.损失是由于小张未尽到安全保障义务,由第三人造成的

E.损失是由于物品的自然属性造成的

参考答案:ABCE

41.旅行社责任保险的责任赔偿限额由旅行社与保险公司根据旅行社( )因素来协商确定的。

A.经营范围　　B.经营规模　　C.员工人数

D.风险管控能力　　E.自身需要

参考答案:ABDE

42.债权是因( ),权利人请求特定义务人为或者不为一定行为的权利。

A.合同　　　B.侵权行为　　C.无因管理　　D.不当得利

E.法律法规的其他规定

参考答案:ABCD

43.纳入"旅游不文明行为记录"的旅游从业人员行为主要包括( )。

A.强迫旅游者交易　　　　B.不尊重旅游者的饮食习惯

C.与旅游者争吵　　　　　D.向旅游者宣传迷信思想

E.殴打旅游者

参考答案:ADE

44.旅游主管部门对下列哪些人员不予颁发导游证( )。

A.无民事行为能力人　　　　B.限制民事行为能力人

C.患有传染性疾病的人　　　D.受过刑事处罚的人

E.被吊销导游证的人

参考答案:ABCE

45.总书记强调乡村振兴是包括( )的全面振兴。

A.产业振兴　　　B.人才振兴　　　C.文化振兴

D.生态振兴　　　E.组织振兴

参考答案:ABCDE

46.根据《中华人民共和国食品安全法》规定,保健食品声称保健功能,应当具有科学依据,不得对人体产生( )危害。

A.急性　　　　　B.亚急性　　　　C.慢性

D.生物性　　　　E.化学性

参考答案:ABC

47.旅游者小赵游览某景区时,故意在国家保护的文物上刻画"到此一游"。对此,由公安机关对小赵实施治安管理处罚说法正确的有( )。

A.处警告或者200元以下罚款

B.处警告或者500元以下罚款

C.处5日以上10日以下拘留,并处500元以下罚款

D.处5日以上10日以下拘留,并处200元以上500元以下罚款

E.情况较重的,处5日以上10日以下拘留,并处200元以上500元以下罚款

参考答案:AE

48.旅游主管部门向上级主管部门报告旅游突发事件的内容应当包括( )。

A.事件发生的时间、地点、信息来源

B.简要经过、伤亡人数和姓名、影响范围

C.事件涉及的旅游经营者、其他有关单位名称

D.事件发生原因及发展趋势的初步判断

E.报告人姓名、单位及联系电话

参考答案:ACDE

49.根据《最高人民法院关于审理旅游纠纷案件适用法律若干问题的规定》,下列属于"旅游经营者有权要求旅游者支付合理费用"的情形是( )。

A.为旅游者安排的另行付费的项目

B.为老年旅游者提供的与其他游客相同的服务项目

C.旅游者转让旅游合同

D.旅游者单方解除合同

E.因不可抗力等客观因素变更旅游行程

参考答案:CDE

50.申请世界遗产须具备以下( )前提。

A.真实性和完整性　　　　　　　B.稀缺性和杰出性

C.制定相关法律法规 D.设立保护机构

E.有经费

参考答案:ACDE

51.某旅行社将旅游业务委托给不具有相应资质的旅行社。那么,由旅游主管部门对该旅行社实施行政处罚说法正确的有(　　)。

A.责令改正

B.没收违法所得

C.处2万元以上10万元以下罚款

D.情节严重的,责令停业整顿1个月至3个月

E.情节严重的,吊销旅行社经营许可证

参考答案:ACD

52.当情况紧急或者发生重大、特别重大旅游突发事件时,导游可直接向发生地、旅行社所在地(　　)报告。

A.县级以上旅游主管部门

B.县级以上安全生产监督管理部门

C.市级以上旅游主管部门

D.市级以上安全生产监督管理部门

E.负有安全生产监督管理职责的其他相关部门

参考答案:ABE

53.旅游者小赵报名参加某旅行社组织的赴国内某城市观看足球比赛的旅游活动,在体育场不听工作人员制止,向场内投掷矿泉水瓶多只。对此,由公安机关对小赵实施治安处罚说法正确的有(　　)。

A.警告

B.500元以下罚款

C.情节严重的,处5日以下10日以下拘留,可以并处500元以下罚款

D.情节严重的,处5日以下10日以下拘留,可以并处2000元以下罚款

E.被处以拘留的可同时责令12个月内不得进入体育场馆观看同类比赛

参考答案:ACE

54.根据《中华人民共和国旅游法》规定,旅游者与旅游经营者发生纠纷,可以通过(　　)途径解决。

A.双方协商

B.向消费者协会、旅游投诉受理机构或者有关调解组织申请调解

C.根据达成的仲裁协议提请仲裁机构仲裁

D.向监察机关提出申诉

E.向人民法院提起诉讼

参考答案:ABCE

55.《最高人民法院关于民事诉讼证据的若干规定》中列举的当事人无须举证证明的事实包括(　　)。

　　A.当事人承认的事实

　　B.众所周知的事实

　　C.自然规律以及定理、定律

　　D.已为仲裁机构的生效裁决所确认的事实

　　E.根据已知的事实和日常生活经验法则推定出的另一事实

　　参考答案:BCDE

56.旅游目的地风险提示信息应当包括(　　)。

　　A.风险类别　　　B.提示级别　　　C.已经影响的区域

　　D.应采取的措施　　E.发布机关

　　参考答案:ABDE

57.旅游者小赵在某温泉酒店洗浴中心更衣时摔成重伤,经查是由于中心雇用的保洁员小王清洁不彻底,地面湿滑导致小赵摔倒,导游小张在入住酒店时已尽安全提示义务,那么下列说法错误的是(　　)。

　　A.酒店和旅行社对小赵的损害承担连带责任

　　B.酒店和小王对小赵的损害承担连带责任

　　C.酒店对小赵的损害承担赔偿责任

　　D.小王对小赵的损害承担赔偿责任

　　E.小张对小赵的损害承担赔偿责任

　　参考答案:ABDE

58.导游在带团过程中,因违反(　　),造成严重社会不良影响的行为属于旅游不文明行为。

　　A.法律法规　　　B.工作规范　　　C.公序良俗

　　D.职业道德　　　E.等级制度

　　参考答案:ABCD

59.根据《旅游安全管理办法》,旅游经营者应当遵循下列要求(　　)。

　　A.服务场所、服务项目和设施设备符合有关安全法律、法规和强制性标准的要求

　　B.配备必要的安全和救援人员、设施设备

　　C.建立旅游目的地安全风险提示制度

　　D.建立安全管理制度和责任体系

　　E.保证安全工作的资金投入

　　参考答案:ABDE

60.公民申请普通护照,应当提交本人的相关材料包括(　　)。

　　A.居民身份证　　　　　　　　　　B.居民户口簿

C.近期免冠照片 D.申请事由的相关材料

E.银行存款证明

参考答案:ABCD

61.《导游管理办法》第17条规定,有下列情形之一的,所在旅游主管部门应当注销导游证:(　　)

A.导游死亡的

B.导游证有效期届满未申请换发导游证的

C.导游证依法被撤销、吊销的

D.取得导游证后出现无民事行为能力或限制行为能力的

E.取得导游证后受过刑事处罚,过失犯罪的除外

参考答案:ABCDE

62.(　　)等经营场所、公共场所的经营者、管理者或者群众性活动的组织者,未尽到安全保障义务,造成他人损害的,应当承担侵权责任。

A.宾馆　　　　B.机场　　　　C.娱乐场所

D.体育场馆　　E.银行

参考答案:ABCDE

63.某旅行社安排导游小张为在境内旅游的某旅行团提供导游服务,同时要求小张先行垫付旅游活动过程中的团队餐、住宿等费用。对此,由旅游主管部门对该旅行社实施行政处罚正确的有(　　)。

A.责令改正

B.没收违法所得

C.处3000元以上3万元以下罚款

D.情节严重的,吊销旅行社业务经营许可证

E.情节严重的,责令停业整顿或者吊销旅行社业务经营许可证

参考答案:ABE

64.《文化和旅游部关于实施旅游服务质量提升计划的指导意见》指出,实施导游和领队业务素质研培计划,不断提升导游和领队(　　),增强主动传承和弘扬社会主义核心价值观的意识。

A.文化底蕴　　B.理解能力　　C.表达能力

D.外语能力　　E.信息素养

参考答案:ABCD

65.深化"互联网+旅游"推动旅游业高质量发展的重要任务包括(　　)。

A.加快建设智慧旅游景区　　　　B.完善旅游信息基础设施

C.创新旅游企业服务模式　　　　D.加大线上旅游营销力度

E.保障旅游数据安全

参考答案:ABDE

66.中国出境旅游者在境外购物时,领队应( )。

  A.鼓励大家在地接社导游带去的商店购物

  B.控制购物的次数和时间

  C.提醒游客注意货物的真伪和质量

  D.提醒游客注意货物的产地和价格

  E.尽量延长购物时间

  参考答案:BCD

67.旅游经营者组织、接待出入境旅游,发现旅游者从事违法活动,未及时向公安机关、旅游主管部门或者我国驻外机构报告的,下列由旅游主管部门对其实施的行政处罚说法正确的是( )。

  A.责令改正   B.没收违法所得

  C.处5000元以上5万元以下罚款 D.处1万元以上10万元以下罚款

  E.情节严重的,责令停业整顿或者吊销旅行社业务经营许可证

  参考答案:CE

68.2020年1月19日至21日,习近平在云南看望慰问各族民族干部群众时发表讲话,他指出要巩固依法整治旅游市场乱象的成果,推动旅游产业持续健康发展,要树牢"绿水青山就是金山银山"的理念,驰而不息打好( )三大保卫战。

  A.晴空   B.蓝天   C.碧水

  D.净土   E.森林

  参考答案:BCD

69.国家根据旅游活动的风险程度,对旅行社、住宿、旅游交通以及高风险旅游项目等经营者实施责任保险制度,其中高风险旅游项目包括( )。

  A.高空   B.高速   C.户外

  D.潜水   E.探险

  参考答案:ABDE

70.景区开放应当具备( )条件,并听取旅游主管部门意见。

  A.有必要的旅游配套服务和辅助设施

  B.有必要的安全设施及制度

  C.有必要的环境保护设施和生态保护措施

  D.有必要的门票价格优惠制度

  E.法律、行政法规规定的其他条件

  参考答案:ABCE

71.依法成立的旅游行业组织,实行自律管理,具体承担的职责包括( )。

  A.制定行业经营规范和服务标准 B.对会员进行自律管理

  C.组织开展职业道德教育和业务培训 D.提高从业人员素质

  E.承担部分行政管理职能

  参考答案:ABCD

72.某旅行社经营境内旅游和入境旅游业务,在未获取出境旅游经营许可的情况下经营欧洲出境旅游业务。对此,旅游主管部门对该旅行社实施行政处罚正确的有(　　)。

　　A.责令改正

　　B.没收违法所得

　　C.并处10万元以上50万元以下罚款,违法所得50万元以上的,并处违法所得1倍以上5倍以下罚款

　　D.责令停业整顿

　　E.情节严重的,责令停业整顿或吊销旅行社业务经营许可证

　　参考答案:ABDE

高知识测试

导游业务题库

一、判断题(判断描述正确请选A,判断描述错误请选B)

1. 旅游行业的核心价值观是"游客为本、服务至诚"。（　　）
参考答案：A

2. "专职导游"是指旅行社正式导游,他们与旅行社签有正式的用工合同。（　　）
参考答案：B

3. 一旦发现游客有中风征兆,导游应立即将其搀扶到旅游车上去休息。（　　）
参考答案：B

4. 导游服务是脑力劳动和体力劳动的高度结合,没有大专以上文化程度是做不好导游工作的。（　　）
参考答案：B

5. 在疫情没有完全终结的情况下团队出游,导游要提醒客人乘车时佩戴口罩,间隔一定距离就座。（　　）
参考答案：A

6. 接待中小学研学旅行团队时导游需要格外注意安全管理,要编制安全手册,制定各种安全预案。（　　）
参考答案：A

7. 导游接受游客委托办事,不宜说"我办事、你放心""没问题,肯定办好"之类的话。（　　）
参考答案：A

8. 旅游者患一般性疾病,导游可建议其离团休息,并告知医疗费用自理。（　　）
参考答案：B

9. 导游讲解的虚实结合法,要求导游不能只讲故事和传说,还应当进一步说明故事和传说反映的历史事实或者科学的原理。（　　）
参考答案：A

10. 根据民航局的规定,出生不足14天的婴儿和醉酒的旅客不得乘坐民航客机。（　　）
参考答案：A

11. 参加海外大学面试的学生和旅居国外的侨民,可向我国外事部门申请办理中华人民共和国护照。（　　）

参考答案:B

12.在汽车行进途中,导游要多与司机闲聊,避免司机疲劳驾驶。(　　)

参考答案:B

13.高质量导游服务的三要素是语言、知识和态度。(　　)

参考答案:B

14.导游职业道德三大意识是政治意识、敬业意识和服务意识。(　　)

参考答案:A

15.若有游客中暑,导游应立即将其送至阴凉通风处,并采取相应的处置措施。(　　)

参考答案:A

16.导游不能向游客推销商品,更不能向商家索要回扣。(　　)

参考答案:A

17.2016年8月国家旅游局下发《关于深化导游体制改革加强导游队伍建设的意见》,宣布取消导游资格证三年有效的规定,明确导游资格证终身有效。(　　)

参考答案:A

18.全陪作为国内组团社的代表,负责保证旅游计划的落实,在整个旅游活动中起主导作用。(　　)

参考答案:A

19.导游服务质量的优劣,直接影响着旅游产品的销售,这是导游服务具有信息反馈作用的具体体现。(　　)

参考答案:B

20.在旅游过程中,导游人员要以身作则,遵守文明旅游规范,并引导旅游者开展文明旅游活动,这是导游人员的基本职责。(　　)

参考答案:A

21.导游人员可以适当使用香水,但应注意适量,以3米左右的距离内能闻到香味为宜。(　　)

参考答案:B

22.穿西装时,衬衫的袖子最好露出西服袖口1厘米左右。(　　)

参考答案:B

23.握手时间的长短可根据握手双方的关系亲密程度灵活掌握,初次见面一般握手不应超过2秒钟。(　　)

参考答案:B

24.导游带团时绝对不允许喝酒。(　　)

参考答案:B

25.在涉外交往中,一旦涉及位置的排列,原则上都讲究左尊右卑、左高右低。

参考答案:B

26.西餐礼仪规范中,男客人应帮助其左边的女宾挪动一下椅子。( )

参考答案:B

27.地陪在接团前要与旅行社计调人员核实该团客人所住房间的数目、类别、用房时间是否与旅游接待计划相符,核实房费内是否含早餐。( )

参考答案:A

28.地陪到机场接团,应提前10分钟到达。( )

参考答案:B

29.地陪接到旅游团集合登车后,应用手指逐一清点人数,清点无误后方可示意司机开车。( )

参考答案:B

30.游客肌肉拉伤,24小时内不可对伤处进行热敷和按摩,只能进行冷敷。( )

参考答案:A

31.散客包价旅游在我国是指10人以下不提供全陪服务的包价旅游。( )

参考答案:B

32.为了防止地接社向导游下达接待任务时出现失误,在接团前导游应先与全陪核对各自的行程安排。( )

参考答案:B

33.旅游者进入酒店后,地陪应陪同到前台办理住店手续,并将房卡分发给旅游者,告诉全陪和领队自己的房间号,以便联系。( )

参考答案:B

34.旅游者上下车时,导游应恭候在车门旁,热情地搀扶和协助每一位旅游者。( )

参考答案:B

35.抵达景点后在导览图前,地陪应讲明游览线路、游览所需时间、集合时间和地点,以及参观游览中的注意事项。( )

参考答案:A

36.旅游者抵达后才提出饮食禁忌,导游应尽量满足,如果处理确有困难,导游可将餐费退还旅游者,让其自行解决。( )

参考答案:B

37.导游送海外客人离境,应该提前90分钟到达机场,以便办理出境手续。( )

参考答案:B

38.对于常去的景区,全陪可以将客人交地陪安排,自己不一定非得随团活动。( )

参考答案:B

39.导游分配标间,如果团队中有夫妻,而且在旅游合同中已声明必须安排在一起,导游应该无条件满足。( )

参考答案:A

40.购物是旅游者的一项重要活动,导游人员不得私自收取商家给予的购物"回扣"。( )

参考答案:A

41.旅行团在向异地城市移动过程中,全陪主要的任务是提醒旅游者注意人身和财物的安全。( )

参考答案:B

42.在景点游览时,全陪与地陪应分工协作。全陪带团前行,地陪应殿后,招呼滞后的旅游者,并不时清点人数,以防走失。( )

参考答案:B

43.伸出食指往下弯曲,在中国表示数字"9",在墨西哥表示"钱",在日本则表示"偷窃"。( )

参考答案:A

44.导游人员对游客的发问或要求不正面表示意见,而是绕过问题从侧面予以回应或回绝,这是柔和式回绝。( )

参考答案:B

45.某旅游团内两名游客产生矛盾,其中一名游客要求单独用餐,地陪应耐心做好劝说工作,并请领队协调。( )

参考答案:A

46.如果游客看中客房内的某种摆设或物品,要求购买,导游应委婉拒绝,说明饭店的摆设是不能购买的。( )

参考答案:B

47.有旅游者要求将已预订好的火车票换为飞机票,导游人员应尽量满足其要求,但需说明差价由其本人承担。( )

参考答案:B

48.在人际知觉中,最后给人留下的印象因时间距离最近而对人有着强烈的影响,这在心理学中称为"近因效应"。( )

参考答案:A

49.现代导游服务是一种专业化、职业化的服务,不以营利为目的。( )

参考答案:B

50.如果晚上安排自由活动,全陪应给客人规定返回酒店的时间,以保证客人的安全。(   )

参考答案:A

51.旅游者在境外滞留不归,领队应及时向旅行社和当地的中国使领馆报告。(   )

参考答案:A

52.大巴车在高速公路上行驶时,原则上导游不应站在前排进行讲解。(   )

参考答案:A

53.欣赏齐白石的画,游客感受到的不只是草木鱼虾,而是一种悠然自得、鲜活洒脱的情思意趣。这种审美感受是悦耳悦目。(   )

参考答案:B

54.苏轼《题西林壁》诗中的"横看成岭侧成峰,远近高低各不同",说明观景赏美要注意观赏角度。(   )

参考答案:A

55.按照国际惯例,导游人员带团乘坐任何交通工具时,都应最后一个下,第一个上,以便于照顾游客。(   )

参考答案:B

56.导游在与游客交往时应充分尊重对方,尽力与游客保持亲密无间的关系。(   )

参考答案:B

57.导游接待青少年研学旅行团队,应将实践性放在第一位。(   )

参考答案:B

58.处理游客个别要求的基本原则是"合理而可能"原则。"合理"和"可能"这两个条件要同时满足。(   )

参考答案:A

59.游客要求去不对外开放的地区(或机构)参观游览,导游人员可以协助办理相关手续后,带领团队前往。(   )

参考答案:B

60.为增进与旅游车司机的友情,导游人员在行车途中应多与司机聊天。(   )

参考答案:B

61.旅游团的游览活动结束后,游客要求延长逗留期限,一般情况下可满足其要求。(   )

参考答案:B

62.旅游活动中若有旅游者突然生病,通常情况下由全陪及患者亲友将其送往

医院,地陪则带团继续游览。(　　)

参考答案:A

63.所谓错接,是指导游人员接了不应该由他接的旅游团(者)的现象。如果错接的是另一家旅行社的团时,导游应立即向旅行社汇报,设法尽快交换旅游团,并向旅游者说明情况并致歉。(　　)

参考答案:A

64.如果发生空接事故,经过核实是旅游团(者)推迟抵达,地陪便可自行离开。(　　)

参考答案:B

65.如果已经造成误机(车、船)事故,导游人员和旅行社应该做好事故补救工作,使损失和影响减少到最低程度。(　　)

参考答案:A

66.有些旅游事故是由不可抗力造成的,因此旅游事故的发生是不可能完全杜绝的。(　　)

参考答案:A

67.如果错接发生在本社的两个旅游团之间,两名导游又同是本社的地陪,那么就将错就错,继续接团。(　　)

参考答案:A

68.导游要有强烈的证件安全意识,必要时全陪、地陪可以替旅游者保管证件。(　　)

参考答案:B

69.一场西式正式宴会如果有餐前鸡尾酒,正餐的时间至少应比请柬上规定的时间晚1个小时;若不招待鸡尾酒,晚30分钟就可以。(　　)

参考答案:B

70.旅游者要求转递的物品中有食物时,导游人员应婉言拒绝,请其自行处理。(　　)

参考答案:A

71.误机(车、船)属重大事故,它不仅给旅行社带来巨大的经济损失,而且也会让旅游者蒙受经济方面还有其他方面的损失,严重影响旅行社声誉。(　　)

参考答案:A

72.一名日本游客因某个要求得不到满足而提出提前离团时,导游可以让其自行办理分离签证及其他离团手续,所需费用由旅游者自理。(　　)

参考答案:B

73.游客患病死亡,其遗物应由家属清点。如果家属不在现场,由地陪导游清点。(　　)

参考答案:B

74.我国旅游饭店分为五个星级,即一星级、二星级、三星级、四星级、五星级(含白金五星级)。最低为一星级,最高为白金五星级饭店。( )

参考答案:A

75.有一名游客向导游投诉同房团友睡觉打鼾、使其无法正常休息,提出住单间,导游请领队内部调整未成,告知游客单间房费由其本人及打鼾团友各付一半。( )

参考答案:B

76.当代旅游需求发生较大变化主要表现在个性化旅游产品和自助游占绝大部分。( )

参考答案:A

77.大陆居民须持有效的《大陆居民往来台湾通行证》,并办理旅游签注赴台旅游。( )

参考答案:A

78.某韩国旅游团赴长白山旅游,由于连续阴雨天,在山顶未能如愿看到天池,游客要求更改行程,多停留一天参观,导游人员原则上应满足游客要求。( )

参考答案:B

79.游客入住酒店后要求调换房间朝向,导游原则上应予拒绝。( )

参考答案:B

80.如果游客患一般疾病,导游应劝其及早就医,注意休息,不要强行游览。( )

参考答案:A

81.旅游团一名游客旅游期间不小心患上感冒,导游可将自己随身携带的感冒药送给游客服用。( )

参考答案:B

82.游客的要求不违法,不违反旅游协议,就是合理的,旅行社就应该予以满足。( )

参考答案:B

83.按照有关规定,境外游客在退税定点商店购买的退税物品,其金额达到800元时才可享受退税。( )

参考答案:B

84.外国旅游者在签证有效期内,可以在中国任何地区内自由旅行,但他们必须尊重当地的风俗习惯。( )

参考答案:B

85.由于饭店超额预订而使客人不能入住的,饭店应该主动替客人安排本地同

档次或高于本饭店档次的饭店入住,所产生的费用由饭店承担。( )

参考答案:A

86.2014年8月,中国民航局规定旅客携带充电宝的额定能量是100-160瓦特小时。( )

参考答案:A

87.游客在野外或山地旅游时被黄蜂蜇伤,导游应帮助游客轻轻挑出蜂刺,可用醋清洗伤口,因为黄蜂的毒液属于酸性毒液。( )

参考答案:B

88.世界三大国际航空客运联盟中总部设在美国的是星空联盟。( )

参考答案:B

89.按照铁路部门发布的火车票退改签规定,无论是网上订票还是窗口订票,每位旅客只能改签2次。( )

参考答案:B

90.导游的人格魅力主要体现为微笑和热情,让客人有宾至如归的感觉。( )

参考答案:B

91.普通旅客乘坐火车,可以免费携带物品的重量是30千克。( )

参考答案:B

92.游客携带外币现钞金额等值5000美元至1万美元出境时,海关凭携带外汇出境许可证查验放行。( )

参考答案:A

93.团队在远离城市的某大型山地景区游览过程中发生意外,导游应当第一时间拨打景区救援电话而不是110。( )

参考答案:A

94.从事领队工作必须在取得导游证基础上加试领队资格证并合格,才能办理领取证。( )

参考答案:B

95.若游客被蜈蚣刺伤,导游应立即用肥皂水帮其冲洗伤口。( )

参考答案:A

96."不识庐山真面目,只缘身在此山中",说明观赏位置不同也会影响到观赏效果。( )

参考答案:B

97.《中华人民共和国护照法》规定,护照持有人的年龄未满16周岁,护照有效期为5年。( )

参考答案:A

98.成人旅客购买卧铺车票乘车时,可以免费携带一名身高不足1.3米的儿童。( )

参考答案:B

99.车次前冠以字母"G"的列车为高铁列车。( )

参考答案:A

二、单选题(只有一个选项是正确的,多选、错选、不选均不得分)

1.新中国成立前,我国成立的首家旅行社是( )。
A.中国国际旅行社　　　　　B.中国旅行社
C.中国现代旅行社　　　　　D.中国汽车旅行社

参考答案:B

2.景区讲解员在从事讲解服务时,必须( )。
A.持有正式的导游证　　　　B.接受旅行社的委派
C.携带并使用话筒　　　　　D.在限定的景区内服务

参考答案:D

3.我国和一些国际组织对导游服务实行规范化管理的主要目的,是( )。
A.加强对导游的管理　　　　B.维护导游的权益
C.保护消费者的权益　　　　D.保障经营者的利益

参考答案:C

4.旅游团队入住饭店,如果需要叫早,原则上应由( )通知饭店?
A.领队　　　B.全陪　　　C.地陪　　　D.旅游者

参考答案:C

5.领队职责与全陪职责最大的不同是领队应该( )
A.维护好团队团结　　　　　B.保护游客的安全
C.协助办理通关手续　　　　D.监督各地接待旅行社完成接待计划

参考答案:C

6.1949年11月19日,新中国第一家旅行社( )在厦门成立。
A.中国旅行社　　　　　　　B.中国国际旅行社
C.华侨服务社　　　　　　　D.中国青年旅行社

参考答案:C

7.成为一名合格导游人员的首要条件是( )
A.热情　　　B.勤奋　　　C.爱国　　　D.开拓

参考答案:C

8.国家旅游局从( )开始组织导游人员资格考试。

A.1985年 B.1988年 C.1989年 D.1994年

参考答案:C

9.导游人员应将( )放在导游服务第一位,它是衡量导游人员是否履行职责的基本尺度。

A.落实接待计划规定的内容 B.一视同仁、平等对待游客
C.维护游客的合法权益 D.提供个性化服务

参考答案:A

10.全国导游公共服务监督平台正式上线是在( )。

A.2014年 B.2016年 C.2017年 D.2018年

参考答案:B

11.旅行社所称"半包价旅游"是在全包价旅游的基础上没有包含( )服务的一种旅游包价形式。

A.午、晚餐 B.住房 C.早餐 D.城市间交通

参考答案:A

12.在未来社会,人们的文化修养更高,对知识的更新更加重视,尤其文化旅游、专业旅游、生态旅游的发展让导游业务呈现出( )的发展趋势。

A.导游手段科技化 B.导游职业自由化
C.导游方法多样化 D.导游内容高知识化

参考答案:D

13.根据规定,导游人员资格证书应由( )颁发。

A.当地导游协会 B.县级旅游行政管理部门
C.市级旅游行政管理部门 D.省级旅游行政管理部门

参考答案:D

14.取得导游人员资格证,并与旅行社订立劳动合同或者在旅游行业组织注册的人员,可以通过( )向所在地旅游主管部门申请取得导游证。

A.全国旅游监管服务信息系统 B.地方导游协会
C.地方旅游行政管理部门官网 D.导游自由执业平台

参考答案:A

15.导游证的有效期为( )。

A.2年 B.3年 C.4年 D.5年

参考答案:B

16.旅游者在华期间生病治疗,其住院和医疗费用一般由( )支付。

A.接团社 B.组团社 C.旅游者 D.导游

参考答案:C

17.在取得初级导游等级以后,具有大专以上学历且取得导游证满( )年,报

考前3年内实际带团不少于( )个工作日,经笔试导游知识专题、汉语言文学知识或外语,合格者晋升为中级导游。

A.3,80 B.3,90 C.2,80 D.2,90

参考答案:D

18.导游在讲解北京故宫的建造时间时,对美国游客说:"故宫在哥伦布发现新大陆七十年之前就已建成";对英国游客说:"故宫的建造时间是在莎士比亚诞生之前的一百四十年"。这里导游运用的讲解方法是( )。

A.制造悬念法 B.故事法 C.类比法 D.分段讲解法

参考答案:C

19.2016年国家旅游局为导游自由执业划定了门槛:参与自由执业的导游应该具有导游自由执业责任保险,每次事故个人责任限额应不低于( )人民币。

A.5万元 B.10万元 C.20万元 D.50万元

参考答案:D

20.导游带团购物,非必须提供的服务是( )。

A.到文物商店购买古玩时请海外客人保留发票和火漆印

B.告诉海外旅游者我国海关准许带出境的商品限额

C.如实介绍商品特色,帮助客人洽谈价格

D.按合同规定时间和地点安排购物

参考答案:C

21.发生误机事故后,导游首先应该( )

A.安抚游客 B.报告旅行社

C.联系最近的航班送走客人 D.及时通知下一站调整行程

参考答案:B

22.导游执业方式自由化是导游自由执业的核心,目前导游执业主要有五种模式,下列选项中不属于五种模式的是( )。

A.旅游公司委派模式 B.游客直联模式

C.旅行社委派模式 D.旅行社预订模式

参考答案:A

23.地陪导游在阅读接待计划时,应对其中的重点内容做好( )。

A.汇报 B.记录 C.分析 D.统计

参考答案:B

24.1845年,托马斯·库克组织350人赴利物浦旅游途中第一次聘请了地方导游游览的景点是( )。

A.达拉谟城堡 B.爱德华国王城堡

C.圣乔治城堡 D.卡那封城堡

参考答案:D

25.北京时间为零点时,当地时间为16:00的城市是( )。
A.伦敦　　　B.纽约　　　C.首尔　　　D.巴黎
参考答案:A

26.地陪在接团前想核实团队用房情况是否与旅游接待计划相符,应联系旅行社( )部门。
A.计调　　　B.外联　　　C.公关　　　D.账务
参考答案:A

27.导游人员必须遵守的基本道德规范是( ),也是社会主义各行各业必须遵守的基本行为准则。
A.爱国爱企、自尊自强　　　B.遵纪守法、敬业爱岗
C.公私分明、诚实善良　　　D.克勤克俭、游客至上
参考答案:A

28.中餐赴宴礼仪规范要求,按时出席宴请是礼貌的体现,一般可按规定时间提前或延后不超过( )到达。
A.3分钟　　　B.5分钟　　　C.8分钟　　　D.10分钟
参考答案:B

29.因天气原因,旅游团所乘航班需推迟2小时才能起飞,游客仍滞留在上一站,而全陪和领队又没有及时通知下一站接待社。下站导游不知道这种临时变化,仍按原计划接站,造成了空接,该导游应该首先( )。
A.若推迟时间不长,坚持在机场等候
B.推迟时间较长,重新落实接团事宜
C.尽量与该团全陪取得联系
D.地陪应立即与本旅行社有关部门联系查明原因
参考答案:D

30.旅游者因抢救无效死亡,导游应留存由主治医师签字和医院盖章的《抢救经过报告》和( )。
A.《尸体解剖报告》　　　B.死亡诊断证明
C.死亡公证书　　　　　D.因病死亡证明
参考答案:B

31.我国最早的导游服务质量国家标准是( )制定的。
A.1993年　　　B.1995年　　　C.1997年　　　D.1999年
参考答案:B

32.导游等级考试制度的建立始于( )。
A.1992年　　　B.1994年　　　C.1998年　　　D.2000年

参考答案:B

33.地陪接了一旅游团,出发前到旅行社计调部领取相关票证、表格和费用。以下不属于领取内容的是( )。

 A.旅游合同   B.旅游团名单

 C.住宿结算单   D.旅游服务质量反馈表

参考答案:A

34.导游讲解与旅行生活服务之间是( )的关系

 A.相互独立又互为因果   B.互为条件又互相补充

 C.相互联系又相互包含   D.相互独立又互相替代

参考答案:B

35.地陪前往机场接机,到达机场经询问旅游团乘坐的航班晚点5小时,地陪应该( )。

 A.原地等候   B.报告旅行社,听从安排

 C.回家等候   D.先完成其他工作

参考答案:B

36.地陪认找旅游团的时候,要核实团队除了( )外的基本信息,以防接错。

 A.旅游团团名   B.领队、全陪的姓名

 C.旅游者人数   D.旅游者年龄

参考答案:D

37.2016年8月,原国家旅游局、交通部联合规范"导游专座",规定( )为导游专座,旅游者不能抢占导游专座,以保障导游在工作中的人身安全。

 A.司机背后第一排靠窗位   B.司机背后第一排靠过道位

 C.开门侧第一排靠窗位   D.开门侧第一排靠过道位

参考答案:D

38.地陪在旅游团面前的首次亮相指的是( )

 A.入店服务   B.迎接服务   C.致欢迎辞   D.首次沿途导游

参考答案:B

39.旅游团商定好第二天的集合出发时间后,由( )通知饭店总台办理旅游团的叫早手续。

 A.地陪   B.全陪   C.领队   D.行李员

参考答案:A

40.核对商定日程的时候,有部分游客提出与原日程有较大变动且涉及接待规格调整的要求时,导游应( )。

 A.婉拒   B.报告地接社   C.报告组团社   D.与领队协商

参考答案:A

41.地陪手中的接团计划与领队的计划有部分出入时,地陪首先应( )。
A.依照领队的计划　　　　　B.坚持地陪的计划
C.报告组团社　　　　　　　D.报告地接社
参考答案:D

42.地陪服务工作的中心环节是( )。
A.迎接服务　　B.住店服务　　C.参观游览服务　　D.送行服务
参考答案:C

43.每日参观游览服务中,地陪应该提前( )到达集合地点。
A.5分钟　　　　B.10分钟　　　C.20分钟　　　D.30分钟
参考答案:B

44.导游服务的政治属性是由( )决定的。
A.价值观念　　B.文化传统　　C.经济制度　　D.社会制度
参考答案:D

45.在扩大旅游客源上,一种比广告宣传更有效的宣传方式是( )。
A.营销人员的促销　　　　　B.导游的介绍
C.互联网上的推介　　　　　D.游客的"口头宣传"
参考答案:D

46.针对旅游团参观游览项目的不同,地陪导游应重点做好相关( )和语言的准备。
A.旅游物质　　B.活动计划　　C.专业知识　　D.外在形象
参考答案:C

47.旅游接待计划是组团旅行社委托地方接待旅行社落实团队活动的( )文件。
A.指导性　　　B.意向性　　　C.契约性　　　D.建议性
参考答案:C

48.在核对和商定日程时,若领队提出新增旅游项目,地陪应当( )。
A.婉言拒绝　　　　　　　　B.及时向组团社反映
C.原则同意　　　　　　　　D.及时向地接社反映
参考答案:D

49.地陪在接小型旅游团或无领队、无全陪的散客旅游团时,要在接站牌上写上( ),以便客人能主动与地陪联系。
A.接待社名称　　B.组团社名称　　C.地陪导游姓名　　D.游客姓名
参考答案:D

50.外国旅游团抵达饭店后,分配房间的工作应由( )来完成。
A.地陪　　　　B.全陪　　　　C.领队　　　　D.团长

参考答案:C

51.在下面旅行社四大业务中,属于产品消费的是( )。
A.旅游产品开发　　B.旅游产品销售　　C.旅游服务采购　　D.旅游者接待
参考答案:D

52.旅游接待计划是地陪了解旅游团基本情况和安排当地活动日程的( )。
A.主要依据　　　B.指导原则　　　C.工作标准　　　D.参考意见
参考答案:A

53.( )第十二届全国人民代表大会常务委员会第二十四次会议通过了修改《中华人民共和国旅游法》的决定,我国实施近十年的领队证审批制度正式被取消。
A.2016年11月7日　　　　　　　B.2016年10月7日
C.2017年11月7日　　　　　　　D.2017年1月7日
参考答案:A

54.导游服务在连接各项接待服务中起( )作用。
A.强化　　　　B.先导　　　　C.纽带　　　　D.黏合
参考答案:C

55.如果旅游团乘坐火车、轮船离站,建议导游提前( )抵达车站或码头。
A.2小时　　　B.90分钟　　　C.1小时　　　D.半小时
参考答案:C

56.全陪导游准备带一个四川省的旅游团去陕西旅游,他应准备的专业知识主要是( )。
A.少数民族方面　　B.历史文物方面　　C.石窟艺术方面　　D.风景名胜方面
参考答案:B

57.旅游团中某位旅游者希望带其在华亲友的孩子随团活动,导游应该( )。
A.婉言拒绝　　　　　　　　　　B.表示同意
C.首先征求领队及团员的意见　　D.首先向领导汇报
参考答案:C

58.地陪在迎接旅游团时所致欢迎词的内容应简洁,一般应控制在( )左右。
A.15分钟　　　B.10分钟　　　C.8分钟　　　D.5分钟
参考答案:D

59.在导游讲解中,较为理想的语速应控制在每分钟( )左右。
A.150字　　　B.200字　　　C.250字　　　D.300字
参考答案:B

60.旅游团下榻饭店后,如发现客房未打扫干净、卫生设备不符合清洁标准、空调器发生故障或房间有蟑螂等问题,且饭店不能及时予以解决,导致旅游者出现严重不满时,地陪应要求饭店方面( )。

A.为旅游者更换房间　　　　　　B.向旅游者致歉并限期改正
C.双倍赔偿旅游者损失　　　　　D.退还旅行社所预交的房款
参考答案：A

61.境外旅游团客人登车后,地陪要做的第一件事是(　　)。
A.致欢迎词　　　　　　　　　　B.调整时差
C.清点人数　　　　　　　　　　D.通报前往的目的地
参考答案：C

62.旅游者的法律救援权是指其合法权益受到侵害而又得不到满意的解决时,有(　　)的权利。
A.向其他旅游者诉说　　　　　　B.向旅游行政管理部门提出控告
C.向法院提出诉讼　　　　　　　D.向社会公示
参考答案：C

63.导游在介绍杭州西湖时,先从其概况、传说、成因讲起,继而讲解湖中景物。这种讲解方法称为(　　)。
A.突出重点法　　B.分段讲解法　　C.画龙点睛法　　D.虚实结合法
参考答案：B

64.在征得旅游团及领队、全陪同意的情况下,地陪可以对(　　)做适当调整。
A.旅游价格　　　B.旅游计划　　　C.团队人数　　　D.活动日程顺序
参考答案：D

65.如果旅游者要求地陪代购商品并帮助托运,地陪一般应(　　)。
A.积极配合　　　B.予以婉拒　　　C.履行承诺　　　D.坚决推辞
参考答案：B

66.旅游者上车后,导游应有礼貌地清点人数,最好采用(　　)的方式进行。
A.念客人姓名　　　　　　　　　B.请客人自我介绍
C.用手指点数　　　　　　　　　D.默数
参考答案：D

67.在接待入境旅游团时,全陪一般应提前(　　)到达接站地点,与首站接待的地方导游人员一起迎接旅游团。
A.15分钟　　　　B.半小时　　　　C.45分钟　　　　D.1小时
参考答案：B

68.在陪同国内旅游团时,全陪应提前(　　)到达组团社事先与旅游者约定的集合地点,等候他们的到来。
A.10分钟　　　　B.2小时　　　　C.1小时　　　　D.半小时
参考答案：D

69.按照接待计划,一个来自云南的旅游团将于次日乘6点的早班飞机离开上海,但是饭店餐厅无法提早供应早餐,地陪导游应该( )。

A.与餐厅经理交涉,要求餐厅提早开餐

B.帮助游客提前在外卖店代购

C.请客人自行解决早餐

D.请餐厅提前准备简便餐食

参考答案:D

70.游客提出住更高标准的房间时,导游的正确做法是( )。

A.告知游客超标,不能满足

B.如有房间,可予以满足,但游客要交付退房损失费和房费差价

C.婉言拒绝

D.请全陪报告组团社,由组团社决定

参考答案:B

71.下列不属于现代旅游业三大支柱产业的是( )。

A.旅游资源　　B.旅游饭店　　C.旅行社　　D.旅游交通

参考答案:A

72.导游工作的服务性要求导游人员( )。

A.不卑不亢,一视同仁　　　　B.求同存异,实事求是

C.认清角色,摆正位置　　　　D.不计名利,乐于奉献

参考答案:C

73.导游人员下列接机服务程序,不符合要求的是( )。

A.提前10分钟到达机场

B.站在显著位置,手持接站牌等候对方领队或全陪前来认找

C.核实对方旅行社名称、团号及准确到达人数

D.集合登车,并采用默数的方法清点人数

参考答案:A

74.团队参观游览出发后,地陪首先要做的工作是( )。

A.致欢迎词　　B.介绍当日行程　　C.沿途风光介绍　　D.活跃气氛

参考答案:B

75.下列工作不属于全陪导游职责范围的是( )。

A.维护游客安全　　B.处理团队事务　　C.景点讲解　　D.致欢送词

参考答案:C

76.下列哪种情况下,导游人员可以同意游客自由活动的要求( )。

A.团队离开本地前2小时游客要求自由活动

B.游客要求在游泳区游泳

C.游客要求在江河湖泊划小船

D.游客想单独骑自行车去陌生地方

参考答案:B

77.旅游团中一游客与同室客人发生矛盾,要求住单间,导游人员的下列做法不正确的是( )。

A.导游人员先请领队调解或内部调整

B.饭店如有空房,可满足其要求

C.委婉拒绝游客的要求,请客人忍耐几天

D.如果住单间,告知游客房费由提出方自理

参考答案:C

78.一名海外游客在离境前一天晚上找导游,希望导游帮她把一件贵重礼品转交给当地的朋友。面对此要求,导游首先应( )。

A.向旅行社汇报,经领导同意后按规定办理

B.为游客着想,立即答应游客的要求

C.婉拒并帮助游客联系快递公司上门接件

D.请游客把礼品带回,下次来再带来

参考答案:C

79.旅游者的下列要求中,导游必须满足,否则构成违约的是( )。

A.旅游者在旅游协议中已声明的饮食禁忌

B.旅游者要求退、换餐

C.旅游者想换个档次更高的酒店

D.旅游者要求品尝风味餐

参考答案:A

80.全国所有旅客列车从( )1月1日起实行车票实名制。

A.2002年　　　B.2004年　　　C.2006年　　　D.2012年

参考答案:D

81.不可抗力会造成旅游计划的被迫改变。导游下列做法中,不正确的是( )。

A.实事求是地将情况向旅游者说清楚求得其谅解

B.提出替代方案,与旅游者协商,并告知有关法律法规规定

C.立即给旅游者一定的物质补偿

D.以精彩的导游讲解、热情的服务吸引旅游者的注意力

参考答案:C

82.导致错接事故的主要原因是( )。

A.组团社与接待社之间工作衔接失误

B.导游安排行程不当

C.导游没有核实团队信息

D.游客在上一站或途中滞留,不能准时到达

参考答案:C

83.对于旅游者在旅游过程中提出的特殊饮食要求,下列说法正确的是( )。

A.已订妥的风味宴,旅游者在临近用餐时不想去,导游表示无所谓,立即退餐

B.旅游者提出推迟用餐,导游应告知其不能超过用餐时间,否则将自动取消用餐,餐费不退

C.旅游者患病要求在客房内用餐,地陪告知旅游者,客房不提供任何送餐服务

D.旅游者坚持自己单独用餐,导游可协助其与餐厅联系,告之餐费自理,原餐费不退

参考答案:D

84.领队小宋带领旅游团24人赴泰国旅游。飞机抵达机场后,地陪就向小宋要求增加该团的自费项目,领队小宋下列回应最妥当的是( )。

A.告之上车后由地陪直接向客人说明并收取费用

B.直接拒绝,说明此团不参加任何自费项目

C.报告组团社,由组团社与地陪所在地接社协调

D.告之先进行计划内的活动,找适当机会征求全团成员意见,以客人自愿参加为原则

参考答案:D

85.发生漏接事故后,导游首先应做好的工作是( )。

A.到旅游者下榻的饭店向他们说明情况并道歉

B.查找原因,避免类似事件再次发生

C.宣布给予旅游者一定的物质补偿

D.与旅游者下榻的饭店联系客人是否已前往入住

参考答案:D

86.地陪导游讲解景区游览线路的最佳时机是( )。

A.大巴车出发时 B.大巴车接近景区时

C.景区入口处 D.景区游览途中

参考答案:C

87.如果游客遇到登机前身份证丢失的情况,可在航班起飞前( )到候机楼公安民警值班室申请办理临时身份证明。

A.120分钟 B.90分钟 C.60分钟 D.30分钟

参考答案:C

88.1982版到2014版的熊猫金银纪念币标注的重量单位都是"盎司",2016版纪念币将计量单位改为"克"。1盎司等于( )。

A.31.1035克　　　B.30.1035克　　　C.31.0235克　　　D.30.0235克

参考答案：A

89.位于东8区的北京迎来了早上6点钟的太阳,而此时纽约应该是(　　)。

A.当天17时　　　B.前一天17时　　　C.当天16时　　　D.前一天16时

参考答案：B

90.乘坐从中国境内机场始发的国际航班的游客,其携带的液体物品每件容积不超过(　　)。

A.150毫升　　　B.120毫升　　　C.100毫升　　　D.80毫升

参考答案：C

91.下列事故中属于治安事故的是(　　)。

A.游客财物被盗　　　　　　B.发生交通事故

C.食用野生蘑菇中毒　　　　D.旅游者意外受伤

参考答案：A

92.根据我国民航部门对行李破损赔偿的规定,被托运的行李全部或者部分损坏、丢失赔偿金额每公斤不超过人民币(　　)。

A.50元　　　B.80元　　　C.90元　　　D.100元

参考答案：D

93.旅游者突发重病,在急救过程中需要手术签字时,地陪应请(　　)签字。

A.领队　　　B.公证人员　　　C.团长　　　D.全陪

参考答案：A

94.导游发现旅游者食物中毒后,首先应(　　)。

A.将患者送往就近医院抢救　　　B.设法进行催吐

C.报告旅行社及相关部门　　　　D.取消旅游活动

参考答案：B

95.重症中暑会出现昏倒、痉挛、皮肤干热、体温超出(　　)等症状。

A.38℃　　　B.39℃　　　C.40℃　　　D.42℃

参考答案：C

96.当旅游团入住饭店时发生了火灾,导游首先应(　　)。

A.通知领队并协助通知全体成员　　　B.组织救援,疏散旅游者

C.报警,拨打119　　　　　　　　　　D.寻找灭火器灭火

参考答案：C

97.下列情况中游客提出换房,导游人员应该满足其要求(　　)。

A.客房内发现蟑螂和老鼠　　　　B.客房朝北光线不好

C.客房在走廊尽头离电梯近　　　D.客人要求住高档客房又拒付差价

参考答案：A

98.旅游团在一地的旅游活动全部结束并前往机场,地陪( )即可离开机场。

A.在进行完交通票据和行李卡移交工作之后

B.在旅游者安检结束之后

C.在旅游团所乘航班起飞之后

D.在将客人带至机场大厅并说明办理程序和办理柜台位置之后

参考答案:B

99.游客携带中药材、中成药前往港澳地区的,总限值为人民币( )。

A.250元　　　　　B.200元　　　　　C.150元　　　　　D.100元

参考答案:C

100.导游人员没有按预定航班(车次、船次)时刻迎接旅游团,导致旅游团到达后无导游人员迎接的现象,称为( )。

A.错接　　　　　B.误接　　　　　C.漏接　　　　　D.空接

参考答案:C

101.旅游者要求的下列自由活动行为中,导游应予劝阻的是( )。

A.游客要求自行参观博物馆　　　　B.游客要求自行游览景点

C.游客要求离站去购物　　　　　　D.游客要求独自拜访名人故居

参考答案:C

102.作为地陪,在确定叫早时间时应与( )商量。

A.领队和全陪　　B.所有客人　　　C.领队　　　　　D.全陪

参考答案:A

103.某旅游团在购买了某地特产的瓷器后发现有瑕疵,经有关部门认定为不合格的商品,旅游者纷纷要求退货,此时,经营者( )。

A.可以坚持"出售商品,概不退货"

B.应当负责退货

C.可以坚持不退款,但可更换同类商品

D.可以坚持不退款,但可购买等额其他商品

参考答案:B

104.导游人员带团时遇到了一位处处刁难的领队,地陪下列做法中欠妥当的是( )。

A.对于领队的刁难,要有理、有利、有节地据理力争

B.在做好工作的前提下,争取大多数人的同情和谅解

C.不予理睬,按既定方案办

D.与其进行个别交谈,指出其要求的不合理性

参考答案:C

105.在旅游途中如果有游客被毒蛇咬伤,导游应该马上用绳、布带或其他植物

纤维在伤口上方超过一个关节处结扎。为免组织坏死,最好每隔( )放松一次。

A.10分钟　　　　B.15分钟　　　　C.20分钟　　　　D.25分钟

参考答案:B

106.一位年迈的旅游者随旅游团抵达苏州故地重游,当晚老人向地陪提出希望探望当地一位失散多年的朋友,这时地陪应该( )。

A.对老人说:您与朋友失散多年,地址很难找,这事没办法解决

B.对老人说:明天您可以不随团活动,去找那位朋友

C.设法予以满足,可在第二天通过旅行社请公安户籍部门帮助寻找

D.为了能让老人如愿以偿,决定第二天亲自去帮助寻找,把工作委托全陪代理

参考答案:C

107.巴黎位于东一区,北京为东八区,日本东京为东九区,当北京时间上午10时,巴黎和东京时间分别是( )。

A.5点和11点　　B.3点和11点　　C.0点和9点　　D.3点和9点

参考答案:B

108.入境游客可免税携带烟草制品的限量是( )。

A.香烟200支　　B.香烟400支　　C.雪茄50支　　D.烟丝400克

参考答案:B

109.对出入境人员进行的( ),不存在任何特殊免检对象。

A.海关检查　　　B.安全检查　　　C.边防检查　　　D.卫生检疫

参考答案:B

110.一位7岁的小学生购买机票,可以按照同一航班成人普通票价的( )购买儿童票。

A.10%　　　　　B.20%　　　　　C.30%　　　　　D.50%

参考答案:D

111.根据中国民航局的规定,乘坐经济舱的旅客,其登机手提行李限额为( )。

A.不限制携带行李件数,限重5千克　　B.只能携带一件,不限重量

C.只能携带一件,限重5千克　　　　　D.可以携带两件,限重5千克

参考答案:C

112.根据中国民航局的规定,旅客随身携带的手提行李尺寸不得超过( )。

A.20×30×45厘米　　　　　　　　B.25×30×50厘米

C.20×40×55厘米　　　　　　　　D.25×40×55厘米

参考答案:C

113.成年游客购买铁路旅客人身意外伤害保险的费用是3元,最高赔付额是( )。

A.5万元　　　　　B.10万元　　　　C.20万元　　　　D.55万元

参考答案:D

114.导游运用虚实结合手法讲解古建筑,其中"实"是指有关建筑物的( )。

A.历史沿革,名人轶事　　　　B.建筑布局,功能用处

C.结构风格,名人轶事　　　　D.神话故事,民间传说

参考答案:B

115.中国国际航空公司的英文代码是( )。

A.MF　　　　　B.CZ　　　　　C.CA　　　　　D.MU

参考答案:C

116.入住饭店后,客人反映电视机没有遥控器,地陪的正确做法是( )。

A.安慰客人,将就一晚,反正明天就离店

B.告诉客人这种小问题可以找领队来解决

C.立即报告旅行社,请示处理办法

D.找楼层服务员解决

参考答案:D

117.下列关于散客旅游者的描述中,不正确的是( )。

A.通常文化层次较高　　　　B.有较丰富的旅游经验

C.对服务的要求不高　　　　D.自主旅游能力较强

参考答案:C

118.送外国旅游团出境时,全陪和地陪可在( )离开机场。

A.旅游团所乘航班起飞后　　　　B.旅游团办理登机手续时

C.与旅游团成员交接完行李后　　D.旅游团进入隔离区后

参考答案:D

119.某旅行团乘今天16:00的航班离开北京飞往香港,地陪小李至少应在( )之前把旅游团带到机场。

A.13:00　　　　B.14:00　　　　C.14:30　　　　D.15:00

参考答案:B

120.某旅游团一行15人抵达杭州,地陪小王在客人住进饭店之后开始与领队商定第二天的日程安排。小王发现领队和自己的计划有出入,这时地陪小王应( )。

A.按照领队计划执行　　　　B.按照自己计划执行

C.跟领队协商解决　　　　　D.及时报告旅行社,查明原因,分清责任

参考答案:D

121.某旅行团定于当日乘21:00起飞的航班离开桂林,晚餐后部分旅游者提出

再看一下市容,地陪应( )。

A.提醒旅游者不要太晚回来,以免误机

B.与全陪分头陪同前往

C.劝阻旅游者不要前往

D.告诉旅游者如误机,责任自负

参考答案:C

122.旅游团因故推迟离开某市一天,该市地陪首先应( )。

A.适当延长该团在主要景点的游览时间

B.酌情为该团增加游览景点

C.及时将该团行程变化通知组团社

D.为该团重新落实用餐、用房、用车事宜

参考答案:D

123.导游在进行导游活动时,( )以上的旅游团应举接待社社旗。

A.6人　　　　　　B.8人　　　　　　C.9人　　　　　　D.10人

参考答案:C

124.旅游团乘旅游车外出游览时,由于司机不慎,发生交通事故造成游客重伤。在交通事故的善后处理中,应遵循( )为第一位的原则。

A.保护旅行社的利益　　　　　　B.保护旅游者的基本权益

C.保护旅游车公司的利益　　　　D.协商解决

参考答案:B

125.安排住同一房间的旅游者,如因睡眠、起居习惯等原因要求另开房间,其房费应由( )。

A.组团社承担　　　　　　B.地接社承担

C.要求单独居住的游客承担　　　D.同一房间游客分担

参考答案:C

126.下列旅客中可以免交民航发展基金的是( )。

A.持公务护照的旅客　　　　B.12周岁以下的儿童

C.持外交护照的旅客　　　　D.48小时内过境旅客

参考答案:B

127.地陪接待一个来自新加坡的VIP团,接待社的领导随同前往机场迎接。当宾主双方见面时,地陪正确的介绍方式是( )。

A.先自我介绍再将接待方领导介绍给客人

B.先自我介绍再将客人介绍给接待方领导

C.先将领导介绍给客人再自我介绍

D.先将客人介绍给领导再自我介绍

参考答案:C

128."四川有座峨眉山,离天只有三尺三;湖北有座黄鹤楼,半截插在云里头"。导游在这里运用了( )修辞手法。
A.夸张　　　　B.引用　　　　C.双关　　　　D.映衬
参考答案:A

129."不识庐山真面目,只缘身在此山中"。说明观景赏美要注意保持一定的( )。
A.心理距离　　B.时间距离　　C.空间距离　　D.物理距离
参考答案:A

130.下列事故中,完全因导游工作失误造成的是( )。
A.旅游者在游览中走失　　　　B.旅游者丢失行李
C.错接　　　　　　　　　　　D.空接
参考答案:C

131.下列预防和处理游客晕车问题的做法中,错误的是( )。
A.提醒游客坐车前一定要吃得很饱
B.提醒游客坐车前不要吃得太油腻
C.建议游客提前服用晕车药
D.建议游客坐在大巴前排靠窗的位置
参考答案:A

三、多选题(至少有两个选项是正确的,多选、少选、错选、不选均不得分)

1.导游平等服务原则需要导游( )。
A.平均分配和游客交流的时间　　B.对游客一视同仁,保持平等距离
C.对游客不能有亲疏贵贱之分　　D.与游客平等交流
E.对任何游客不能有超常服务
参考答案:BCD

2.富强、民主、文明、和谐、自由、平等、公正、法治、爱国、敬业、诚信、友善,是社会主义核心价值观的基本内容,其精辟概括了( )
A.国家的价值目标　　　　B.道德的价值标准
C.社会的价值取向　　　　D.文化的价值取向
E.公民的价值准则
参考答案:ACE

3.旅游团在抵达旅游景点游览之前,地陪应向游客讲清的问题有( )。
A.游览结束后的集合时间和地点　　B.旅游车的型号、颜色、标志和车号

C.进入景点后的游览路线　　　　D.游览景点的位置及其周边情况

E.游览中的注意事项及安全

参考答案:ABCE

4.陪同游客前往景区途中,地陪服务的主要内容有(　　)。

A.安排好酒店叫早服务　　　　B.介绍当日活动安排

C.沿途风情、风光导游　　　　D.活跃气氛

E.到达前介绍景区概况

参考答案:BCDE

5.导游人员要搞好与领队的关系,应该(　　)。

A.支持领队的工作　　　　　　B.服从领队的领导

C.尊重领队的人格　　　　　　D.坚持原则,避免正面冲突

E.遇事主动与领队沟通与商量

参考答案:ACDE

6.接机后前往饭店的途中,地陪的服务包括(　　)。

A.致欢迎词　　　　　　　　　B.说明前往地点

C.介绍本地概况　　　　　　　D.分发"游客意见表"

E.介绍下榻饭店的情况

参考答案:ABCE

7.地陪服务准备工作中的熟悉接待计划,包括下列内容(　　)。

A.旅游团的基本信息　　　　　B.旅游团成员情况

C.旅游团抵离本地情况　　　　D.旅游团上下站地接社信息

E.旅游团特殊要求

参考答案:ABCE

8.下列物品中,属于中华人民共和国海关禁止出境的有(　　)。

A.伪造的货币　　B.虎骨　　C.犀牛角　　D.音响电子制品

E.珍贵文物及其他禁止出境的文物

参考答案:ABCE

9.旅游者突患重病,导游处理得正确的是(　　)。

A.立即送往医院抢救　　　　　B.请领队或患者亲属留在医院

C.注意保存医疗档案　　　　　D.告诉患者住院、治疗费用自理

E.病人安顿后地陪可带领其他客人继续旅行

参考答案:ABCDE

10.下列对导游工作纪律描述正确的有(　　)。

A.导游应按照旅游计划安排游客参观游览

B.导游不能接受游客主动给予的小费

C.导游不得参与黄、赌、毒等违法活动

D.导游不得购买旅游者的物品

E.导游不得接受商家给予的"回扣"

参考答案：ACDE

11.地陪导游应该熟悉团队情况。以下说法正确的是( )。

A.导游应该熟悉团员的基本情况

B.导游应该熟悉团队的特点

C.导游应该熟悉旅游接待计划

D.导游应该熟悉交通路况

E.导游应该熟悉团队费用结算的方式

参考答案：ABC

12.部分游客提出不想随团去景区,想在市内某商场购物,地陪导游处理正确的是( )。

A.尽量动员他们随团参观

B.征得全陪同意后可以放行

C.必要时请全陪陪同他们去购物

D.动员其他游客去该商场购物

E.善意地欺骗游客该商场正在装修,不营业,以打消其购物的念头

参考答案：ABC

13.某外国旅游者因个别要求得不到满足而执意要求退团,导游人员应该( )。

A.设法弥补过错,耐心解释

B.因需办理分离签证手续,原则上应予拒绝

C.直接满足其要求

D.报告旅行社同意后协助安排其返程

E.建议客人向所在国家驻华使领馆求助

参考答案：ABD

14.地陪导游服务程序中的接站服务包括( )等内容。

A.旅游团抵达前的业务准备　　B.旅游团抵达后的接站服务

C.赴饭店途中服务　　　　　　D.核商日程

E.景点导游讲解

参考答案：ABC

15.游客丢失证件、物品的预防措施有( )。

A.游览时导游可帮助游客保管重要物品

B.入住酒店时导游应提醒游客将贵重物品存放到酒店贵重物品保管室

C.离开旅游车时导游应提醒游客勿将贵重物品放在车上

D.导游应做好行李物品的清点、交接工作

E.出发前劝游客尽量不要随身携带重要证件

参考答案：BCD

16.地陪接站服务程序主要有下列哪些步骤?(　　)

A.提前半小时到达接站点　　　　B.手持接站牌站在显著位置迎候客人

C.核实团队　　　　　　　　　　D.集合登车

E.清点人数

参考答案：ABCDE

17.在审核旅游活动日程时,如果地陪发现地接社发给他的接待计划与旅游团领队或全陪出示的旅游计划之间存在明显差异,应迅速查明原因,以便(　　)。

A.减少损失　　B.分清责任　　C.规避风险

D.及时调整　　E.追究责任

参考答案：BD

18.导游讲解"虚实结合法"中的"虚"是指与景观有关的(　　)。

A.艺术价值　　B.民间传说　　C.历史事实

D.趣闻轶事　　E.神话故事

参考答案：BDE

19.散客旅游团队具有的特点有(　　)。

A.旅行社服务承诺的差异　　　　B.客人性别的差异

C.参团价格的差异　　　　　　　D.成员社会地位的差异

E.客人期望值的差异

参考答案：ACDE

20.全陪应做好必要物质准备,主要包括(　　)。

A.身份证件　　B.少量现金　　C.接团资料

D.游客信息　　E.个人物品

参考答案：ABCE

21.旅游团在各站停留期间,全陪的工作主要有(　　)。

A.协助地陪导游的各项工作　　　B.提供导游讲解服务

C.保障游客的安全　　　　　　　D.检查各站的服务质量

E.安排旅游团的活动日程

参考答案：ACD

22.对于地陪在景区的服务,下列说法正确的有(　　)。

A.首先请客人记住所乘车辆的车号或特征、集合时间和地点

B.应要求客人随团参观游览,不能单独行动

C.可以聘请景区讲解员进行讲解

D.导游可以脱离团队,让客人自行游览

E.注意观察,防止客人走失

参考答案:ACE

23.全陪分房时团队出现单男或单女现象,可采取的分房措施是( )。

A.让客人和非本团队的陌生人合住一间房

B.安排一个三人间

C.安排标间加床

D.请客人入住专门的驾导房

E.问客人是否愿意住单间,根据合同由其支付另一半费用

参考答案:BCE

24.全陪在陪同游客参观游览的过程中,可通过下列哪些措施行使其安全职责?( )

A.禁止客人自发的探险行为

B.主动走在团队最后

C.在前带队,督促大家紧跟团队

D.随时清点人数

E.多观察周围环境和动向,提醒游客注意人身财产安全

参考答案:ABDE

25.在国外住店过程中,领队应提醒游客注意( )。

A.不在公共场所吸烟

B.讲话声音不能影响到其他人

C.不要穿拖鞋、睡衣在酒店内串房

D.不要随意带走酒店的设施和挂件

E.不要随地吐痰

参考答案:ABCDE

26.地陪预防游客走失的措施有( )。

A.让游客记住接待社的名称、旅游车车号或标志、下榻饭店名称、电话

B.做好每天行程预报工作,包括游览景点及用餐地点

C.讲清旅游路线、所需时间,不断强调集合时间和地点

D.地陪、全陪和领队要分工协作、密切配合、各司其职

E.自由活动时提醒游客不要走得太远,不要太晚回饭店

参考答案:ABCDE

27.若接待计划中有地陪不熟悉的景点,地陪在接团前应了解该景点的( )。

A.所在位置　　B.开放时间　　C.主要设施

D.游览线路　　　　E.厕所位置

参考答案：ABDE

28.导游服务是旅游服务中具有代表性的工作,具有(　　)的特点。

A.独立性强　　　B.脑体高度结合　C.客观要求复杂多变

D.跨文化性　　　E.导游个性化鲜明

参考答案：ABCD

29.全陪在末站服务时,应做到(　　)。

A.提醒游客保管好自己的物品和证件

B.征求游客的意见和建议

C.致欢送词

D.协助游客清点行李,以防遗失

E.请游客填写"游客意见表"

参考答案：ABCE

30.导游到机场接到应接的散客后,要做好的工作有(　　)。

A.介绍所代表的旅行社和自己的姓名,对其表示欢迎

B.询问游客在机场是否有需要办理的事情

C.询问游客托运的行李件数,并进行清点

D.帮助游客提取行李并引导其上车

E.介绍当地的风情和下榻的饭店的情况

参考答案：ABCD

31.接团前,地陪应到旅行社领取的表单有(　　)。

A.接待计划表　　　　　　B.旅游团名单

C.旅游服务质量反馈表　　D.物品借用表

E.费用结算单

参考答案：ABCE

32.参加我国导游资格考试的条件,正确的有(　　)。

A.中华人民共和国公民

B.具有大专或者以上学历

C.身体健康

D.具有适应导游需要的基本知识和语言表达能力

E.参加国家旅游局或地方旅游行政管理部门组织的考试培训

参考答案：ACD

33.决定导游讲解语言快慢的因素有(　　)。

A.游客的类型　　B.讲解的方式　　C.讲解的内容

D.游客的情绪　　E.讲解的地点

参考答案:AC

34.导游处理好与旅游团领队关系的方法主要有( )。

A.多同领队磋商　　　　　　　　B.多给领队"面子"

C.多按领队的意见办　　　　　　D.多支持领队的工作

E.多给领队一些好处

参考答案:ABD

35.下列关于导游人员相关礼仪规范的说法中,正确的有( )。

A.女导游可以佩戴耳环、手镯等饰物

B.带团时最好不要吃葱、蒜、韭菜等有异味的食物

C.坐下时不应高跷二郎腿

D.始终以微笑来面对游客,为游客提供微笑服务

E.不随意进入游客房间,确有事需要进入时,应事先电话约定并准时抵达

参考答案:BCDE

36.导游人员着装的TPO原则分别是指( )。

A.风格　　　B.品位　　　C.场合

D.时间　　　E.地点

参考答案:CDE

37.地陪导游接旅游团前的业务准备包括( )。

A.落实住房　　　　　　　　B.熟悉接待计划

C.落实旅游车辆　　　　　　D.做好有关知识准备

E.与全陪联系

参考答案:ABCE

38.在地陪带团过程中,要随时提醒游客记住旅游车的( )等信息。

A.司机姓名　　　B.座位数　　　C.车牌号、

D.车型　　　　　E.颜色

参考答案:CDE

39.游客的下列行为中,属于违法行为的有( )。

A.嫖娼　　　　B.贩毒　　　　C.信教

D.讲黄段子　　E.套购外汇

参考答案:ABE

40.导游与司机的协作应该包括( )。

A.及时向司机通报相关信息

B.征求司机对日程安排的意见

C.行车中与司机闲聊

D.遇到险情,由司机保护车辆和游客,导游去寻求援助

E.协助司机做好行车安全工作

参考答案：ABDE

41.下列关于导游沿途导游的做法中,正确的有（　　）。

A.面带微笑站在车的前部、司机的右后侧

B.对重要的内容要重复讲解或加以解释

C.高速公路上要站稳抓牢进行导游讲解

D.旅游者如果比较疲劳,导游可少讲解,多让旅游者休息

E.长距离行驶时,导游可以穿插进行一些游戏和娱乐内容

参考答案：ABDE

42.关于用餐时的导游服务,下列描述中正确的有（　　）。

A.地陪应介绍餐厅的设施、菜肴特色、酒水类别和洗手间的位置

B.告知旅游者餐饮标准所含范围与自费项目

C.巡视用餐不少于3次,随时解答旅游者在用餐中提出的问题

D.让有特殊饮食习惯的旅游者单独用餐

E.监督、检查餐厅是否按标准提供服务

参考答案：ABE

43.旅游团在住店期间遇到火灾,导游正确地处理火灾的方法是（　　）。

A.立即拨打110报警

B.迅速通知领队和全体成员,疏散旅游者

C.导游应告知旅游者用湿毛巾捂住口鼻

D.千万不要让旅游者乘电梯或者跳楼逃生

E.若着火点在本楼层,导游应率领旅游者逃向楼顶平台

参考答案：BCD

44.接待好残障游客,关键在于导游要（　　）。

A.耐心解答问题　　　　　　B.预防游客走失

C.给以适时、恰当的关照　　D.给以具体、周到的服务

E.做好提醒工作

参考答案：CD

45.导游在讲解的时候要根据（　　）的不同来调节音量。

A.旅游者数量　　　　　　　B.旅游者理解能力

C.导游讲解地点　　　　　　D.导游讲解内容

E.旅游者年龄

参考答案：ACDE

46.导游人员与旅游者目光接触的向度是指视线接触的方向。视线向下接触一般有（　　）等含义。

A.期盼 B.爱护 C.宽容 D.理性

E.轻视

参考答案:BCE

47.从中国山水画与西方油画的比较,就能明显感觉到东方人与西方人的思维差异,西方人的思维方式一般是( )。

A.从抽象到具体 B.从具体到抽象 C.从远到近 D.从近到远

E.由小到大

参考答案:BDE

48.下列关于概述法的说法,正确的是( )。

A.是一种将典故、故事、传说等与景物介绍有机结合起来的讲解方法

B.概述法是对景点的景物布局、特色等基本情况进行轮廓性介绍的方法

C.通常适用于游览较大的景点之前在入口处示意图前进行的讲解

D.使游客对景点有一个整体认识

E.介绍时突出大景点中具有代表性的景观

参考答案:BCD

49.导游在接待高龄游客时,下列做法正确的是( )。

A.日程安排不要太紧,活动量不宜过大

B.适当增加休息时间和上厕所的次数

C.采用激将法激发游客的游兴

D.重要事项要反复提醒

E.晚间活动不要回酒店太晚

参考答案:ABDE

50.调节游客情绪的主要方法有( )。

A.诱导法 B.精神补偿法 C.分析法

D.物质补偿法 E.转移法

参考答案:BCDE

51.游客在( )情况下要求调换房间,导游应予以满足。

A.房间有老鼠 B.楼层不好 C.房间看不到风景

D.夏天空调不制冷 E.浴缸有污迹

参考答案:AD

52.心肺复苏可用于旅游者因( )而导致的呼吸中止和心跳停顿。

A.心脏病 B.溺水 C.中风

D.触电 E.高血压

参考答案:ABDE

53.如果游客要求增加游览项目,导游人员的正确操作应该是( )。

A.告诉游客增加游览项目需要增加费用,如果游客对费用没有意见就积极安排

B.看时间是否允许,如果没问题要先请示接待社

C.请接待社有关部门报价,将报价报给游客

D.游客认可报价后,地陪应陪同前往,并将费用收取后按实际花销支付给司机

E.将游客所交费用的收据交给游客

参考答案:BCE

54.入境旅游团中一游客希望购买几件古玩,导游人员正确处理方法是( )。

A.告诉游客古玩商店价格较高,可考虑在地摊上选购物美价廉的仿古艺术品

B.如游客从私人手上购买古玩,应提醒游客鉴别真伪

C.首先要建议游客去正规的古玩商店

D.提醒游客保存好发票

E.提醒游客保留古玩上的火漆印

参考答案:CDE

55.游客请导游人员代为购买某商品并快递时,导游人员应( )。

A.尽最大所能帮助游客

B.一般应婉拒

C.请示旅行社领导,看是否接受委托

D.如旅行社同意,则收取足够的钱款

E.快递后给对方预留的手机号留言,以示所委托之事已办妥

参考答案:BCD

56.外国游客丢失护照和签证后,导游应该协助其( )。

A.向其所在国驻华使馆挂失

B.到当地接待社开具遗失证明

C.到当地公安机关申领"护照遗失证明"

D.再持"护照遗失证明"到其驻华使馆申报新护照

E.再到当地公安机关申报签证

参考答案:BCDE

57.导游带领游客到高原地区旅游,为预防他们发生高原反应,导游应提前告知游客( )等。

A.不宜喝酒 B.要多喝水

C.不宜急速行走、跑步 D.前几天少洗澡或不洗澡

E.可服用抗高原反应药物

参考答案:ABCDE

58.前往景区游览途中,地陪应做的工作有( )。

A.重申当日活动安排 B.了解游客生活需求

C.沿途风光讲解　　　　　　　D.调整时差

E.活跃气氛

参考答案:ACE

59.某国内旅游团离站前请地陪导游帮助转递一包裹给其在当地的亲友,该导游经接待社同意后接受了旅游者的委托,其办理的程序包括(　　)。

A.打开检查　　　　　　　　B.请客人写委托书

C.收据交给旅行社　　　　　D.收取一定的费用

E.签收人确认签字

参考答案:ABCE

60.当旅游车到达景点,地陪应当在游客下车前提醒大家注意(　　)。

A.旅游车的标志或车号　　　B.返回旅游车的时间

C.司机的姓名电话　　　　　D.景区游览线路

E.带走贵重物品

参考答案:ABE

61.导游在接待亲子旅游团时,对儿童的正确做法应是(　　)。

A.不讨好儿童而给其买食物、玩具

B.不在旅游活动中突出儿童,而冷落其他游客

C.家长同意后,可单独带儿童外出活动

D.儿童生病,应及时建议家长请医生诊治

E.不能提供药品给儿童服用

参考答案:ABDE

62.因导游自身原因造成旅游团漏接后,导游应采取的补救措施有(　　)。

A.尽量满足游客的要求

B.给游客一定的物质补偿

C.提供更优质的讲解服务

D.诚恳赔礼道歉,求得游客谅解

E.必要时请接待社领导出面赔礼道歉

参考答案:BCDE

63.地陪导游到机场迎接入境旅游团时,如发现该团人数减少了,其正确做法有(　　)。

A.察看旅游团入境时是否办理了未到游客的签证注销手续,没有办理请领队马上办理

B.立即通知接待社有关人员变更该团住房、用餐和交通票的数量

C.提醒接待社有关人员通知各地接社该旅游团人数变更的情况

D.应及时报告接待社,在接待社征得组团社同意后才能迎接旅游团

E.联系组团社,查明缺少原因

参考答案:ABC

64.境外旅游团游客在我国境内丢失了行李,导游应在事后向旅行社写出书面报告,主要内容有( )。

A.行李丢失情况　　　　　　B.自己的分析判断
C.行李查找过程　　　　　　D.行李丢失处理结果
E.失主和其他游客的反映

参考答案:ACDE

65.旅游意外保险保障的内容有( )。

A.人身意外保障　　　　　　B.医疗费用保障
C.个人财物保障　　　　　　D.精神损失保障
E.个人法律责任保障

参考答案:ABCE

66.导游领队"一岗双责"是指( )。

A.为旅游者提供服务　　　　B.引导旅游者理性购物
C.讲好中国故事,弘扬社会正气　　D.加强团队安全管理
E.引导旅游者文明旅游

参考答案:AE

67.出境游客丢失护照和签证后,导游正确的处理措施是( )。

A.协助失者去当地接待社开具遗失证明
B.协助失者到就近警察机构报案,取得警察机构开具的报案证明
C.协助失者到所在国移民局补办护照和签证
D.向中国驻当地使领馆通报
E.回国后携带有关证件申请补办新护照

参考答案:ABE

68.重大旅游事故处理完后,导游应写出书面报告,其主要内容有( )。

A.事故发生的情况与原因　　B.事故处理过程与进展情况
C.事故对旅游活动的影响　　D.事故善后处理情况
E.应吸取的经验教训

参考答案:ABDE

69.在带团过程中,若出现游客烫伤的意外事件,导游可以( )。

A.用温酒冲洗,减轻疼痛　　B.用冷水为伤者做冷敷处理
C.用紫药水为伤者做创口外敷　　D.挑破伤者的水泡
E.用冰袋冰敷烫伤处

参考答案:BE

70.为防止游客在景点游览时走失,地陪应做好的工作有(　　)。

A.在景点下车前告知旅游者旅游车的停车地点、车型和车号

B.在景点示意图前向旅游者介绍游览路线、所需时间、集合时间和地点

C.在游览时以丰富的讲解内容和高超的讲解技巧吸引游客

D.在导游讲解中防止他人跟团听讲

E.在游览中要注意游客动向,提醒掉队的游客跟上团队

参考答案:ABCE

71.导游在带团中遭遇泥石流,应采取的紧急措施有(　　)。

A.跑在泥石流前面　　　　　　　B.跑向人多的地方

C.躲进旁边建筑物　　　　　　　D.尽量远离河道

E.带领旅游团向山坡上坚固的高处跑

参考答案:DE

72.在室内遇到地震发生时,导游应指导游客(　　)。

A.不要逃出后又返回房中取财物

B.迅速进电梯,撤至室外

C.不在楼道躲避

D.应就地躲在桌、床等结实的家具下

E.尽量躲在窄小的空间内,如卫生间、厨房或内墙角

参考答案:ACDE

73.为防止游客单独外出时走失,导游应告知其记住(　　)。

A.接待社的名称　　　　　　　　B.自己的电话号码

C.下榻饭店的名称　　　　　　　D.下榻饭店的建筑形式

E.下榻饭店的电话号码

参考答案:ABCE

74.住宿时导游进行文明引导包括(　　)等内容。

A.提醒旅游者尊重服务人员　　　B.提醒游客爱护饭店设施

C.提醒游客减少一次性物品使用　D.提醒游客不大声喧哗、不随地吐痰

E.提醒游客集合用餐时不要迟到

参考答案:ABCD

75.公务护照的签发机关为我国的(　　)。

A.外交部　　　　　　　　　　　B.公安机关出入境管理机构

C.驻外使馆、领馆　　　　　　　D.外交部委托的各省、市外事部门

E.外交部委托的其他驻外机构

参考答案:ACDE

76.下列属于普通签证的有(　　)。

A.公务签证   B.留学签证   C.旅游签证

D.工作签证   E.人才签证

参考答案:BCDE

77.台湾居民可以在(　　)地区申领台湾同胞往来大陆通行证。

A.台湾   B.大陆   C.香港

D.日本   E.澳门

参考答案:ABCE

78.某游客在景点游览过程中走失,经全陪和领队分头寻找后仍未找到,此时地陪应该(　　)。

A.立即向该景点管理部门求助,告知走失者的特征

B.与该团下榻的饭店联系,询问走失者是否已回饭店

C.若经过上述努力仍未找到,应及时将情况报告旅行社

D.经旅行社同意后,向公安局报案,并告知走失者的特征

E.将该团其他游客送上旅游车后,自己留下来继续寻找

参考答案:ABCD

79.游客在前往旅游景点途中突患重病,地陪应该(　　)。

A.征得患者同意后,立即送往就近医院救治

B.请全陪、领队和患者亲属陪同前往

C.及时将游客突患重病情况报告旅行社

D.及时将游客突患重病情况报告旅游局

E.自己继续带领其他游客赴景点游览

参考答案:ABCE

80.下列物品中,旅游者在出境时需向海关申报的是(　　)。

A.一台价值8900元的单反相机   B.一部价值5700元的苹果手机

C.5000欧元现金   D.鲜肉月饼、香蕉、火腿肠

E.一件重量为60克的金首饰

参考答案:ABCE

81.旅游团中部分游客不愿看计划安排内的文娱节目,而要求去看另一演出。此时,地陪可采取的措施有(　　)。

A.如时间许可,与计调部联系,尽可能予以更换

B.如无法调换,应耐心向这部分游客做解释工作

C.征求这部分游客意见是否可另外安排时间去看另一演出

D.若这部分游客仍坚持去看另一演出,应讲清费用自理

E.若这部分游客仍坚持去看另一演出,还应讲清未看的文娱节目票款不退

参考答案:ABDE

82.为预防交通事故的发生,导游对司机应该(　　)。

A.在天气不好、交通拥挤的情况下提醒其注意安全,谨慎驾驶

B.在日程安排上留有余地,不催促司机为抢时间而超速行驶

C.在确保旅游者人身安全的情况下,奉劝其慢速行驶

D.提醒其开车前不要饮酒,不要让非本车人员开车

E.出车前提醒其检查车辆,若有隐患及时修理或换车

参考答案:ABDE

83.发生重大交通事故,导游应该(　　)。

A.立即组织现场人员抢救受伤游客

B.保护好现场,立即报案

C.迅速将发生交通事故情况报告接待社

D.如实向受伤游客家属介绍受伤情况

E.做好未受伤游客的安抚工作

参考答案:ABCE

84.游客购买并携带出境的文物,海关凭(　　)查验放行。

A.文物古籍部门加盖的鉴定标志

B.文物古籍外销统一发票

C.文化行政管理部门开具的"文物出境许可证"

D.文化行政管理部门加盖的鉴定标志

E.有游客签名的付款证明

参考答案:BD

85.某老年游客进客房时,因客房内地毯凸起不慎摔伤,其女儿告知地陪,要求饭店赔偿。经地陪从中协调后,双方达成一致,此时该地陪应做好的工作还有(　　)。

A.提醒双方将一致的意见形成文字　　B.请领队在形成文字的意见上签字

C.请全陪在形成文字的意见上签字　　D.将形成文字的意见复印一份留存

E.事后将复印件交旅行社保存

参考答案:ADE

86.为防止游客的财物被盗,导游应(　　)。

A.提醒游客将贵重物品存放在饭店前台保险柜里

B.提醒旅游者外出时应将现金放在客房里,不要随身携带

C.提醒游客在路上行走时随时注意身边可疑的人

D.提醒游客不要将房号告诉陌生人,晚上睡觉时要将房门锁好

E.在旅游车到达景点后,提醒司机在游客下车后关好车门、车窗

参考答案:ACDE

87.加入国际航空天合联盟的中国航空公司有（　　）。

A.中国国航　　B.东方航空　　C.厦门航空

D.深圳航空　　E.国泰航空

参考答案：BC

88.导游忌讳与外国游客谈论的话题有（　　）。

A.工作性质　　B.工资收入　　C.女性年龄

D.婚姻状况　　E.旅游感受

参考答案：BCD

89.为防止客房治安事故的发生，导游应提醒游客（　　）。

A.将贵重物品存入饭店保险柜　　B.不要让陌生人进入房间

C.不要让服务员随意进入房间　　D.出入房间时锁好门

E.不要将房号告诉陌生人

参考答案：ABDE

90.导游在接待游客投诉时，应耐心倾听，让其把话说完，这样做的好处有（　　）。

A.有利于缓和其激动的情绪　　B.有利于消除其心中的不满

C.有助于导游思索解释的办法　　D.有助于导游采取处理的措施

E.有助于导游和其达成和解

参考答案：AC

91.食物中毒的常见症状有（　　）。

A.恶心　　B.呕吐　　C.头痛

D.腹痛　　E.腹泻

参考答案：ABDE

92.因大雪封山，导致旅游团被迫变更旅游活动计划时，导游应采取的措施是（　　）。

A.向游客耐心解释，求得原谅

B.提出替代方案，与游客协商

C.请旅行社领导出面，向游客表示歉意

D.报告组团社并通知下一站

E.以精彩的讲解、热情的服务激起游客的游兴

参考答案：ABCE

93.下列导游做法中正确的是（　　）。

A.不代游客保管证件　　B.协助境外游客托运购买的大件物品

C.免费带亲友随团活动　　D.即将离开本地时，劝阻游客自由活动

E.为有困难的游客转递食品

参考答案:ABD

94.一旦发现旅游者疑为细菌性食物中毒,导游应该(　　)。

A.立即让游客停止进食,同时协助患者反复催吐

B.若旅游者集体中毒,应报告卫生防疫部门、接待社和旅游行政管理部门

C.封存患者所食用的食物和呕吐物,带到医院协助诊断

D.记录医生的救治过程

E.送医院救治时,要求医生开具诊断证明,写明中毒原因

参考答案:ABCE

95.旅游团出机场时,一游客发现自己的行李箱丢失,导游应该(　　)。

A.询问上一站旅行社行李运送情况

B.询问机场工作人员该团行李是否全部运到

C.带失主到失物登记处办理行李丢失认领手续

D.若行李确已丢失,协助失主向航空公司索赔

E.将失主行李丢失情况报告旅行社

参考答案:CDE

96.导游在接受散客接待任务后,应当详细阅读接待计划,明确(　　)。

A.旅游车的档次

B.抵达本地的日期(时间)、航班(车次)

C.下榻的饭店

D.所接游客姓名

E.提供哪些服务项目

参考答案:BCDE

97.为了保证旅游者在发生火灾时能尽快疏散,导游应(　　)。

A.熟悉饭店楼层安全出口的位置

B.熟悉饭店楼层电梯间的位置

C.提醒游客阅读客房内的安全避险线路示意图

D.提醒游客阅读客房内的服务指南

E.掌握领队和全体游客的房间号码

参考答案:ACE

第三部分　自选导游词创作

　　受篇幅所限,本部分选取近三年导游服务赛项一等奖获奖导游词各1篇作为范例,供备赛师生参考。

司城旧址雄荆南　唐崖胜景遗沉浮

2021年全国职业院校技能大赛高职组导游服务赛项一等奖作品

获奖学生：耿紫嫣
指导教师：丁洁

各位同学大家好，今天我们文化探秘之旅的第一站是世界遗产地——唐崖土司城遗址，这里也是目前已知城市功能格局最完整、保存最完好的土司城遗址之一。说起土司，它指的是封建王朝授予少数民族地区首领的世袭官职，历经元明清三代。接下来就让我们一起走进这沧桑古老的唐崖，共同探寻深山中的"土司皇城"。

我们现在所看到的，是土司生活办公的衙署区。六百多年前，土家族世袭土司覃氏，依山就势建造唐崖土司城。至第12代土司覃鼎，因战功显赫被朝廷同意扩建治所，于是以"三街十八巷三十六院落"的格局，配以城墙，建成这固若金汤的唐崖土司城。大家请看，这条东西向的主干道与南北向的横街交会，形成上、中、下三街，纵横交错的36条小巷随地势相互连接，四通八达。整座土司城中的街巷与自然和谐共生，既有象征"皇权"的中轴对称，又体现出"天人合一"的道家思想。

大家请看，衙署区最前端是一座石牌坊，这是明熹宗为表彰土司覃鼎的战功而立，也被称为"镇城之宝"。牌坊的横额上正面刻有"荆南雄镇"，背面是"楚蜀屏翰"，这八个大字都是皇帝亲笔所写，体现了明熹宗对土司平定叛乱、安邦荆南的褒奖。同学们再看牌坊上的雕刻，土王出巡的浮雕反映了土王巡查时的盛况，极具土家文化特色，而渔、樵、耕、读这四幅浮雕体现的则是文武兼修、农商结合的汉文化。可以说，这座功德牌坊既是土司走向权力中心的起点，更是土家族和汉族人民勤劳智慧的重要结晶。

同学们有没有发现，土司的生活区设计得非常精妙，那他死后的归属地又是怎样的呢？我们一起去看看。土司陵位于司城最后方，整个墓室为仿汉殿堂式，重檐庑殿顶，五柱四开间，用石头雕刻出斗拱、鸱吻等仿木构件，周围刻有瑞兽、云纹等汉地风格图案，这座陵墓是目前我国已知的规模最大、等级最高、形制最独特的土司墓，土家族的墓葬将生与死两个空间放在了一个区域，国内罕见，又用土汉文化的融合将其特点体现得淋漓尽致。

同学们，漫步土司城，脚下的青石街像被翻开的王朝史书。土司制度秉承的是因地制宜、因俗而治的多民族管理智慧，唐崖司城遗址，则见证了中华民族融合发展、文化自信的璀璨与辉煌。

阿 者 科

2022年全国职业院校技能大赛高职组导游服务赛项一等奖作品

获奖学生:珠海城市职业技术学院　张启龙
指导教师:珠海城市职业技术学院　周丽君

"七彩云南,梦想红河"！各位游客,大家好！欢迎您来到红河州元阳县阿者科村旅游考察。

先来做个小调查:各位是从哪里知道我们阿者科的呢？是从电影《无问西东》？还是从去年的高考试卷？又或是从纪录片《中国减贫密码》里呢？大家是不是很好奇,我们这里究竟有什么样的魅力呢？接下来,请您跟随我,让我为您揭晓。

我看各位已经被眼前的梯田给吸引了。没错,梯田的确是我们这里的一大魅力,我们村位于世界文化遗产——红河哈尼梯田的核心区,同时,也是梯田申遗的五个重点村落之一。

大家想想看,这世界上大多数的文化遗产是不是早就已经走进历史,成为过去了呢？而我们的哈尼梯田1300年来一直生生不息,沿用至今。各位请看,这一片片的山坡,通过一代代哈尼先民们勤劳的双手才铺成了这一道道的阶梯,有些地方甚至多达3000级。我们眼前看到这泛着波光的梯田在不同的季节又会几番变身:春天披花衫,夏天着绿纱,秋天穿金衣,冬天揽镜妆。一年四季之中,哈尼梯田最美的时候是冬天,灌满水的梯田倒映着天空的颜色。

如果您是2018年以前来到这里,看到的可不是现在这个样子。那时候村里的年轻人都外出打工,梯田没人种,房子没人住,村里卫生没人管,公路还不通,是云南省挂得上名的深度贫困村。

直到2018年1月,中山大学保继刚教授团队应元阳县政府邀请,为我们村编制了"阿者科计划"。由政府和高校分别派出驻村干部,共同指导村民们建立旅游公司,通过门票以及几十种旅游体验项目获得收入。这些收入的三成用作公司的日常运营以及后续建设,剩下的七成全都拿来给村民分红。计划实施这5年来,已经成功分红了6次。最近的一次,全村65户人家,分得最少的一户都拿到了两千多元。您可别嫌少,要知道在计划实施以前,这里的每户人家一年的收入也不过三千来元。

有家的地方有工作,那谁不愿意回家呢？我呀,就是我们村的返乡青年。我们阿者科村已经实现了旅游脱贫,相信在党和政府的领导下,有了科研团队的帮助,还有游客们的支持,我们阿者科更能通过发展旅游来保护世界遗产,实现乡村振兴。让我们阿者科的孩子也能"看得见山,望得见水,记得住乡愁"!

为了表达我们的感谢,接下来请您加入我们哈尼族传统的长街宴,品尝与梯田同样具有1300年历史的红米做成的"红米饭、红米线、红米粑粑、红米果"等哈尼族传统美食,同时聆听习近平总书记也提过的非遗——哈尼古歌四季生产调。

好嘞,咋咗咋咗,额补伙咋嘛(哈尼语),请大家随我入席!

上海四行仓库抗战纪念馆

2023年全国职业院校技能大赛高职组导游服务赛项一等奖作品

获奖学生：上海旅游高等专科学校　王伟
指导教师：上海旅游高等专科学校　刘堂

（口琴苏州河）

上海晋元中学的同学们，大家好，刚才的这段口琴呢，是电影《八佰》的片尾曲。欢迎来到"上海红色之旅"的第二站——四行仓库抗战纪念馆。

现在我们所看到的四行仓库呢，创建于1931年，原来是大陆银行和北四行的联合仓库，也是抗战期间中国军队在上海的最后一处据点。

1937年淞沪抗战打响了，时任中国军队第88师524团副团长的谢晋元，率领400多人，据守四行仓库。同学们有没有想过，为什么昨天看的电影叫《八佰》呢？没错，当时为了迷惑敌人，壮大声势，他们对外宣称四行仓库内有八百人，所以外界称他们为"八百壮士"。

面对数十倍的日寇，谢晋元将军带领"八百壮士"孤军奋战四天四夜，击毙敌军200多人，直到接到撤退命令后，才冲出重围。这场战役不仅沉重地打击了日本侵略者的嚣张气焰，也让全世界看到了中国人民抗战的决心与勇气。

同学们，请随我进入馆内，下面，我要向你们展示一封特殊的家书，现在看到的，就是谢晋元将军写给妻子的一封家书，也是一封遗书。

今天，作为晋元中学的同学们，请大家和我一起朗读这封家书，来致敬将军："我神州半壁河山，日遭蚕食，亡国灭种之祸，发之他人，操之在我，为国杀敌，是革命军人素志也。"

谢晋元将军还让每一位留守的战士们给家人写一封家书。他勉励战士们不要怕流血牺牲，要挽救国家民族于危亡，并嘱托道："只要还有一个人，就要同敌人拼到底！四行仓库就是我们的埋骨之处！"在场的战士大多岁数不大，小的和你们一样十六七岁，大的也不过二十出头，很多人没想到，这一生所写的第一封家书竟是自己的遗书。

八十六年前的那场战斗，让全世界看到了我们中华民族抵御外敌的决心。和平来之不易啊，珍惜和平，铭记历史，更要铭记那些为了国家和民族牺牲的英雄们。

好，同学们，下面我们的研学任务开始了，请大家在馆里寻找更多的英雄事迹，写到你的研学手册中。自由活动期间，请大家注意安全。1小时后，我们将前往第三站——中共一大纪念馆。

第四部分　现场导游词创作

　　题库中1—15号主题各进行了2个团型的创作,全部团型均有涉及,16—50号主题不区分团型,只提供范例供参赛师生参考。

2023年全国职业院校技能竞赛导游服务赛项题库

第二部分 现场导游词创作及讲解题库

一、旅游文化主题（50个）

中国书法	中国篆刻	中国画	中国刺绣
中国酒文化	中国剪纸	中医针灸	中国茶文化
中国传统制茶技艺	中国四大菜系	四大年画	良渚文化
儒家文化	青花瓷	景泰蓝	藏族唐卡
太极拳	宣纸传统制作技艺	端午节	藏族雪顿节
傣族泼水节	彝族火把节	云南普洱茶	蒙古族那达慕大会
北京烤鸭	四川火锅	三星堆遗址	周口店北京猿人
殷墟甲骨文	秦始皇陵兵马俑	上海石库门	都江堰水利工程
湖北曾侯乙编钟	辛亥革命	红军长征精神	"两弹一星"
红旗渠精神	成昆铁路	青藏铁路	港珠澳大桥
北京四合院	福建土楼	皖南古村落	藏族碉楼
苏州园林	北京颐和园	承德避暑山庄	京剧
川剧变脸	二十四节气		

二、团型（5种）

1. 政务考察团　　2. 商务考察团　　3. 记者采风团
4. 亲子旅游团　　5. 中(小)学生研学团

1 【中国书法】

政务考察团

各位领导(嘉宾):

  这边请,马上就要进入展馆的书法展区了,提起书法,相信现场的各位中不乏书法爱好者。在这里,请允许我浅显地介绍中国书法的发展历史。

  中国书法,随着汉字的演变而发展,经过三千多年的历程,从甲骨文、金文演变为大篆、小篆、隶书,至东汉、魏、晋的草书、楷书、行书诸体,已经成为中国文化的代表性象征。2009年,"中国书法"被列入了联合国教科文组织非物质文化遗产名录。

  从象形文字到甲骨文,商周、春秋还有汉代的简帛朱墨手迹,唐楷的法度,宋人尚意,元明尚态,清代的碑帖之争等书法演进。书法也是中国及深受中国文化影响过的周边国家和地区特有的一种文字美的艺术表现形式。如在日本、韩国等国家,书法艺术也很流行。

  书法是世界上少数几种文字所有的艺术形式,包括汉字书法、蒙古文书法、阿拉伯文书法等。中国书法最初以图画记事的形式出现,先人在沙地上画漂亮的图画符号,形成了书法雏形,直至发明毛笔,便产生了书法,也有其他如硬笔书法、指书等。

  从狭义讲,书法是指用毛笔书写汉字的方法和规律。包括执笔、运笔、点画、结构、布局等内容。例如,执笔指实掌虚,五指齐力;运笔中锋铺毫;点画意到笔随等。从广义讲,书法是指按照文字特点及其含义,如汉字的基本形态为方形,通过点画的伸缩、轴线的扭动,形成各种不同的形态,组合成富有美感的作品。

  随着文化事业的发展,在我国出现了现代书法。它在传统书法基础上,加以创新,突出"变"字,融诗书画为一体,力求形式和内容统一,使作品成为"意美、音美、形美"的三美佳作。这些佳作不仅具有欣赏价值,而且通过展出、拍卖的形式,带动了艺术市场的繁荣。

  接下来,很荣幸陪同各位领导(嘉宾)一同品鉴休会。

作者:张潇潇

中(小)学生研学团

同学们:

  在以前以笔墨为主要书写工具的时代,民间常说"字如其人、文如其人",究竟是不是这样呢? 科学研究表明,人类的大脑与双手息息相关,与其说手在写,不如说是大脑在指挥手做运动,一笔一画都能反映出书写者的个性,因此,通过笔迹,确实可以挖掘一个人的内心世界。我们马上就要进入展馆的书法展区了,先带大家了解中国书法的发展简史。

汉字是迄今为止连续使用时间最长的主要文字,也是上古时期各大文字体系中唯一传承至今的文字。是不是很骄傲?中国书法,随着汉字的演变而发展,经过三千多年的历程,从甲骨文、金文演变而为大篆、小篆、隶书,至东汉、魏、晋的草书、楷书、行书诸体,已经成为中国文化的代表性象征。2009年,"中国书法"被列入了世界非物质文化遗产名录。

从象形文字到甲骨文,商周、春秋还有汉代的简帛朱墨手迹,唐楷的法度,宋人尚意,元明尚态,清代的碑帖之争等书法演进。书法也是中国及深受中国文化影响过的周边国家和地区特有的一种文字美的艺术表现形式。有同学知道除了中国还有哪些国家吗?对了,是日本、韩国等国家。

书法,包括汉字书法、蒙古文书法、阿拉伯文书法等,是世界上少有的几种文字的艺术表现形式。中国书法最初以图画记事的形式出现,先人在沙地上画漂亮的图画符号,形成了书法雏形,后来发明毛笔,便产生了书法,也有其他如硬笔书法、指书等。

从狭义讲,书法是指用毛笔书写汉字的方法和规律,包括执笔、运笔、点画、结构、布局等内容。例如,执笔指实掌虚,五指齐力;运笔中锋铺毫;点画意到笔随等。从广义讲,书法是指按照文字特点及其含义,如汉字的基本形态为方形,通过点画的伸缩、轴线的扭动,形成各种不同的形态,组合成富有美感的作品。

随着文化事业的发展,我国出现了现代书法。它在传统书法基础上,加以创新,突出"变"字,融诗书画为一体,力求形式和内容统一,使作品成为"意美、音美、形美"的三美佳作。

大家还知道哪些著名书法家吗?让我们一起去寻找自己喜欢的书法作品,探寻书法家的内心世界,并将心得体会写在今天的学习总结中。

作者:张潇潇

2 【中国篆刻】

记者采风团

亲爱的媒体朋友们：

欢迎来到中国篆刻之乡考察采风，希望通过我的介绍能加深您对篆刻艺术的了解。

篆刻是一种传统的艺术形式，因古代印章多采用篆书入印而得名，它是书法和镌刻结合来制作印章的艺术。篆刻三法为篆刻术语，指篆法、章法、刀法。就制作工艺而言，它是指将在平面上设计好的纹样或文字镌刻在金属、石头、牙、角等材质上，由古代的印章制作技艺发展而来的一门独特的镌刻艺术，距今已有3000多年的历史。篆刻已在2009年被列入联合国教科文组织非物质文化遗产名录。

印章起源于阶级社会，开始作为一种凭证的信物，之后印章又成为权益的证物。春秋战国时期，印章的用途逐渐广泛，有器物记名用印、金币用印、标准器量器用印等。秦汉进入繁盛时期，至汉代形制更为多样，印文多采用缪篆。魏晋南北朝基本上依循秦汉印章的传统。唐代官印体积增大，印文采用小篆，镌刻多为朱文。

宋元私印范围开始扩大，收藏印、斋馆印、词句印兴起。印章在形制、用材、印文的镌刻、章法布局皆有显著变化。特别是文人、书法家、画家参加刻印，镌刻由工匠扩大到文人，这样印章进入篆刻艺术时代。自明代中叶，印章已从实用品、书画艺术的附属品，而发展成为独立的艺术。"篆刻"一词原为比喻书写和精心为文的意思，"篆谓篆书，刻谓雕刻文章也"，后来却成为镌刻印章这一艺术的名称。明代中叶到晚清的近500年中出现了各种风格的流派，把中国古代篆刻艺术推向了又一繁荣时期。除了被奉为篆刻之祖的明代文彭的吴门派、以何震为代表的徽派之外，影响较大的还有首任杭州西泠印社社长吴昌硕的吴派，现代篆刻家齐白石的齐派，等等。

篆刻艺术作品不仅具有文化承载和审美欣赏价值，而且具有文化交流价值。印章本身就有不菲的价值，而名家古画的鉴定，通过印章又能提供支持佐证。中国篆刻艺术的繁盛其中一个重要的因素是入印文字的形体美在起作用。各位媒体朋友您请看，文字的书体复杂多变，从体式来看分为真、草、隶、篆，每种体式又有不同的书写风格。真可谓方寸之间显华章，细微之处见乾坤。希望通过您的镜头和笔尖，使篆刻文化得到更好的宣传。

作者：张潇潇

商务考察团

各位企业家、商界精英们：

欢迎来到中国篆刻之乡，共同探讨中国篆刻艺术的商业价值。

这是一种传统的艺术形式，因古代印章多采用篆书入印而得名。它是书法和镌刻结合来制作印章的艺术。篆刻三法为篆刻术语，指篆法、章法、刀法。就制作工艺而言，它指将在平面上设计好的纹样或文字镌刻在金属、石头、牙、角等材质上，由古代的印章制作技艺发展而来的一门独特的镌刻艺术，距今已有3000多年的历史。篆刻已在2009年被列入联合国教科文组织非物质文化遗产名录。

印章起源于阶级社会，开始作为一种凭证的信物，之后印章又成为权益的证物。春秋战国时期，印章的用途逐渐广泛，有器物记名用印、金币用印、标准器量器用印等。秦汉进入繁盛时期，至汉代形制更为多样，印文多采用缪篆。魏晋南北朝基本上依循秦汉印章的传统。唐代官印体积增大，印文采用小篆，镌刻多为朱文。

宋元私印范围开始扩大，收藏印、斋馆印、词句印兴起。印章在形制、用材、印文的镌刻、章法布局皆有显著变化。特别是文人、书法家、画家参加刻印，镌刻由工匠扩大到文人，印章进入篆刻艺术时代。自明代中叶，印章已从实用品、书画艺术的附属品，而发展成为独立的艺术。"篆刻"一词原为比喻书写和精心为文的意思，"篆谓篆书，刻谓雕刻文章也"，后来却成为镌刻印章这一艺术的名称。明代中叶到晚清的近500年中出现了各种风格的流派，把中国古代篆刻艺术推向了又一繁荣时期。除了被奉为篆刻之祖的明代文彭的吴门派、以何震为代表的徽派之外，影响较大的还有首任杭州西泠印社社长吴昌硕的吴派，现代有篆刻家齐白石的齐派，等等。

篆刻艺术作品不仅具有文化承载和审美欣赏价值，而且具有文化交流价值。印章本身就有不菲的价值，而通过印章又能为名家古画的鉴定提供支持佐证。真可谓方寸之间显华章，细微之处见乾坤。本地的篆刻艺术颇具规模，希望通过各位企业家的点金之手，整合完善的文化产业链，为产业的商业价值赋能，将其推向更大的国际市场。

作者：张潇潇

3 【中国画】

亲子旅游团

亲爱的家长们、可爱的小朋友们：

1500年前，有个叫左思的人，搬家到洛阳后写了一篇文章《三都赋》，由于写得太好了，全洛阳城的读书人抢着买纸去抄录，搞得后来纸都没得买了，这就是洛阳纸贵的故事。他还写过一句诗"非必丝与竹，山水有清音"，意思是说，你别闷在家里学什么乐器了，应该到自然中去，到山水中去，大自然会给你很多惊喜。当我们领略到美丽的大自然时，不免想要把它们记录下来，如果没有照相机，我们还能通过什么途径呢？对了，画画！

今天咱们来现场了解学习中国画，用中国画是最能表达大自然的美丽的，它可是超过2000岁了，在战国时期就出现了帛画，这之前又有原始岩画和彩陶画。中国画是中国传统民族绘画的统称，也称国画或水墨画。它是以墨为主要颜料，以水为调和剂，以毛笔为主要工具，以宣纸和绢帛为载体的具有民族特色的特有画种。

对中国绘画而言，中国文化的启智性很重要。明代心学家王阳明在《传习录》中提到："你未看此花时，此花与汝心同归于寂。你来看此花时，则此花颜色一时明白起来。"意思是说，一朵花在深山开放，我不知道它存在，可是当我看到这朵花的时候，这朵花的颜色、形态就渐渐明白起来。这也就是说天地大美只有通过你的感悟才能转化为人类的美感。

小朋友们，要考考你们了，想学中国画，工具有什么啊？家长可以提示帮忙作答。

对了，有笔墨纸砚颜料，还有其他工具，如调色瓷盘、吸水海绵、印章等。

在这里，我要告诉小朋友们一个秘密，做到形神兼备，是中国画特别是人物画创作的关键。关于"形神"的关系，民间流传着这样一个故事"画龙点睛"，下次再为大家讲解。中国画的美是简洁丰润的，它是中国魂的完美展现。要看懂、画好中国画，就要好好地了解中国的哲学和文化。

作者：张潇潇

政务考察团

各位领导、嘉宾：

很荣幸陪同讲解并学习中国画，大家这边请。

中国画是中国传统民族绘画的统称，也称国画或水墨画。它是以墨为主要颜料,以水为调和剂,以毛笔为主要工具,以宣纸和绢帛为载体的具有民族特色的特有画种。它植根于华夏浓厚的文化沃土之中,跨越不同时空,形成了融汇民族文化素养、思维方式、审美意识和哲学观念的完整的艺术体系,与西方的油画形成了两座并峙的艺术高峰。

国画产生于中国文化之中。对中国绘画而言,中国文化的启智性很重要。《庄子·外篇·知北游》中讲"天地有大美而不言,四时有明法而不议,万物有成理而不说"。中国画就是要去体会这种美、这种内在目的性,然后将其运用笔墨表现出来,而不需要问"这树长在这对不对"。另一方面,天地大美只有通过感悟才能转化为人类的美感。

相信各位领导已有所了解,国画和西方绘画原则有许多不同的地方,其重在神似不重形似,强调观察总结不强调现场临摹,运用散点透视法不用焦点透视法,重视意境不重视场景等。现代国画的发展也开始吸收西方绘画的一些技巧,如明暗光影的配置、人体结构的准确等,也有画家将国画的意境用于油画创作。

当中国人的智慧和在哲学上感悟用绘画体现的时候,绘画就得益无穷了。中国禅宗讲,"妙悟者不在多言"。王维在《山水诀》将这视作对山水画的要求,即"以少许胜多许",以最简练的语言表现最丰富的内容。八大山人的画就是一种符号性的空前伟岸的语言,他的画已经撇除了一切的繁文缛节、一切的矫揉造作和一切的事功媚俗,剩下的只有"士气"的符号,精微广大、高明中庸。八大山人画的鸟,蜷曲着身子,他寥寥几笔,把鸟的全部内在生命表达得淋漓尽致。

感谢领导们的莅临考察,民族的就是世界的,希望有更多的营商政策扶持国画传承与发展。

作者:张潇潇

4 【中国刺绣】

商务考察团

各位企业家代表、商界精英们：

欢迎来考察中国刺绣名城。刺绣又名"针绣"，俗称"绣花"。以绣针引彩线，按设计的花样，在织物上刺缀运针，以绣迹构成纹样或文字，是我国优秀的民族传统工艺之一。

刺绣，起源于人们对装饰自身的需要。史传黄帝时代就有彩绘花纹的记载，也就是说古代原始人类早已懂得用色彩来美化自己，开始是将颜色涂在身上，称"彰身"，再进一步刺在身上，称"文身"，后来就画在衣服上，再发展成绣在服装上。

传世最早的刺绣，为湖南长沙出土的战国时期楚墓中的两件绣品，其针法，完全用辫子股针法（即锁绣）绣成于帛和罗上，针脚整齐，配色清雅，线条流畅，充分展示了楚国刺绣艺术的成就。

在历史的变迁中，由于市场需求和刺绣产地的不同，刺绣工艺品作为一种商品开始形成了各自的地方特色。而其中苏、湘、粤、蜀四个地方的刺绣产品销路尤广，影响尤大。江苏省苏州市的苏绣，代表作有双面绣《猫》；湖南省湘绣以狮、虎为主要题材，有"苏猫湘虎"之说；广东省粤绣代表作有《百鸟朝凤》；四川省蜀绣代表作有《熊猫》《芙蓉鲤鱼》等，既传承古艺又有创新，极具特色，被誉为我国"四大名绣"。

刺绣的魅力不仅仅在于它精湛的技艺和华美的外观，更在于它所传递的文化内涵和艺术价值。每一幅刺绣作品都是对传统文化的传承和演绎，同时也是对美好生活的向往和追求，具有极高的文化价值和市场价值。在刺绣的过程中，手工艺人们将情感、信仰和习俗融入其中，使得每一幅作品都充满了生命力。

如今，刺绣已经成为世界非物质文化遗产，不仅是中国，世界各地的手工艺人们都在用自己的方式传承和发扬刺绣这门古老的艺术。我们也希望通过今天的考察活动，借助各位的宣扬，开拓国际市场，让千万条彩线轻盈穿梭，传承这古老优秀的技艺，绣出中国独有的绚烂。

作者：张潇潇

中（小）学研学团

各位同学：

今天的研学课堂来到了中国刺绣名城，让我们一起感受中国传统技艺的魅力。

刺绣又名"针绣"，俗称"绣花"。以绣针引彩线，按设计的花样，在织物（比如丝绸、布帛)上刺缀运针,以绣迹构成纹样或文字,是我国优秀的民族传统工艺之一。刺绣,起源于人们对装饰自身的需要。史传黄帝时代就有彩绘花纹的记载,也就是说古代原始人类早已懂得用色彩来美化自己,开始是将颜色涂在身上,称"彰身",再进一步刺在身上,称"文身",后来就画在衣服上,再发展成绣在服装上。

同学们,遇到知识点要随听随记在研学手册上哦。

传世最早的刺绣,为湖南长沙出土的战国时期楚墓中的两件绣品,其针法,完全用辫子股针法(即锁绣)绣成于帛和罗上,针脚整齐,配色清雅,线条流畅,充分展示了楚国刺绣的艺术成就。

唐代以前的绣品,多为实用或装饰,刺绣内容与生活上的需要和风俗有关。宋代刺绣之作,除为实用品外,尤致力于绣画。自晋唐以来,文人士大夫热爱书法及绘画,书画乃当时最高的艺术表现,至宋更及于丝绣,书画风格直接影响到刺绣的风格。迄清各时代的绣画皆与绘画密不可分。

江苏省苏州市的苏绣,代表作有双面绣《猫》;湖南省湘绣以狮、虎为主要题材,有"苏猫湘虎"之说;广东省粤绣代表作有《百鸟朝凤》;四川省蜀绣代表作有《熊猫》《芙蓉鲤鱼》等,既传承古艺又有创新,极具特色,被誉为我国"四大名绣"。这也是一个知识点,同学们请记录。

刺绣的魅力不仅在于精湛的技艺和华美的外观,更在于传递的文化内涵和艺术价值。每一幅刺绣作品都是对传统文化的传承和演绎,同时也是对美好生活的向往和追求,具有极高的文化价值和市场价值。在刺绣的过程中,手工艺人们将情感、信仰和习俗融入其中,使得每一幅作品都充满了生命力。

如今,刺绣已经成为世界非物质文化遗产,不仅是中国,世界各地的手工艺人们都在用自己的方式传承和发扬刺绣这门古老的艺术。有兴趣的同学们通过今天的研学活动,也可以尝试亲手学习传承。

作者:张潇潇

5 【中国酒文化】

商务考察团

各位企业家代表、商界精英们：

欢迎莅临考察，今天的考察主题是中国酒文化，提到酒，相信各位都不陌生。

中国是世界上较早的酿酒国家，早在5000年前就已开始。

中国酒根据酿酒方法分类，有蒸馏酒、发酵酒和配制酒。根据酒精含量分类，有高度酒（一般在40%vol以上）、中度酒，低度酒。根据商业习惯，分为白酒、黄酒、葡萄酒、啤酒、果酒、露酒和药酒等。其中，白酒按香型可分为酱香型，以贵州茅台酒为代表，又称茅型；清香型，以山西汾酒为代表，又称汾型；浓香型，以四川泸州老窖特曲酒为代表，又称泸型，或窖香型；米香型，以广西桂林三花酒为代表；其他香型，如贵州董酒、陕西西凤酒等，具有各自独特的生产工艺和口感风味，其主体香及香型尚未确定。

酒是一种文化的载体，在几千年的文明史中，几乎渗透到政治、经济、文化教育、文学艺术和社会生活等各个领域。

中国传统文化，最讲究敬天地礼神明，沐浴更衣，以最好的酒，配上最高规格的礼仪，为向上苍、祖灵祈求福祉。此刻的酒文化，庄严而又厚重，扮演着神圣的祭品，承载着人们的希望和对未来的美好祝愿。

酒文化是中华民族饮食文化的重要组成部分。酒是人类较古老的食物之一，它的历史几乎是与人类文化史一道开始的。自从酒出现之后，作为一种物质文化，酒的形态多种多样，其发展历程与经济发展史同步，而酒又不仅仅是一种食物，它还具有精神文化价值。作为一种精神文化，它体现在社会政治生活、文学艺术，乃至人的人生态度、审美情趣等诸多方面。在这个意义上讲，饮酒不是就饮酒而饮酒，它也是在饮文化。

酒文化，上得了帝王高雅殿堂，亦可出入寻常百姓家，颇有种多元博大的思想境界。它在传统与时尚中寻找平衡，在开放与坚守中独具个性，和而不同，兼容并蓄。随着文化的沉淀，稳重庄严、豪爽不羁、自然喜气……统统化为它的风骨气质。当地气质最好的酒都在这里了，各位贵宾稍后可以亲自品鉴挑选，以酒为媒，预祝打开商业交流的新篇章。

作者：张潇潇

中(小)学研学团

各位同学们:

今天我们的学习主题是中国酒文化,是不是有同学已经偷偷地有经验了?这可不行,要等成年以后才可以适量饮酒,不然对身体会造成很大的伤害。

中国是世界上较早的酿酒国家,早在5000年前就已开始。

中国酒根据酿酒方法分类,有蒸馏酒、发酵酒和配制酒。根据酒精含量分类,有高度酒(一般在40%vol以上)、中度酒,低度酒。根据商业习惯,分为白酒、黄酒、葡萄酒、啤酒、果酒、露酒和药酒等。其中,白酒按香型又可分为酱香型、清香型、浓香型、米香型和其他香型等。

除了白酒,同学们还知道有什么酒吗?是的,还有浙江绍兴最出名的黄酒,电视广告里看到的山东烟台葡萄酒,青岛夏天走在大街上人手拎着一塑料袋的啤酒等等。

酒是一种文化的载体,在几千年的文明史中,几乎渗透到政治、经济、文化教育、文学艺术和社会生活等各个领域。

中国传统文化,最讲究敬天地礼神明,酒扮演着神圣的祭品,承载着人们的希望和对未来的美好祝愿。中国是酒文化的极盛地,不少文人学士写下了品评鉴赏美酒佳酿的著述,留下了斗酒、写诗、作画、养生、宴会、饯行等品酒佳话。饮酒的意义远不只满足口腹之欲;在许多场合,它都是作为一个文化符号,一种文化消费,用来表示一种礼仪,一种气氛,一种情趣,一种心境;酒与诗,从此就结下了不解之缘。有酒的地方,就有江湖。烈酒配豪杰,更彰侠风义胆。

酒文化,上得了帝王高雅殿堂,亦可出入寻常百姓家,颇有种多元博大的思想境界。它在传统与时尚中寻找平衡,在开放与坚守中独具个性,和而不同,兼容并蓄。随着文化的沉淀,稳重庄严、豪爽不羁、自然喜气……统统化为它的风骨气质。有人说,中国人的气质都在酒中,中国酒的气质就是中国人的气质。

同学们,我们虽然不能亲口品尝,但是可以通过观察色泽、闻其味道,或者看看谁还有更多的方法,来判断酒的种类。

作者:张潇潇

6 【中国剪纸】

记者采风团

各位媒体朋友们：

欢迎大家来采风考察，体验剪纸艺术。在中国，剪纸具有广泛的群众基础，交融于各族人民的社会生活，是各种民俗活动的重要组成部分。2009年，中国剪纸入选联合国教科文组织人类非物质文化遗产代表作名录。下面，我们一起走进非遗剪纸的世界，感受这门古老艺术的独特魅力吧！

中国剪纸是一种用剪刀或刻刀在纸上剪刻花纹，用于装点生活或配合其他民俗活动的民间艺术，经由千百年的锤炼，饱含浓郁民俗气息，它源于历代劳动人民对生活的热爱和对自然的敬畏，是中华民族传统美学和哲学观念的重要体现之一。

剪纸主要用来做窗花、喜花、礼花和门笺等。人们在传统节日和重要场合，喜欢用剪纸来装饰房屋或赠送亲友，以表达喜庆和祝福之意。此外，剪纸还常常用于庆祝新生儿、婚礼和生日等重要日子，具有吉祥的寓意。20世纪50年代中期，新疆吐鲁番市阿斯塔那墓葬群出土了世界上最早的剪纸实物，这是约1500年前南北朝时期丧俗使用的剪纸。中国是世界剪纸的故乡，20世纪丝绸之路东段中国境内考古发现的剪纸文物，印证了这样一个事实。

不同地区和民族有自己独特的剪纸艺术风格，相关组织通过十多年的多民族剪纸调查发现，中国有33个民族在日常传统习俗中使用了剪纸或非纸材的剪形。

纸的制造技术是从中国开始的。中国向世界传播了造纸术，为世界剪纸的普及提供了可能。另一个影响剪纸的因素就是制作剪纸的工具——剪刀的历史，剪刀形制的发展也是影响剪纸发展的重要因素。中国剪刀的历史可追溯至铁器时代的西汉早期，广州淘金坑发现的铁剪刀，是考古发现最早的剪刀，那时是无轴的"8"字股或"U"字股剪刀，唐代以前的剪纸，就是用这样的剪刀剪制的。

中国民间剪纸的传承主体是妇女群体，剪纸也是古代女红传统中比较普及的技艺之一，在传统乡村社会中，剪纸的传承模式主要是家庭式传承。记者朋友们，为了让这种古老的技艺传承下去，受众更广，影响更大，拜托大家多做宣传，多做推广！

作者：张潇潇

亲子旅游团

各位家长和小朋友们：

欢迎来体验剪纸艺术。在中国，剪纸具有广泛的群众基础，交融于各族人民的社会生活,是各种民俗活动的重要组成部分。2009年,中国剪纸入选联合国教科文组织人类非物质文化遗产代表作名录。下面,我们一起走进非遗剪纸的世界,感受这门古老艺术的独特魅力吧!

中国剪纸是一种用剪刀或刻刀在纸上剪刻花纹,用于装点生活或配合其他民俗活动的民间艺术,经由千百年的锤炼,饱含浓郁民俗气息,它源于历代劳动人民对生活的热爱和对自然的敬畏,是中华民族传统美学和哲学观念的重要体现之一。各位家长在参观的过程中,请留意小朋友,眼看手勿动,注意安全。

剪纸主要用来做窗花、喜花、礼花和门笺等。人们在传统节日和重要场合,喜欢用剪纸来装饰房屋或赠送亲友,以表达喜庆和祝福之意。此外,剪纸还常常用于庆祝新生儿、婚礼和生日等重要日子,具有吉祥的寓意。不同地区和民族有自己独特的剪纸艺术风格。例如,北方地区的剪纸艺术风格多以线条简洁、图案明快著称;南方地区的剪纸艺术则偏向于色彩鲜艳、细腻多变;在西南地区,剪纸以其线条流畅、造型简单、寓意深刻而闻名。

相关组织通过10多年的多民族剪纸调查发现,中国有33个民族在日常传统习俗中使用了剪纸或非纸材的剪形。

20世纪50年代中期,新疆吐鲁番市阿斯塔那墓葬群出土了世界上最早的剪纸实物,这是约1500年前南北朝时期丧俗使用的剪纸。中国是世界剪纸的故乡,20世纪丝绸之路东段中国境内考古发现的剪纸文物,印证了这样一个事实。

纸的制造技术是从中国开始的。中国向世界传播了造纸术,为世界剪纸的普及提供了可能。另一个影响剪纸的因素就是制作剪纸的工具——剪刀的历史,剪刀形制的发展也是影响剪纸发展的重要因素。现在,体验环节到了,请家长们拿好工具,注意照看好小朋友,一起制作一件剪纸作为留念吧!

作者:张潇潇

7 【中医针灸】

政务考察团

各位领导、嘉宾：

国之瑰宝，医之精髓。2010年，中医针灸成功入选人类非物质文化遗产代表作名录，标志着"关于生命与自然界认知智慧结晶"的中医针灸得到了国际社会的普遍认同，进一步打开了我国中医药传统文化多样性的新局面。

针灸对于治疗神经系统疾病、骨关节疾病等有很好的治疗效果。当人体经络中的气循环出现异常时，经络可能发生堵塞，从而引起各种疾病，而通过针刺穴位，可使气的循环恢复正常，从而疏通经络，达到治疗的目的，这也是针灸的原理所在。

针灸包括针法与灸法。针法即在中医理论的指导下将毫针按照一定的角度刺入患者皮肤，并运用提插、捻转等手法来刺激特定的部位，帮助疏通经络，从而达到治疗目的的一种治疗方法。刺入的点即穴位，人的身体一共有300多个穴位，不同的疾病所选取的穴位是不同的。

各位领导，请移步这边。灸法，这是指在穴位上用灸柱进行烧灼、熏熨的一种治疗方法，它主要是利用热的刺激达到治疗疾病的目的，由于大多选用艾草，因此也称为艾灸。此外，还有桑枝灸、灯芯灸、柳条灸、隔药灸等方法。

数千年来，古代医家从扁鹊、华佗到张仲景、孙思邈等，都曾通过针灸解除病痛，甚至挽救生命，于是，这一行之有效的疗法世代相传。针灸疗法有广泛的适应性，疗效迅速显著，具有操作简便、费用经济、极少副作用的独特优势。迄今为止，针灸已经传播至世界140多个国家和地区。

从某种意义上说，中医针灸既扮演着复兴中国传统文化的先锋角色，也担负着推动中医药事业发展的重任，因此，中医针灸文化精髓的传承和发展是一项利在当代、功在千秋的自信自强工程。恳请社会各界更多关注和投入中医青年人才培养，多加宣传和倡导，打破"中医是老的吃香"的固有观念，让更多的年轻人投入到中医药行业中来，成为祖国医疗卫生事业的生力军。

作者：张潇潇

商务考察团

各位企业家、商界精英们：

到了一定的年龄，有些血脉自然觉醒，比如中医养生。各位嘉宾，今天咱们来了解中国的针灸文化。

传说针灸起源于三皇五帝时期,伏羲发明了针灸,直至2010年,中医针灸成功入选联合国非物质文化遗产名录,标志着"关于生命与自然界认知智慧结晶"的中医针灸得到了国际社会的普遍认同,进一步打开了我国中医药传统文化多样性的新局面。

针灸对于治疗神经系统疾病、骨关节疾病等有很好的治疗效果。当人体经络中的气循环出现异常时,经络可能发生堵塞,从而引起各种疾病,而通过针刺穴位,可使气的循环恢复正常,从而疏通经络,达到治疗的目的,这也是针灸的原理所在。

针灸包括针法与灸法。针法即在中医理论的指导下将毫针按照一定的角度刺入患者皮肤,并运用提插、捻转等手法来刺激特定的部位,帮助疏通经络,从而达到治疗目的的一种治疗方法。刺入的点即穴位,人的身体一共有300多个穴位,不同的疾病所选取的穴位是不同的。灸法则是指在穴位上用灸柱进行烧灼、熏熨的一种治疗方法,它主要是利用热的刺激达到治疗疾病的目的,由于大多选用艾草,因此也称为艾灸。另外还有桑枝灸、灯芯灸、柳条灸、隔药灸等方法。

数千年来,古代医家从扁鹊、华佗到张仲景、孙思邈等,都曾通过针灸解除病痛,甚至挽救生命,于是,这一行之有效的疗法世代相传。中医针灸的文化精髓是"仁、顺、活、和",也是中医针灸赖以生存和延续的土壤。针灸疗法有广泛的适应性,疗效迅速显著,具有操作方法简便易行、医疗费用较低、极少副作用的独特优势。

最珍贵的就是健康,各位嘉宾想必感同身受,创造财富更要需要健康的体魄。从某种意义上说,中医针灸既扮演着复兴中国传统文化的先锋角色,也担负着推动中医药事业发展的重任,其蕴含着大量的实践观察、知识体系和技术技艺,凝聚着中华民族强大的生命力与创造力,是中华民族智慧的结晶,也是全人类文明的瑰宝,应该得到更好的保护与利用。

作者:张潇潇

8 【中国茶文化】

中(小)学研学团

各位同学们：

5000多年前，神农氏遍尝百草，发现了可以用来解毒的茶，《神农百草》记载"茶味苦，饮之使人益思、少卧、轻身、明目"。茶的利用史大致可分为四个阶段：药用、食用、饮用、品用。实际上中国的饮茶历史只有2700年左右，而真正的饮茶风俗，是在秦吞并巴蜀后由蜀地对外传播的。文史上记载有"秦人取蜀，而后始有茗饮之事"。

知识点来了，请做好记录。茶文化有广义和狭义之说，广义的茶文化是指整个茶业发展历程中有关物质和精神的总和，包括制度、物态、行为和心态四个层次；狭义的茶文化专指精神财富这一项，包括行为和心态文化。

茶通"琴、棋、书、画、诗、曲"六艺，谓之形而上；茶融"柴、米、油、盐、酱、醋"六味，谓之形而下，雅俗共赏。

同学们，我们一起来尝试理解一下茶文化的内涵。茶把"三教合一"的文化精华融合起来。茶与道通，古代茶人常把温盏、投茶、沏泡、品饮、收杯、洁具、复归视为一次与大自然亲近融合的历程，其实是把大自然恩赐之茶作为人和天地融合的一种体验；茶与儒通，以茶礼人，客来敬茶，是中国传统文化的重要内容之一；茶与佛通，对于僧人来说，饮茶不仅仅是为了醒神和增加营养物质，重要的是能否端起茶杯悟出一颗平常心来。

茶圣陆羽给茶人定义：喝茶，最宜"精行俭德"之人；"当代茶圣"吴觉农也给茶人定义：勤勤恳恳，埋头苦干，清廉自守，无私奉献，具有君子操守。所以，世人得出了"人品即茶品，品茶即品人"的精辟妙言，这句话意在告诉人们，人要像茶一样有历经磨难而不屈的奉献精神，继而走向奉献人生的道路。

目前，在众多的茶类划分中，运用最广泛、最权威、认知度最高的当属六大茶类，即绿茶、红茶、青茶、黑茶、白茶、黄茶。

同学们，在接下来的课程中，继续深入了解每类茶的特点，找到适合自己和亲友的一款好茶吧！

作者：张潇潇

记者采风团

媒体朋友们：

欢迎考察了解中国茶文化，《神农百草》中记载"茶味苦，饮之使人益思、少卧、轻身、明目"。茶由神农氏发现并利用，其利用史大致可分为四个阶段：药用、食用、饮用、品用。实际上中国的饮茶历史有2700年左右，而真正的饮茶风俗，是在秦吞并巴蜀后由蜀地对外传播。文史上记载有"秦人取蜀，始知茗饮事"。

广义的茶文化，是指整个茶业发展历程中有关物质和精神的总和，包括制度、物态、行为和心态四个层次；狭义的茶文化，专指精神财富这一项，包括行为和心态文化。茶通"琴、棋、书、画、诗、曲"六艺，谓之形而上；茶可下，融"柴、米、油、盐、酱、醋"六味，谓之形而下，雅俗共赏。

中国茶文化，源头在道家，核心为儒家，发展在佛家。故茶与道通，通在自然；茶与儒通，通在中庸；茶与佛通，通在神合。把"三教合一"的文化精华融合起来，便是中国茶文化的核心"和合"思想。茶与道通：古代茶人常把温盏、投茶、沏泡、品饮、收杯、洁具、复归视为一次与大自然亲近融合的历程，其实是把大自然恩赐之茶作为人和天地融合的一种体验，"天人合一""道法自然"是道家思想的重要内容。茶与儒通，以茶礼人，客来敬茶，是中国传统文化的重要内容之一，有人说，中国人的待客之礼是通过茶来培养的，此话有一定的道理。茶与佛通，对于僧人来说，饮茶不仅仅是为了醒神和增加营养物质，重要的是能否端起茶杯悟出一颗平常心来。

茶文化是中国传统文化的核心力量，茶文化作为精神文明的载体，可以反映在许多层面。各位媒体朋友们，请坐下来，品尝一杯清茶。我代表茶乡人民感谢大家的宣传力量。

作者：张潇潇

9 【中国传统制茶技艺】

政务考察团

各位领导、嘉宾：

大家好！报告一个好消息，2022年11月29日晚，我国申报的"中国传统制茶技艺及其相关习俗"在联合国教科文组织保护非物质文化遗产政府间委员会第17届常会上通过评审，列入联合国教科文组织人类非物质文化遗产代表作名录。

中国传统制茶技艺及其相关习俗涉及的非遗领域包括：社会实践、仪式和节庆活动，有关自然界和宇宙的知识和实践，传统手工艺。例如，茶园管理、茶叶采摘、茶的手工制作，以及茶的饮用和分享的知识、技艺和实践等。

传统制茶技艺主要集中于秦岭淮河以南、青藏高原以东的江南、江北、西南和华南四大茶区，包括浙江、江苏、江西、湖南、安徽、湖北、河南、陕西、云南、贵州、四川、福建、广东、广西等地，相关习俗在全国各地广泛流布，为多民族所共享。

制茶师根据当地的风土，使用炒锅、竹匾、烘笼等工具，运用绿茶的"杀青"，黄茶的"闷黄"，黑茶的"渥堆"，白茶的"萎凋"，乌龙茶的"做青"，红茶的"发酵"，花茶的"窨制"等核心技艺，制作发展出2000多种茶品。以乌龙茶制作的过程为例："萎凋"，目的是蒸发水分；"做青"是乌龙茶制作的核心技艺，通过反复多次摇动、静置，使茶叶持续失水，生发出乌龙茶的香气；制茶师再使用炒锅进行"杀青"；然后进行"揉捻"，挤出叶汁，使之凝于叶表；此后是"烘焙"，制茶师用炭灰包裹火炭，将茶叶放在烘笼上缓慢干燥，完成初制。

与该遗产项目相关的知识和技艺主要通过家族传承、师徒传承和社区传承等传统方式进行传承，并与正规教育有所融合。

下面，请制茶师现场展示制作乌龙茶的部分核心技艺，请贵宾们移步观看。

作者：张潇潇

记者采风团

媒体朋友们：

大家好，报告一个好消息，2022年11月29日晚，我国申报的"中国传统制茶技艺及其相关习俗"已通过评审，列入联合国非物质文化遗产名录。至此，我国共有43个项目列入联合国教科文组织非物质文化遗产名录、名册，居世界第一。

中国传统制茶技艺及其相关习俗涉及的非遗领域包括：社会实践、仪式和节庆活动，有关自然界和宇宙的知识和实践，传统手工艺。例如，茶园管理、茶叶采摘、茶的手工制作,以及茶的饮用和分享的知识、技艺和实践等。

传统制茶技艺分布在北纬18°—37°、东经94°—122°范围内,主要集中于中国秦岭淮河以南、青藏高原以东的江南、江北、西南和华南四大茶区,包括浙江、江苏、江西、湖南、安徽、湖北、河南、陕西、云南、贵州、四川、福建、广东、广西等地,相关习俗在全国各地广泛流传,为多民族所共享。

制茶师根据当地的风土,使用炒锅、竹匾、烘笼等工具,运用杀青、闷黄、渥堆、萎凋、做青、发酵、窨制等核心技艺,发展出绿茶、黄茶、黑茶、白茶、乌龙茶、红茶六大茶类及花茶等再加工茶,2000多种茶品。

下面请制茶师以乌龙茶制作的过程为例演示部分核心技艺,各位嘉宾边看我边解说。

"萎凋",目的是蒸发水分;"做青"是乌龙茶制作的核心技艺,通过反复多次摇动、静置,使茶叶持续失水,生发出乌龙茶的香气;制茶师再使用炒锅进行"杀青";然后进行"揉捻",挤出叶汁,使之凝于叶表;此后是"烘焙",制茶师用炭灰包裹火炭,将茶叶放在烘笼上缓慢干燥,完成初制。

与该遗产项目相关的知识和技艺主要通过家族传承、师徒传承和社区传承等传统方式进行传承,并与正规教育有所融合。

媒体朋友们,感谢各位对中国传统制茶技艺的关注,我们期待中国传统制茶技艺登上更大的舞台。

作者:张潇潇

10 【中国四大菜系】

亲子旅游团

亲爱的家长和小朋友们：

大家好！到我们最喜欢的环节了——品尝美食。我先来介绍一下中国四大菜系，稍后看哪个小朋友知道今天吃什么？

菜系，也称"帮菜"，是指在选料、切配、烹饪等技艺方面，经长期演变而自成体系，具有鲜明的地方风味特色，并为社会所公认的中国饮食的菜肴流派。早在春秋战国时期，中国传统饮食文化中南北菜肴风味就表现出差异。到唐宋时，南食、北食各自形成体系。发展到清代初期时，鲁菜、苏菜、粤菜、川菜，成为当时最有影响的地方菜，被称作"四大菜系"。

1.鲁菜

鲁菜，即山东菜，是我国北方影响最大的一个菜系，有北方代表菜之称。讲究调味醇正，口味偏咸鲜，具有鲜、嫩、香、脆的特色。烹调技法以爆、炒、扒、熘见长，善用酱、葱、蒜调味和用清汤、奶汤增鲜。代表名菜有九转大肠、油爆双脆、葱烧海参等。

2.苏菜

苏菜，又称淮扬菜。主要特点是用料广泛，以江河湖海水鲜为主；刀工精细，烹调方法多样，擅长炖、焖、煨、焐，追求本味，清鲜平和，适应性强；菜品风格雅丽、形质均美。

苏菜是由淮扬菜（扬州、淮安）、江宁菜（南京、镇江）、苏锡菜（苏州、无锡）等几部分组成，以淮扬菜为代表。代表名菜有松鼠鳜鱼、叫花鸡等。

3.粤菜

粤菜历来以选料广博奇杂、菜肴新颖奇异而闻名。它由广府（以广州菜为代表）、客家（又称东江风味，以惠州菜为代表）、潮汕（以潮州菜为代表）三种风味组成，以广府风味为代表。代表名菜有白灼海虾、脆皮乳猪等。

4.川菜

川菜具有用料广博，味道多样，菜肴适应面广等特点，其中尤以味型多样、变化巧妙而著称，具有"一菜一格""百菜百味"的特殊风味。代表名菜有鱼香肉丝、宫保鸡丁等。

好了，上菜啦，小朋友们快去洗手哦！

作者：张潇潇

中(小)学研学团

同学们,如果我说中国菜是全世界最棒的,没有人不同意吧?

中国烹饪与法国烹饪、土耳其烹饪被认为是"世界三大烹饪流派代表"。

中国烹饪经历了夏商周的"铜烹时期"、西汉以后的"铁烹时期",发展到现在,烹饪工艺不断改进和完善,形成富有中国特色的风味体系。早在明清时期,我国就形成了鲁、苏(淮扬)、粤、川"四大菜系"。菜系,也称"帮菜",是指在选料、切配、烹饪等技艺方面,经长期演变而自成体系,具有鲜明的地方风味特色,并为社会所公认的中国饮食的菜肴流派。

1.鲁菜

鲁菜即山东菜,是我国北方历史悠久、影响最大的一个菜系,有北方代表菜之称。讲究调味醇正,口味偏咸鲜,具有鲜、嫩、香、脆的特色。烹调技法以爆、炒、扒、熘见长,善用酱、葱、蒜调味和用清汤、奶汤增鲜。代表名菜有九转大肠、油爆双脆、葱烧海参等。

2.苏菜(又称淮扬菜)

主要特点:用料广泛,以江河湖海水鲜为主;刀工精细,烹调方法多样,擅长炖、焖、煨、焐,追求本味,清鲜平和,适应性强;菜品风格雅丽、形质均美。代表名菜有松鼠鳜鱼、响油鳝糊、大煮干丝等。

3.粤菜

粤菜选料广博奇杂、菜肴新颖奇异。它由广府(以广州菜为代表)、客家(又称东江风味,以惠州菜为代表)、潮汕(以潮州菜为代表)三种风味组成,以广府风味为代表。代表名菜有白灼海虾、脆皮乳猪、白云猪手等。

4.川菜

川菜用料丰富,味道多样,菜肴适应面广,其中尤以味型多样、变化巧妙而著称。代表名菜有鱼香肉丝、宫保鸡丁等。

说到这里,有同学知道八大菜有哪些吗?请记录刚刚讲过的知识点入册哦。

作者:张潇潇

11 【四大年画】

亲子旅游团

亲爱的家长和小朋友们：

咱们来讨论一个热闹的话题——过年。请问小朋友们，过年的时候最喜欢和爸爸妈妈一起玩什么？是放烟花还是贴年画呢？今天我们一起来看看好看的年画是怎么来的。

年画和春联一样，都起源于"门神"。为什么叫"年画"呢？因为大都在新年时张贴，用于装饰环境，含有吉祥喜庆祝福新年之意。苏州桃花坞、天津杨柳青、山东潍坊杨家埠和四川绵竹，是我国著名的四大民间木刻年画产地。

桃花坞木版年画，因曾集中在苏州城内桃花坞一带生产而得名。它以木版雕刻，用一版一色的传统水印法印刷，具有构图精巧、形象突出、主次分明、优美清秀、严密工整的独特风格，民间画坛称之为"姑苏版"。

天津杨柳青版画，有"家家会刻版，人人善丹青"之誉。它将木刻水印和手工彩绘相结合，保留了民间绘画的技法，并受清代画院的影响，多取材于旧戏剧、美女、胖娃娃等，构图丰满，线条工整，色彩艳丽，人物头脸多粉金晕染。其与苏州桃花坞年画并称"南桃北柳"。

潍坊杨家埠版画，体现一个词"淳朴"，其全以手工操作并用传统方式制作，制作年画时，先用柳枝木炭条、香灰作画，名为"朽稿"，再完成正稿，描出线稿，分别雕出线版和色版，手工印刷。年画印出后，再手工补上各种颜色并进行简单描绘。不受自然的约束，以丰富的想象力和寓意的手法表现主题。

四川绵竹年画以彩绘见长，具有浓厚的民族特征和鲜明的地方特色。构图讲求对称、完整、色彩红火、热烈，被誉为"四川三宝""绵竹三绝"。一般分红、黑货两类。其题材分为避邪迎祥、历史人物、戏曲故事、民俗民风、花鸟虫鱼等。门神画是绵竹传统年画的主要品种。

家长朋友们，接下来我们一起分辨一下几种年画，比一比哪个家庭最快、最准？

作者：张潇潇

记者采风团

亲爱的媒体朋友们：

欢迎大家来考察，今天采风的主题活泼又热烈，说的是年画。中国存世最早的年画是宋版《隋朝窈窕呈倾国之芳容图》。年画始于古代的"门神画"，从早期的自然崇拜和神祇信仰逐渐发展为驱邪纳祥、祈福禳灾和欢乐喜庆、装饰环境的节日风俗活动,表达了民众的思想情感和向往美好生活的愿望。

苏州桃花坞、天津杨柳青、山东潍坊杨家埠和四川绵竹,是我国著名的四大民间木刻年画产地。

桃花坞木版年画,继承了宋代的雕版印刷工艺,兼用人工着色和彩色套版,以门画、中堂、条屏为主要形式,题材多为时事风俗、戏曲故事等。它的制作技艺主要由画稿、刻版、印刷工艺组合而成,一版一色、线条劲健。其色彩鲜艳、造型夸张,具有浓郁地方特色。

杨柳青年画保留了民间绘画的技法,并受清代画院的影响,多取材于旧戏剧、美女、胖娃娃等,构图丰满,线条工整,人物头脸多粉金晕染,风格严谨,背景简洁,注重人物神情的刻画。您看,这幅画中的胖娃娃是不是看着就喜庆?它与南方著名的苏州桃花坞年画并称"南桃北柳"。

山东潍坊杨家埠年画全以手工操作并用传统方式制作,先用柳枝木炭条、香灰作画,名为"朽稿",再完成正稿,描出线稿,分别雕出线版和色版,手工印刷。印出后,再手工补上各种颜色并进行简单描绘,直观地展现淳朴农民的简单愿望。

四川绵竹年画以彩绘见长,构图讲求对称、完整、主次分明、多样统一。其题材包含避邪迎祥、历史人物、戏曲故事、民俗民风、花鸟虫鱼等。按制作方法分为"捶墨""落墨"和"填色"三大类。门神画是绵竹传统年画的主要品种。

记者朋友们,欢迎以您专业的眼光赏鉴年画并和制作艺人畅谈交流,将中国的年画推向更广阔的天地。

作者:张潇潇

12 【良渚文化】

各位领导、贵宾：

大家好！可以这么说，放眼公元前3000年左右的世界，良渚文明足以与美索不达米亚（两河流域）的苏美尔文明并驾齐驱了。后者被认为创造和发明了世界上最早的城市、文明和文字，同时也可能是《圣经》中大洪水事件的起源地，从而被西方人视为经典的文明样本，在整个人类文明发展史上享有崇高的地位。

现在，请允许我自豪地讲解良渚文化。

1936年，施昕更是良渚遗址的第一个发现者。1959年，夏鼐先生正式提出"良渚文化"的名称。2007年，考古学家发现以莫角山宫殿为中心的四周还有一圈环绕的城墙。标志着良渚文明的确立。良渚人的食物以谷物类为主，辅以肉食与蔬菜瓜果，主食是稻米，肉食的主要来源是人工饲养的猪、鸡、鸭等各种家畜，及野猪等狩猎获取的野生动物。除此之外，还有各种水生动物。多处良渚文化墓葬中出土有鲨鱼牙齿，这恐怕暗示良渚先民捕鱼业的触手甚至已伸向了浩瀚大海。

良渚文化分布区域主要在钱塘江流域和太湖流域，包括余杭良渚，嘉兴南、上海东、苏州、常州、绍兴、宁波一带；扩张区，西到安徽、江西，往北一直到江苏北部，接近山东；影响区，直到山西南部地带。玉琮是良渚文化的典型玉器，在良渚文化玉器中，地位最为突出。

习近平总书记指出，良渚遗址是中华五千年文明史的实证，是世界文明的瑰宝。国家文物局认为，良渚遗址群将成为实证中国境内的1万年旧石器时代人类文化史的圣地。2019年7月6日，联合国教科文组织将中国世界文化遗产提名项目"良渚古城遗址"列入世界遗产名录。申遗成功标志着中华五千年新石器时代文化史得到国际社会认可。

各位领导，参观告一段落，现在请移步至文化馆进一步了解首届"良渚论坛"的相关信息，感谢您的聆听。

作者：张潇潇

13 【儒家文化】

商务考察团

各位企业家、商界精英代表们：

过去四十年，中国是世界上经济增长最快的国家，我们探讨发现廉价劳动力、人口红利以及全球化东风下的出口带动等因素都无法充分解释中国增长之谜。随后，又有人区分了经济增长的根本动因——地理、制度与文化等以及直接动因——投资、教育与技术进步等。发现也不能"解密"。于是，我们提出，儒家文化或许才是真正的差异化因素，进而分析了中国经济增长的三个直接动因，并据此推论：中国（以及其他受儒家文化影响的东亚经济体）之所以能迅速积累物质资本和人力资本，很可能得益于勤劳节俭和重视教育的儒家文化传统。也正因为如此，中国才能比其他发展中国家更好地吸收西方的现有技术，提升本土的创新能力，促成经济的快速崛起。

说到这里，您是不是感同身受？

儒家文化是以儒家思想为指导的文化流派。儒家学说为春秋时期孔丘所创，倡导血亲人伦、现世事功、修身存养、道德理性，其中心思想是恕、忠、孝、悌、勇、仁、义、礼、智、信，其核心是"仁"。

在文化维度，崇尚"礼""仁"，注重秩序。在模式维度，坚守和而不同，秉持兼容并包。在教育维度，弘扬尊师重教，主张有教无类。在社会维度，倡导"温良恭俭让"，认同"家国同构"。在决策者维度，注重个人修为，推崇精英主政。儒商信奉"修己以安人""其身正，不令而行；其身不正，虽令不从"，管理者注重树立正确的世界观、人生观、价值观和名利观，培养良好的职业操守和品格。在劳动力维度，甘于吃苦耐劳，崇尚勤奋好学。

中国经济发展的比较优势在于强调勤劳、储蓄、教育、信任和仁政的儒家文化。文化兴则国运兴，文化强则经济强、民族强。各位企业家代表们，我在各位业界成功者的身上感受到了儒家文化的气息以及成大事者沉静平稳的气质品格，向您致敬学习。

作者：张潇潇

亲子旅游团

各位家长和小朋友们：

家长们想必关注到了，国学在孩子们的教育中的分量越来越重了。是的，中华文化源远流长,其中儒家学派以其特有的魅力绵延至今。把"儒"字拆开,是一个人字和一个需字。人们需要的,人们想要的,这就是儒家文化。战国时期,儒家是诸子百家中影响最大的一个学派,产生于春秋时期,创始人为孔子。孔子、孟子、荀子是儒家学派三位重要的代表人物。孔子的思想以"天命论""中庸"之道和"仁""礼"为核心。孟子主要继承了孔子"仁"的思想,并提出了"性善论",发展形成"王道"和"仁政"学说和"民贵君轻"的民本思想。

在海外,"儒学"已经成为中华民族传统文化的代名词。儒家文化的内核是求美,求善,求仁义;忧国,忧民,忧天下;重文,重礼,重气节;畏天,畏地,畏天命。"仁"是孔子思想的核心内容,后来孟子将"仁"的思想发展为"仁政"。

"仁"就是"爱人",即爱别人、爱众人,尤其要体恤百姓。孔子认为统治者要做到"仁"就要爱护百姓。主张"节用而爱人,使民以时";"因民之所利而利之"。如何做到"仁",小朋友们知道了吗? 先从爱护身边的家人和朋友做起。

"礼"即周礼,主张"非礼勿视,非礼勿听,非礼勿言,非礼勿动""君君臣臣父父子子""君子和而不同""三人行,必有我师焉""小不忍则乱大谋"等。这个我要来考考家长了,这些都是什么释义呢?

孔子认为学习的目的是成为"君子"。在教学中,提出循循善诱、因材施教、学思结合、知行结合、不愤不启、不悱不发、温故知新、循序渐进、举一反三等教学方法,给教育者做出了示例。

各位家长您看这,儒家思想还奠定了书法文化的理论基础。清代刘熙载在《艺概·书概》中的论述更为精彩:扬子以书为心画,故书也者,心学也。心不若人而欲书之过人,其勤而无所也宜矣。

弘扬国学精髓,传承儒家文化,就靠家长们的引导和小朋友们的努力了,加油。

作者:张潇潇

14 【青花瓷】

中(小)学研学团

"天青色,等烟雨,而我在等你……"

前奏一起,这首歌名"青花瓷"就是本堂课的研学内容了。

青花瓷又称白地青花瓷,简称青花,中国四大名瓷之一。青花瓷属白底蓝花高温釉下彩瓷,以"青"为灵魂,原料为含氧化钴的钴矿,在陶瓷坯体上描绘纹饰后罩上一层透明釉,以1250—1350℃高温一次烧制而成,具有着色力强、发色鲜艳、烧成率高、渲染色彩稳定等特点。

唐朝时的青料是中西亚的钴料,颜色较浓,有结晶斑。一部分唐三彩中有蓝彩,呈正蓝色,或可认为是青花瓷的雏形。

青花瓷在宋代未成为审美主流,用的是国产土料,发色多为灰蓝或灰黑色。

元青花由素瓷向彩瓷过渡,使用波斯进口的苏麻离青,其色蓝艳、易晕散、有铁斑。通过一笔点画的技法,富丽雄浑、画风豪放、成品造型硕大、纹饰丰富。

明永宣时期的青花瓷,以其胎釉精细、色调浓艳、纹饰精美被公认是青花瓷的巅峰之作。明中期造型上由敦厚豪放变得轻巧俊秀。青料开始运用国产的平等青,色调淡雅清新,绘画风格以疏朗为主。

康熙年间,青花瓷工艺达到了历史最高水平。景德镇烧出了被誉为"翠毛蓝""宝石蓝"的青花瓷,"料分五色",用一种青花色料,描绘出景物的阴阳向背、远近疏密,使画面富有立体感,故康熙青花又有"五彩青花"之称。

雍正青花的特色是"秀",采用浙江上等青料,瓷质洁白、胎体精细,釉面光亮莹润,造型俊秀轻巧。

乾隆青花特征鲜明,风格奇巧华丽。之后,由于政治腐败、经济衰退与社会动乱,景德镇瓷业盛极而衰。

现代青花主要是以陶瓷质地的改良、青花料色的丰富、陶瓷造型的创新、水墨画在青花上的运用,及青花综合装饰等形式体现。

了解发展史之后,大家知道青花瓷的主要产地是哪里吗?接下来,让我们带着问题继续学习和探讨。

作者:张潇潇

商务考察团

各位企业家、商界精英们：

青花瓷以"青"为灵魂，以含氧化钴的钴矿为釉色原料，在陶瓷坯体上描绘纹饰后罩上一层透明釉，以1250℃—1350℃高温一次烧制而成，具有着色力强、发色鲜艳、烧成率高、渲染色彩稳定等特点。

青花瓷是源于中国遍及世界的一种白地蓝花高温釉下彩瓷器。青花瓷器起源于九世纪的唐代巩县窑，成熟于十四世纪早期的元代景德镇窑，辉煌于十五世纪初的明代永乐、宣德两朝景德镇珠山御器厂。

一般认为青花起源于唐宋，元代由素瓷向彩瓷过渡，至明永宣时期，青花瓷被公认为达到巅峰。明中期的青花瓷，造型上由敦厚豪放变得轻巧俊秀，色调淡雅清新，绘画风格以疏朗为主。康熙年间，青花瓷成为主流，青花瓷工艺重回巅峰，达到了历史最高水平，康熙青花又有"五彩青花"之称。雍正青花可以用"秀"一字来概括，它采用浙江上等青料，瓷质洁白、胎体精细、釉面光亮莹润、造型俊秀轻巧。乾隆青花特征鲜明，风格奇巧华丽。之后，由于政治经济等社会原因，制瓷业盛极而衰。

从唐宋已见端倪的原始青花瓷，到元代景德镇的湖田窑出现成熟的青花瓷，直至明清时期创烧的青花五彩、孔雀绿釉青花、豆青釉青花、青花红彩、黄地青花、哥釉青花等衍生品种，青花瓷器日渐成为较富有东方民族风情的瓷器品种。青花瓷在元代发展成熟后主要为外销瓷，从明代起成为中国瓷器生产的主流。到清代，青花瓷器仍占主导地位，特别是作为皇家御用之物彰显了其美轮美奂的视觉效果，无论是在工艺技术、绘画水平还是产量方面都达到了历史上的又一高峰，成为中国四大名瓷之一。

各位企业家们，青花瓷作为商务会谈的场地布置、礼物互换、收藏鉴赏，都具有极高的商业和艺术价值。希望刚刚的讲解，可以为您品鉴青花瓷提供一些帮助，感谢您的驻足。

作者：张潇潇

15 【景泰蓝】

政务考察团

各位领导、贵宾们:

不知道您有没有听过这样的民间传说:"家中没有景泰蓝,藏尽天下也枉然","一件景泰蓝,十箱官窑器",可见景泰蓝在收藏界非同一般的地位与影响力。

请允许我简单介绍景泰蓝的背景及制作工艺,景泰蓝,又称"铜胎掐丝珐琅",俗称"珐蓝",又称"嵌珐琅"。是一种在铜质的胎型上,用柔软的扁铜丝,掐成各种花纹焊上,然后把珐琅质的色釉填充在花纹内烧制而成的器物。

它诞生于元末明初,距今已有600多年的历史。在明代景泰年间这种工艺技术达到了最巅峰,制出的工艺品最为精美著名,加之使用的珐琅釉多以蓝色为主,故后人称这种金属器为"景泰蓝"。

"景泰蓝"的命名,早已超出了"大明景泰"这层意义,而被赋予了和谐、高雅、祥和等美好的内涵。"景泰",在我国传统文化中是个祥和与和谐的字眼。

"景泰蓝"的"蓝",则蕴藏着更多的历史印记。铜是人类最早发现和发掘利用的金属,蓝、绿的釉料都是铜的化合物。早在唐宋时期,我国最早提炼出了氧化钴蓝釉料,色泽纯然,蓝中透绿。另外,景泰蓝的"蓝",不单指蓝色调,也不单指蓝釉料,而是把所有釉料统称为"蓝",因此又逐一衍生出"点蓝""补蓝""崩蓝""烧蓝""蓝工"等特有名词。它的制作步骤:经由设计胎图、丝工图纸、蓝图(点蓝的色稿),胎型制作,掐丝,点蓝,烧蓝,磨光,镀金再经水洗冲净干燥处理后,一件绚丽夺目的景泰蓝便脱颖而出了。各位贵宾这边请,这里正在展示景泰蓝的制作过程。

源于元代的西亚、孕育并成长于明清皇宫中的景泰蓝工艺,是京文化,更是中华传统文化中不可忽视的一颗璀璨明星,被称为国宝"京"粹,昔日皇家御用,今朝邦交重礼,景泰蓝曾多次被作为"国礼"送出。

作者:张潇潇

记者采风团

媒体朋友们:

感谢亲临体验报道景泰蓝的制作工艺,我先简单介绍景泰蓝。它诞生于元末明初,距今已有600多年的历史,2006年入选首批国家级非物质文化遗产名录。

源于元代的西亚、孕育并成长于明清皇宫中的景泰蓝工艺,是京文化,更是中华传统文化中不可忽视的一颗璀璨明星。那么,有一个问题出现了,它为什么叫景泰蓝，而不叫景泰绿、景泰红、景泰黄呢？这是因为掐丝珐琅以蓝色基调为主。景泰蓝是外来文化，从中东阿拉伯地区传进中国，阿拉伯文化的主色调崇尚蓝色。他们的建筑中，蓝色是一个非常重要的色调。景泰蓝正名"铜胎掐丝珐琅"，俗名"珐蓝"，又称"嵌珐琅"，是一种在铜质的胎型上，用柔软的扁铜丝，掐成各种花纹焊上，然后把珐琅质的色釉填充在花纹内烧制而成的器物。因其在明朝景泰年间盛行，制作技艺比较成熟，使用的珐琅釉多以蓝色为主，故而得名"景泰蓝"。

"景泰蓝"的命名，早已超出了"大明景泰"这层意义，而被赋予了和谐、高雅、祥和等美好的内涵。"景泰"，在我国传统文化中是个祥和与和谐的字眼。"景泰蓝"的"蓝"，则蕴藏着更多的历史印记。铜是人类最早发现和发掘利用的金属，蓝、绿的釉料都是铜的化合物。早在唐宋时期，我国最早提炼出了氧化钴蓝釉料，色泽纯然，蓝中透绿。另外，景泰蓝的"蓝"，不单指蓝色调，也不单指蓝釉料，而是把所有釉料统称为"蓝"，因此又衍生出"点蓝""补蓝""崩蓝""烧蓝""蓝工"等特有名词。它的制作步骤：经由设计胎图、丝工图纸、蓝图（点蓝的色稿），胎型制作，掐丝，点蓝，烧蓝，磨光，镀金再经水洗冲净干燥处理后，一件绚丽夺目的景泰蓝便脱颖而出了。

各位嘉宾这边请，这里正在展示景泰蓝的制作过程，还需要更详细的资料也可以和制作匠人交流获取。

作者：张潇潇

16 【藏族唐卡】

各位团友们:

经过一晚的休整,我们今天深入藏区感受藏族特色艺术的魅力,在参观的过程中,一定要注意高原反应,如有身体不适请马上告知我协助服务。好了,进入庙宇的大殿,大家抬头看,映入眼帘的就是藏族唐卡。

唐卡,也叫唐嘎,唐喀,系藏文音译,指用彩缎装裱后悬挂供奉的宗教卷轴画。这是藏族文化中一种独具特色的绘画艺术形式,题材内容涉及藏族的历史、政治、文化和社会生活等诸多领域,传世唐卡大都是藏传佛教和本教作品。

您猜猜这幅唐卡用了多久绘制完成?猜不出来吧。传统唐卡的绘制要求严苛、程序极为复杂,制作一幅唐卡短则半年,长则需要十余年。

有朋友问了,为什么用这么长时间呢?因为绘制必须按照经书中的仪轨及上师的要求进行,包括绘前仪式、制作画布、构图起稿、着色染色、勾线定型、铺金描银、开眼、缝裱开光等一整套工艺程序。

您看,这幅唐卡明亮的色彩描绘出佛的世界,颜料传统上全部采用金、银、珍珠、玛瑙、珊瑚、松石、孔雀石、朱砂等珍贵的矿物宝石和藏红花、大黄、蓝靛等植物为颜料以示其神圣。这些天然原料保证了所绘制的唐卡璀璨夺目,历经几百年的岁月,仍是色泽艳丽明亮。唐卡被誉为中华民族绘画艺术的珍品、藏族的"百科全书",也是中华民族民间艺术中弥足珍贵的非物质文化遗产。

唐卡有许多种类。按质地可分为纸质唐卡、布质唐卡和丝质唐卡等。按制作工艺可分为织锦唐卡、缎制唐卡、珍珠唐卡及金汁唐卡等。

其中最珍贵的要数珍珠唐卡和金汁唐卡。珍珠唐卡是将珍珠串起来缝制在布上,组成造型优美的佛像;金汁唐卡分黑墨底色金汁勾绘、金汁底色朱砂勾绘和朱砂底色金汁勾绘三种。

唐卡内容丰富,有反映藏族历史和重大事件的唐卡,有人物传记和人物画像唐卡,有反映生活习俗的风俗画唐卡,有天文历算和藏医藏药唐卡,还有一些唐卡描绘的是自然现象,具有重要的科学研究价值,如《四部医典》中的几十副医药学唐卡就是我国医药学宝库中的瑰宝。

朋友们,进入寺庙后请尊重当地风俗,不要随意拍照和触摸,我们继续参观。

作者:张潇潇

17 【太极拳】

亲爱的团友们：

恰逢春时，天气晴朗，今天的行程安排是体验太极拳。在活动之前，我先来简单介绍下这项在2020年被列入联合国教科文组织的人类非物质文化遗产代表作名录的中国武术瑰宝。

很多外国友人以为中国人都会功夫，这个海外称呼的"功夫"，近代以来曾被称为"国术"，新中国成立后则统称为"武术"。武术是以技击动作为内容，以套路和格斗为运动形式，注重内外兼修的中国传统体育项目。中国武术按照运动形式分为套路、格斗、功法三大类。其中套路按照演练特征来分，主要分为拳术、器械和对练三大类。太极拳是武当武功中拳术的一种。

众所周知，武林中素有"北崇少林，南尊武当"的说法，传说张三丰当年在武当山修道传艺和治病救人，受到群众爱戴和尊敬，被尊为"通微显化真人"。他在研究极阴阳八卦原理的基础上，创立了武当拳，将道家理学内功与民间武术融为一体。

武当武术的特点是相生相克，既对立又统一。将道家的练精化气、练气化神、练神还虚之术融于拳理之中，使武当拳法具有了刚柔相济，以身领手、以意领气、以气运身的武术精华。

太极拳是武当内家以柔克刚的拳术，练拳要求神气鼓荡，两股有力，两肩放松，主宰于腰，腰为太极。上于两膊相合，下于两腿相用，一动式，既轻又灵，一交手，四两拨千斤，先化后发，出奇制胜。

大家看老师演示的动作。其特点：一是轻松柔和，二是均匀连贯，三是圆活自然，四是协调完整。练太极拳时必须以腰为轴，上肢下肢的活动都由躯干来带动，并且相互呼应。太极拳长期练习，能调理任督二脉、肾经、肝经、胆经、心经、膀胱经。太极拳作为中华养生功夫，结合易学阴阳五行之变化，具有内外兼修、刚柔相济的特点。

接下来，让老师教大家一个适合春天调理的动作——云手。云手的动作能舒心、疏肝，使心情舒畅、不易郁结。大家跟着动起来，注意动作轻柔、缓慢，兼顾呼吸。

作者：张潇潇

18 【宣纸传统制作技艺】

亲爱的团友们：

大家都知道中国古代的四大发明吧，是的，今天我们就去参观学习其中一项，于2009年被列入联合国教科文组织发布的非物质文化遗产名录的宣纸传统制作技艺。

造纸术是中国古代四大发明之一，宣纸是传统手工纸品中较为杰出的代表。宣纸以安徽宣城而得名，但宣城本身不产纸，而是周围诸地产纸，以宣城为散集地的原因。

宣纸传统制作技艺即以宣纸为制作对象，以制作过程中原料加工、制浆、捞纸、晒纸、剪纸等环节的知识与实践为核心内容，以安徽泾县为主要流布区域的传统手工造纸技艺。

做宣纸的人常讲一句话：宣纸制造，首在于料。原料加工是宣纸制作过程中历时最长的一个阶段，也是宣纸传统制作108道工序中最为艰辛的部分，是决定宣纸品质的根本所在。宣纸在制作之前，要经过一道皮料制作的工序和一道草料制作的工序。皮料加工包含多道小工序，如砍条、选条、蒸煮、浸泡、剥皮、晾晒、解皮、浆灰等。稻草也要历经8至10个月的日晒、雨淋，草坯到渡草、渡草到青草、青草到燎草的各个阶段都要历时3至4个月左右。皮料和草料要经过选检、碓皮、舂草、切皮、踩料、袋料等工序，完成初步打浆工作。根据所需纸品类别不同，再制浆，按品种进行配比加料后，经过"数棍子"这道必要工序进行融浆，最终形成符合要求的纸浆，再进行老纸、晾晒等工序。

这听起来很复杂，大家可能会有疑问，为什么这项技艺被列入世界非遗名录呢？一为文化载体，二为市场需求。宣纸是中国手工纸在流播过程中注入地方元素诞生的特色纸种，随着中国水墨画的发展，社会对宣纸的需求量显著增多，其知名度、产业规模和从业人数也不断扩大，宣纸传统制作技艺在这一过程中发展成熟。

通过长期传承实践，宣纸制作加工的知识和技术体系不断发展完善，以传统方式制作的宣纸具备百折不损、墨韵万变、不腐不蛀的优良品质，是展示传承东方水墨艺术意境与神韵的最佳载体。宣纸传统制作技艺的活态传承，为中国书画艺术和中国传统文化的传承、发展做出了突出贡献。

作者：张潇潇

19 【端午节】

亲爱的游客朋友们：

过节总是让人欢喜的，亲朋好友也会在节日期间互相问候。但是近年来，有一个节日在问候语方面有点争议，大家知道是哪个节日吗？

是的，就是端午节。有人说问候"端午快乐"不合适，应该问候"端午安康"。究竟是什么原因呢？让我们来了解下这个已于2009年被联合国教科文组织发布的《非物质文化遗产名录》收录的传统节日。农历五月初五为端午节，是汉族民间传统节日，流行于全国大多数地区，除汉族外，蒙古族、回族、藏族、苗族、彝族、壮族、布依族等族也过此节。

端午节起源说法众多，其中以纪念楚国诗人屈原说流传最为广泛，相传屈原于农历五月初五投汨罗江而死。

节日期间主要有赛龙舟、吃粽子、挂钟馗像、挂香袋、饮雄黄酒、插菖蒲、采药等活动，或煮水沐身以祛暑避邪。农历五月，气温逐渐升高，百虫纷纷出现，病毒也滋长起来，所以避毒除害是端午节的主要内容。各地的避毒方式多样，做布老虎、佩戴香囊等皆是应节的驱毒佳方。钟馗原是岁暮时张挂的门神，清代成为端午之神。

端午节吃粽子的风俗，魏晋时盛行，到了唐宋成为名食。关于吃粽子，有趣的说法是毕竟唐宋文人多，为了吃粽子吃得有文化，得找个古人作为由头，于是选择了郁郁不得志的屈原，吃着粽子，寄托着哀思，说着自己的不如意，吟诗作赋……一来二去的，粽子在唐宋时期就成了端午节名食，当然，这也只是戏说。

赛龙舟是端午节中一项重要活动，主要流行于我国南方水乡之地。尤其是在广东，全村举家族之力组建龙舟队，比赛赢了的队伍能收获一年的风光直至来年。

对了，端午节还有一些有意思的别称，如端阳节、天中节、女儿节、五月节等。女儿节？这是怎么回事？原来到了五月端午这天，女孩子要系着五彩丝，戴艾叶和五毒灵符，打扮得漂漂亮亮，另外，嫁出去的女孩子也要回娘家看望家人，因为都是和女孩儿相关，所以叫女儿节。

听完介绍，过端午节的时候怎么问候想必没有争议了吧？

作者：张潇潇

20 【藏族雪顿节】

各位游客朋友们：

欢迎大家走进藏区，了解藏族文化。

藏族分布在中国辽阔的青藏高原上，主要聚居在西藏自治区以及青海省、甘肃省、四川省、云南省等部分地区，以牧业为主，也从事农业。

藏族的医药、天文、历算、戏曲、文学、歌舞、唐卡和热贡艺术等，都有较高水平。藏族人民集体创作的《格萨尔王传》是世界上较长的史诗之一，锅庄舞、藏戏、唐卡、藏医药、雪顿节等被列入国家级非物质文化遗产名录。藏族的节日很多，一年中的主要节日有藏历年、酥油花灯节、雪顿节、采花节、望果节、赛马节等。

我们重点了解的雪顿节，又名藏戏节，"雪"藏语为酸奶子，"顿"藏语为宴的意思，因此，"雪顿"是吃酸奶子的节日，流行于西藏自治区、青海省、甘肃省、云南省等地藏区。每年藏历七月初一举行，连续4—5天。雪顿节最初是一种纯宗教的活动，是藏族世俗百姓向喇嘛们施舍酸奶子以及喇嘛们纵情游玩的节日，17世纪中叶开始演出藏戏，并形成固定的雪顿节。节日期间，各地藏剧团云集拉萨市，先在哲蚌寺，后至罗布林卡，轮流上演传统藏戏。人们身穿节日盛装，会集罗布林卡，看戏饮酒，唱歌跳舞，摆摊设棚，串帷幕做客，主客祝酒，并唱祝酒歌，一直到傍晚才离开罗布林卡回家。

我国55个少数民族都能歌善舞，而且有各自不同的风俗和禁忌。游客朋友们，在游览过程中我们需要注意尊重当地风俗文化，遇到节日活动，除非主人邀请，不要随意打扰当地人的生活，拍照前也要征得对方的同意。

藏族敬酒敬茶也有特殊习俗。到藏族人家里去做客，主人便会敬上青稞酒。客人应先用右手无名指蘸一点酒，配合大拇指弹向空中、半空和地面各一次，意思是先祭天、祭地、祭祖先。然后要遵循"三口一杯"的规矩，即客人轻呷一口酒，主人立即斟满，如此反复三次后，客人再喝干满杯酒。主人敬酥油茶时，会把茶碗捧到客人的面前，这时客人才可以接过来喝，客人不能主动去端茶。

朋友们，藏族人为了欢迎外地的游客，也把他们的节日活动展演搬到了景区的现场，让我们一起去感受节日气氛吧！

作者：张潇潇

21 【傣族泼水节】

各位亲爱的团友：

　　大家早上好！今天，我们要一起穿越到热带雨林，参与一场湿身狂欢——傣族泼水节！想象一下，阳光明媚，鸟语花香，傣家少女身着五彩斑斓的筒裙翩翩起舞，小伙儿们手持金光闪闪的银盆蓄势待发，所有人都在等待那个激动人心的时刻。

　　泼水节，源自傣族人民对水的深深敬畏与热爱。他们相信，水不仅能洗涤尘埃，更能驱邪避害，带来好运。所以在这一天，泼水不再是简单的嬉戏，而是对彼此最真挚、最直接的祝福。泼得越猛，祝福越深沉，被泼得越多，说明您人气爆棚，福气满满！所以，您可要做好心理准备，接下来您可能会被祝福得"透心凉，心飞扬"！泼水节现场，整个西双版纳就像大型水上乐园，泼水广场瞬间变成"水枪大战"现场。友情提示，头部是尊贵部位，不可随意泼水，那是对客人的尊重；背部和肩膀，才是友谊小船翻得"恰到好处"的地方。

　　除了泼水大战，泼水节期间的傣族村寨还会举行各种丰富多彩的活动。比如"赶摆"市集，琳琅满目的手工艺品、特色小吃让人目不暇接；还有"赕佛"仪式，人们虔诚祈福，舞动长龙，祈求来年风调雨顺、五谷丰登；此外，别忘了欣赏傣族传统舞蹈"孔雀舞"，曼妙舞姿犹如孔雀开屏，美轮美奂。

　　泼水节不仅是傣族人民欢庆新年、祈福纳祥的重要节日，也是他们展示民族风情、传承民族文化的大舞台。在这里，您可以尽情释放自我，享受水花飞溅带来的清凉与快乐，同时深度体验傣族独特的民俗风情。记住，参加泼水节，一定要保持开放的心态，准备好随时接受来自四面八方的"祝福水弹"，因为在这个特别的日子里，被泼得越多，说明您越受欢迎！来吧，让我们一起加入这场湿漉漉的狂欢，感受傣族泼水节的独特魅力！

作者：刘夕宁

22 【彝族火把节】

各位旅行家们:

欢迎来到美丽的云南,今晚我们将共赴一场激情四溢、魅力无穷的民族盛会——彝族火把节!火把节,彝语名曰"都则",意为"祭火",堪称彝族年度最大盛典,其重要性不亚于汉族春节,热闹程度堪比"双十一",只是这里的"抢购"是喜庆、吉祥与爱情,无需熬夜,更无需剁手!每年农历六月二十四,整个彝乡仿佛被炽热的火焰唤醒,火把高举,火星纷飞,犹如星辰坠落凡间,照亮人们对美好生活的执着追求。

火把节的起源,充满了神秘的传说色彩。古时,彝族先民遭遇虫害肆虐,庄稼危在旦夕。关键时刻,智者毕摩献计,全族人同日点燃火把,以烈焰震慑害虫,终保丰收。自此,火把节成为彝族人感恩天地、祈福驱邪的重要仪式,兼具传奇与浪漫。

接下来,让我揭秘火把节的精彩环节。首当其冲是庄重的祭火仪式。在毕摩引领下,人们虔诚向火神献祭,祈愿五谷丰登、六畜兴旺。紧接着,高潮来临——火把巡游!男女老少手持象征光明与希望的火把,踏歌而行,沿村寨道路蜿蜒,火光如龙,歌声如潮,气势磅礴,宛如一部现实版"火的交响曲"。

火把节不仅是火的狂欢,更是彝族歌舞艺术的集中展现。身着艳丽民族服装的彝族男女,跳起"阿细跳月""左脚舞"等独特舞蹈,鼓声激昂,舞步灵动,让人忍不住随之摇曳。此外,"抹黑脸"游戏趣味横生,被抹得越黑,代表你越受喜爱,别怕,黑脸也是福气满满!

美食,自然是节日的重头戏。彝族坨坨肉、荞麦饼、酸菜鱼,搭配彝家自酿美酒,定让你回味无穷。特别是火把节特供的烧土豆、烤玉米,香气扑鼻,保你一尝难忘,甚至想打包回家!

朋友们,让我们携手投身这火的海洋,释放激情,共享彝族火把节的欢乐与祥瑞!记住,带上你们的热情,因为这里已备好熊熊之火,只待你加入这场火的狂欢!

作者:刘夕宁

23 【云南普洱茶】

各位尊贵的游客：

欢迎来到云南，今天我们要探索的，是一种被誉为"可以喝的古董"的神秘饮品——云南普洱茶！

普洱茶，绝非寻常茶类可比，它就像一位深藏不露的隐士，低调中蕴含着深厚的历史底蕴与丰富的内涵。它产自云南，尤以普洱、西双版纳、临沧等地最为出众。普洱茶的独特，在于其发酵过程，分为未经人工发酵的生普与经过人工渥堆发酵的熟普。生普如同未经雕琢的璞玉，略带青涩与野性；熟普则如岁月磨砺的宝石，醇厚温和，韵味悠长。

试想一下，身处云雾缭绕的茶山，满目翠绿，茶香弥漫，仿佛连空气都带着清甜。茶农们正细心采摘嫩叶，这是普洱茶的起点。随后，茶叶历经杀青、揉捻、晒干等工艺，开始了迈向"茶中贵族"的旅程。

普洱茶的魅力，不止于味，更在于其变化。生普犹如青春少年，初时茶汤金黄透亮，鲜爽回甘；随时间推移，茶汤渐转红浓，口感醇厚，香气馥郁，如同步入中年的稳重与内敛。熟普则如睿智长者，一出世便"老成持重"，茶汤红褐，滋味醇和，陈香显著。

品普洱茶，如同翻开一本历史长卷。每一次泡茶，都是时间的痕迹，每一次品饮，都是与岁月的对话。无论独酌还是与友共饮，普洱茶总能营造宁静温馨的氛围，且兼具降脂减肥、抗氧化、助消化等功效，养生与享受两不误。

简言之，云南普洱茶，既是饮品，又是文化，亦是生活态度。在此，您将品味时间的味道，感受历史的厚重，体验生活的慢节奏。让我们共同举杯，细品这杯云南"液体黄金"，让心灵在茶香中得以滋养与净化！

作者：刘夕宁

24 【蒙古族那达慕大会】

各位尊贵的游客们:

大家好!欢迎来到广袤无垠的内蒙古大草原,今天我要带你们参加一场集竞技、娱乐、民俗于一体的草原盛宴——蒙古族那达慕大会!那达慕,蒙古语意为"娱乐"或"游戏",堪称蒙古族的"奥林匹克",其地位堪比汉族的春节,热闹程度不输"双十一",而且入场券就是你的热情与好奇心,无需"剁手",只需敞开心扉!每年夏季,草原上的各个部落都会举办那达慕大会,庆祝丰收,祈愿吉祥,展示力量与勇气。

那达慕大会的起源,充满了浓郁的草原风情。传说在远古时期,蒙古族先民为了选拔最英勇善战的勇士,设立了摔跤、赛马、射箭三项竞技。久而久之,这三项运动成为那达慕大会的核心内容,代代相传,直至今日。

接下来,让我带你们一窥那达慕大会的精彩环节。首当其冲的自然是惊心动魄的男子三项竞技。首先是摔跤,又称"搏克",勇士们身着传统摔跤服,光膀赤足,以力量与技巧一决高下,获胜者将被尊为"巴特尔"(英雄)。其次是赛马,骑手们驾驭骏马,如疾风般驰骋草原,展现人马合一的默契,赢得观众阵阵喝彩。最后是射箭,射手们手持弯弓,凝神静气,一箭离弦,直指靶心,那份精准与冷静,让人叹为观止。

除了激烈的竞技项目,那达慕大会还是展示蒙古族传统文化的大舞台。你看,身穿华丽民族服饰的姑娘们翩翩起舞,歌声婉转,仿佛在诉说着草原的美丽传说。还有那悠扬的马头琴声,如泣如诉,如诗如画,将人们带入了辽阔的草原世界。

美食,自然也是那达慕大会不可或缺的一部分。烤全羊、手把肉、奶豆腐、马奶酒……一道道蒙古族特色美食,香气四溢,令人垂涎欲滴。尤其是那热气腾腾的奶茶,醇厚香甜,暖胃暖心,喝上一碗,仿佛就能感受到蒙古族人民的热情好客。

朋友们,让我们一起投身这场草原狂欢,释放激情,共享那达慕大会的欢乐!

作者:刘夕宁

25 【北京烤鸭】

各位亲爱的游客朋友们：

欢迎大家来到文化底蕴深厚的北京城，今天我将化身为您的美食向导，带领大家探寻这座城市最具代表性的美食名片——北京烤鸭。

北京烤鸭，这道誉满全球的中华料理，堪称美食界的"国宝级巨星"，其地位之崇高，就好比京剧中的梅兰芳，电影界的李小龙，无人不知，无人不晓。它的历史源远流长，可以追溯到明朝。相传，当时的宫廷御膳房为了取悦皇帝朱元璋，研制出了一种独特的烹饪技法——挂炉烤鸭。这烤鸭皮脆肉嫩，醇香四溢，深得朱元璋的喜爱，从此成为宫廷御膳的常客。到了清朝，挂炉烤鸭技艺进一步发展，并逐渐传至民间，才使得我们这些寻常百姓也有幸一饱口福。

关于北京烤鸭，还有一个有趣的民间故事。据说在乾隆年间，一次乾隆皇帝微服私访，偶遇一家烤鸭店，被那金黄油亮、香气扑鼻的烤鸭深深吸引。他品尝之后，赞不绝口，于是赐名"天下第一美味"。此后，这家烤鸭店名声大噪，北京烤鸭也随之名扬四海，成为北京美食的一张靓丽名片。

制作北京烤鸭，那可是个技术活儿。首先，主角当然是精选的优质填鸭，它们膘肥体壮，宛如鸭界健美冠军。接着，进入"化妆间"进行"净身"，然后吹气、烫皮、挂糖色，这一系列操作下来，鸭子瞬间变身"金甲战神"。最后，隆重登场的是挂炉烤制环节，鸭子在果木炭火的高温烘烤下，油脂慢慢融化，皮肉分离，香气四溢，此情此景，仿佛在上演一出"鸭生涅槃"的大戏。

吃北京烤鸭，更是一门艺术。片鸭师傅手持利刃，如同舞剑一般，精准地将鸭肉片成大小均匀、皮肉兼顾的鸭片，这刀工，绝对不逊于武侠小说里的绝世高手。食客们则用筷子轻轻夹起一片鸭肉，放在铺好的荷叶饼上，抹上甜面酱，放上几根翠绿的葱段和清脆的黄瓜条，卷起来，一口咬下，让人忍不住大呼："此味只应天上有，人间能得几回尝？"

当然，品尝北京烤鸭，可不只是满足口腹之欲那么简单，它更是一种文化体验。在那些历史悠久的老字号餐馆，如全聚德、便宜坊，一边品尝美食，一边欣赏传统装饰与京味十足的服务，仿佛穿越时空，回到了老北京的蹉跎岁月。此时此刻，您不仅是食客，更是历史的见证者，文化的传承人。

无论你是资深吃货，还是美食探索家，都不能错过这一口"京华烟云，鸭香四溢"的独特体验，让我们的味蕾在这场"鸭"力无穷的盛宴中尽情狂欢吧！

作者：刘夕宁

26 【四川火锅】

各位亲们：

大家好！今天我们要一起揭开四川火锅的神秘面纱，来一场麻辣狂欢！这可是名副其实的美食界"巨星"，其知名度堪比歌坛的周杰伦，影坛的周星驰，无人不晓，无人不爱。而且，你知道吗？尽管四川火锅麻辣劲爆，但却有个"不上火"的秘密，想知道为什么吗？来，听我揭晓！

四川火锅源自明清重庆嘉陵江边，是劳动人民智慧的结晶，麻辣文化的生动写照。灵魂底料来自精选牛油，混搭数十种香料炒制，辣椒、花椒、豆瓣、姜蒜等"麻辣天团"齐上阵，香气扑鼻，色泽红亮。尽管看上去火辣无比，但其不上火的秘密在于：

不上火秘密一：中药配料。底料中融入黄芪、党参、甘草、枸杞等中药材，增添复合香气，更具有清热、滋阴、降火功效，犹如火锅中的"灭火器"。

不上火秘密二：鲜蔬豆制品。涮品阵容中，除了毛肚、鸭肠、黄喉"火锅三巨头"，还有大量蔬菜以及豆制品如豆腐、豆皮、豆腐泡等。这些食材富含膳食纤维，有助于消化，降低火锅对肠胃的刺激，豆制品能中和火锅的燥热，清热解毒。

不上火秘密三：蘸料与饮品。调料中，蒜泥、香菜、葱花、小米椒、花生碎、芝麻酱等自由搭配，油碟堪称点睛之笔，降燥解辣，提香增鲜。搭配冰镇啤酒、酸梅汤或菊花茶等清凉饮品，缓解口腔和肠胃的灼热感。

吃四川火锅，不只是味觉享受，更是一种社交方式和生活态度。围炉而坐，热气腾腾间拉近距离，印证"没有什么是一顿火锅解决不了的，如果有，那就两顿"的生活智慧。无论你是麻辣控还是清淡派，火锅世界总有你的归宿。

简言之，四川火锅集麻、辣、鲜、香于一身，是四川美食瑰宝，中国火锅文化翘楚。别犹豫，此刻就让我们的味蕾在"火辣辣"的狂欢中纵情享受吧！

作者：刘夕宁

27 【三星堆遗址】

各位尊贵的游客们：

大家好！欢迎来到神秘的天府之国四川,今天我要带你们聚焦三星堆遗址的一件重量级展品——青铜神树,一同领略古蜀文明的奇幻魅力!

三星堆遗址,位于四川省广汉市,是中国西南地区较重要的古代文明遗址,距今约3000年至5000年,被誉为"长江文明之源"。这里出土的文物数量众多、种类丰富、造型奇特,尤其是那棵青铜神树,更是以其超凡脱俗的形象,震撼了世人。

这棵"青铜神树",堪称三星堆遗址的"镇馆之宝",高达3.95米,共有九枝、九鸟、九果,树梢还立有一只神鸟,其规模之宏大、细节之精致,让人不得不惊叹古蜀人的艺术才华与工艺水平。如果要用一句话来形容它,那就是现实版的《阿凡达》生命之树! 它仿佛是从另一个世界穿越而来,静静地矗立在那里,等待着我们去解读那隐藏在青铜背后的古蜀神话。

这棵神树的构造极为独特,九枝象征着"九天",九鸟代表着"太阳",九果寓意着"丰收",而树顶那只展翅欲飞的神鸟,可能象征着沟通天地、连接人间与神界的使者。整个神树的设计充满了浓厚的宗教色彩和神秘气息,仿佛在诉说着古蜀人对宇宙的理解、对生命的敬畏以及对神灵的崇拜。

更为惊人的是,青铜神树的铸造工艺极其复杂,需要将多块青铜部件通过精密的嵌合、焊接组装而成,这在几千年前的生产力条件下,堪称奇迹。树干、树枝、果实、鸟儿的每一个细节都被刻画得栩栩如生,仿佛随时都会在你眼前活过来,带你进入那个遥远而神秘的古蜀世界。

站在青铜神树面前,你仿佛能听到它在述说那段失落的古蜀神话,感受到古蜀人对宇宙、生命、自然的深刻理解和独特见解。它不仅是古蜀文明的艺术瑰宝,更是研究古蜀社会宗教观、宇宙观和工艺技术的重要实物资料。

朋友们,让我们一起走近青铜神树,破解那些尘封千年的密码,探寻那段消失在历史长河中的辉煌文明!

作者：刘夕宁

28 【周口店北京猿人】

各位亲爱的游客朋友:

大家好!欢迎来到北京,我是您此次探秘之旅的导游,今天我们要一起穿越回远古时代,探访一位在北京"土生土长"的老祖宗——周口店北京猿人。

首先,让我们聚焦这位"北京原住民"的居住地——周口店遗址。这可不是一座普通的小山沟,而是世界级的考古胜地,堪称人类史上的"五星级豪宅"。几十万年前,当人类的祖先还在世界各地忙于"打野升级"的时候,北京猿人就已经在这片土地上"定居建房",过上了依山傍水、有洞穴有烧烤的"小康生活"。

他们的"房子",就是著名的"龙骨山"。这座山虽然不高,却是北京猿人的天然庇护所。他们选择的洞穴冬暖夏凉,自带空调效果,还有绝佳的"观景阳台",既可以眺望风景,又能防范猛兽入侵。这简直是史前版的"山景别墅",让现代人都羡慕不已。

再来看看他们的饮食文化。北京猿人可不是只会茹毛饮血,他们可是"美食家"呢!考古学家发现,他们的菜单上不仅有各种肉类,如鹿肉、熊掌、鱼虾等,还有丰富的植物性食物,如坚果、野果等,甚至还发现了炭化的竹笋痕迹。下次您品尝北京烤鸭的时候,不妨想一想,这可能是咱老祖宗留下的美食基因在延续。

北京猿人最让人称道的,是他们的手工技艺。您看这些陈列柜里形态各异的石器,有刮削器、砍砸器、尖状器,还有骨针、骨锥等,简直就是一套完整的"史前工具箱"。他们不仅能用这些工具狩猎、采集,还能制作饰品,甚至可能已经掌握了"钻木取火"的技术。您看看,几十万年前的"北京人"就已经玩起了"手工DIY",是不是觉得咱们现代人的"网红手工课"瞬间弱爆了?

最后,我想请大家闭上眼睛,想象一下这样的场景:夕阳西下,北京猿人在洞口燃起篝火,围坐一圈分享猎物,孩子们嬉戏玩耍,大人们讲述着狩猎的英勇事迹。洞穴外,星空璀璨,万物静谧……这就是他们平凡而生动的一天。尽管岁月流转,沧海桑田,但那份对生活的热爱、对家园的守护、对未知的好奇,却在人类血脉中代代相传,直至今日。

再次感谢大家的陪伴,希望这次"史前之旅"能让您收获知识,更收获对人类历史的敬畏与珍视。下一站,咱们继续探索未知,不见不散!

作者:刘夕宁

29 【殷墟甲骨文】

尊敬的游客们：

欢迎大家来到河南安阳，一同探寻神秘而古老的殷墟甲骨文。作为中国最早成熟的文字体系，甲骨文犹如一部跨越时空的通信器，引领我们倾听商朝先民的心声，解读那个遥远时代的秘密。

甲骨文的独特之处首先体现在其载体——龟甲与牛、羊、猪等动物的肩胛骨上。在尚未发明造纸术的商朝，这些硬质材料因耐腐蚀而成为理想的记录媒介，承载着占卜祭祀的神圣信息。从天文气象到农事安排，从疾病诊治到战事预测，再到祭祀祈祷，甲骨文涵盖了商朝社会生活的方方面面，堪称当时的"生活百科全书"。例如，"明日晴，宜耕田"这样的卜辞，揭示了古人对天气的密切关注以及对农业生产的精细规划。

甲骨文的形态之美，展现出古人的非凡创意与艺术才情。字形采用象形、指事、会意、形声等多种造字方法，如"人"字宛如立人之姿，"山"字状若层峦叠嶂，"明"字则巧妙地以"日""月"组合，象征明亮和照耀。每个字仿佛微型画作，蕴含着丰富的视觉魅力。

再来说说甲骨文的惊世发现。清末学者王懿荣偶然在治疗疟疾的"龙骨"药材上，发现了刻有奇异符号的痕迹。凭借深厚的学术素养，他意识到这些符号极有可能是失传已久的古代文字。经深入研究与收集，王懿荣证实了这是商代遗存的甲骨文，从而拉开了系统研究商代文明的序幕。这一重大发现，犹如历史夜空中的一道闪电，照亮了通往商朝文化深处的道路。

此刻，就让我们携手步入这片历史的秘境，共同开启一场文字的探秘之旅，让思绪在古老与现代之间自由翱翔吧！

作者：刘夕宁

30 【秦始皇陵兵马俑】

各位亲爱的游客朋友们：

大家好！我是你们的导游，也是你们今天穿越回秦朝的时光机驾驶员。欢迎来到世界第八大奇迹——秦始皇陵兵马俑！

首先，让我来给大家描绘一下这幅震撼人心的地下画卷。想象一下，您正站在一个巨大的足球场中央，周围密密麻麻排列着一队队兵马俑，个个身披铠甲，手持兵器，威风凛凛。这可不是什么科幻大片的场景，而是实实在在的秦始皇陵陪葬坑！

你们看，这些士兵可不是批量生产的"快餐"，个个都是独一无二的艺术品。瞧那个将军俑，昂首挺胸，神态威严，仿佛刚下完一道攻城拔寨的军令。再看看那弓箭手，弯弓搭箭，蓄势待发，仿佛下一秒就要射出决定战局的一箭。还有那马车兵，驾驭着四匹骏马，气宇轩昂，一看就是秦军中的"豪车一族"。这简直就是古代版的"Cosplay"，只不过演员都是用陶土捏出来的，而且一演就是两千多年，敬业精神绝对满分！

说到这陶土演员的制作工艺，那可真是巧夺天工。据说，当年的工匠们就像现在的3D打印技术一样，先用模具做出各部位的零部件，然后再拼装、烧制，最后还要精雕细琢，涂上鲜艳的彩绘。可惜由于年代久远，大部分色彩已经褪去，但只要稍微发挥一下想象力，就能还原出当年那支栩栩如生的地下军团。哎呀，要是秦始皇知道后世有个叫"美图秀秀"的东西，估计他会把整个陵墓都变成"网红打卡点"。

最后，我要告诉大家一个小秘密。据说，真正的秦始皇陵还深藏在封土堆下，里面除了兵马俑，可能还有水银江河、珠宝山川等等豪华配置。至于那位霸气侧漏的秦始皇本人，是否真的躺在那里，手中紧握着能调动千军万马的神秘"遥控器"，我们就不得而知了。也许有一天，科技发达到能安全无损地打开地宫，到那时，咱们再来个"秦始皇陵深度游"，怎么样？

好了，今天的"秦朝穿越之旅"就到这里。谢谢大家！

作者：刘夕宁

31 【上海石库门】

诸位尊贵的旅友们：

大家好啊！我是你们此行的快乐导航员，即将带领大家走进上海的"心脏"地带，去领略一种既古典又摩登的独特建筑风情——石库门！

首先，让我给你们描绘一下石库门的模样。你们可以把它想象成一位穿着旗袍、头戴礼帽的老克勒（上海话，指讲究生活品质的老派绅士），外表古典优雅，内心却藏着一颗与时俱进的心，石库门建筑，就是这种"新旧交融"的典型代表。它既有江南传统民居的白墙黛瓦、飞檐翘角，又有西方联排住宅的格局和装饰元素，比如罗马柱、券门廊等。这种中西合璧的设计，就好比是上海这座城市的文化名片，诉说着海派文化的包容与创新。

走进石库门，就像翻开一本生动的历史绘本。瞧瞧这窄窄的弄堂，是不是有种"一线天"的感觉？别小看这条"时光隧道"，它可是当年邻里间的社交中心，孩子们在此追逐嬉戏，大人们在此拉家常、晒被子，偶尔还有卖糖粥、修棕绷的小贩穿行其中，热闹非凡。

接下来，我们要参观的就是石库门的灵魂所在——天井。这个看似不起眼的小院子，却是石库门人家的生活舞台。

最后，我想跟大家分享一个关于石库门的小秘密。据说，石库门的名字源于它的大门设计。这门由石头门框、乌漆实心厚木门扇组成，坚固且气派，就如同大户人家的"保险箱"。每次开门关门，都会发出"吱呀"一声，那是石库门特有的欢迎曲，也是岁月流转的见证。所以，下次你们听到这声音，可别以为是闹鬼哦，那是历史在跟你们打招呼呢！

好了，咱们的石库门之旅到此告一段落，期待下次旅行，我们再一同探索更多城市的文化符号！谢谢大家！

作者：刘夕宁

32 【都江堰水利工程】

各位亲爱的游客朋友们：

大家好！欢迎来到举世闻名的都江堰水利工程，我是你们的欢乐导游，今天将带领大家穿越两千多年的时空隧道，探寻这项伟大工程的奥秘，体验一把"水利狂潮"！

首先，我来给大家描绘一下都江堰的"盛世美颜"。都江堰就像是水利界的魔术师，靠的是智慧而非蛮力，它巧妙地运用鱼嘴、宝瓶口和飞沙堰三大法宝，将防洪、灌溉、排沙、航运四大功能完美融合。这哪里是水利工程，分明是大自然与人类共同演奏的生态交响乐嘛！

接下来，我们逐一揭秘这三大法宝。首先是鱼嘴，别误会，不是真的鱼嘴巴，而是形似鱼嘴的一块分水堤。它稳稳地"咬"在岷江江心，将江水分成内江和外江。内江负责灌溉，外江则负责泄洪，两者各行其道，互不干扰。你们看，这鱼嘴是不是很像一位公正无私的裁判员，确保比赛公平进行？

然后是宝瓶口，这个名字一听就有种"瓶中乾坤"的感觉吧？它就像是岷江的咽喉，控制着内江的进水量。为啥叫宝瓶口呢？我猜啊，可能是因为古人觉得这口子像瓶子一样，能装下宝贵的水源，滋养万物。不过，我更愿意认为它是装满了智慧的宝瓶，毕竟，要在这坚硬的山岩上凿出这么个口子，没有超凡的智慧和毅力可不行！

最后出场的是飞沙堰，这名字一听就很酷炫，对不对？飞沙堰的作用就像它的名字一样，专门对付那些淘气的泥沙。当洪水来临时，过量的水流带着泥沙从飞沙堰溢出，由于离心力的作用，大部分泥沙就被甩到外江去了，这就是传说中的"泥沙俱下，唯我独清"。这飞沙堰，简直就是水利界的"扫地僧"，默默无闻却功力深厚。

好了，今天的都江堰之旅就到这里，祝大家愉快并有所收获！

作者：刘夕宁

33 【湖北曾侯乙编钟】

亲爱的游客朋友们：

大家好！欢迎来到历史与音乐交织的奇妙时空，我是你们的快乐导游，今天我们要一同揭开湖北曾侯乙编钟这位"古代音乐巨星"的神秘面纱，感受跨越千年的音符跃动。

首先，让我们把目光投向这座闪耀着青铜光芒的庞大乐器——曾侯乙编钟。瞧瞧这气势，是不是有种"钟鸣鼎食"的豪门范？这可不是普通的钟，而是战国时期曾国国君曾侯乙的陪葬重器，相当于他生前的皇家交响乐团，个个都是"青铜乐师"。整个编钟家族共有65位成员，按大小和音高有序排列，仿佛一支训练有素的青铜合唱团。最大的那个"大哥大"重达203.6千克，最小的"萌新"也有2.4千克。这要是开音乐会，搬道具的兄弟估计得练出一身腱子肉！

编钟的魅力，不仅在于它们的"颜值"和"吨位"，更在于它们能够演奏出完整的五声音阶，甚至十二律齐备，音域跨五个八度，比钢琴还宽广！要知道，这可是公元前400多年的事，那时候欧洲的音乐家还在摸索五线谱的雏形呢。所以，曾侯乙编钟堪称"世界音乐史上的奇迹"，是咱们中国古代音乐文化的"C位担当"。

说到演奏，你们是不是很好奇，这么大个儿的钟是怎么敲响的？别急，这就揭晓谜底。每个编钟都有两个可以敲击的部分，称为"正鼓"和"侧鼓"。敲击不同的部位，就能发出不同的音高，简直就像现代键盘上的黑白键。而且，编钟内部还有精妙的"音槽"设计，使得钟声悠扬悦耳，传播深远。想象一下，当年曾侯乙宴请各国使节，编钟乐团奏响华丽的宫廷乐章，那场面，绝对是春秋战国版的"维也纳新年音乐会"！

当然，编钟不只是乐器那么简单，它们还是权力与地位的象征。每口钟身上都刻满了精美的纹饰和铭文，记录着铸造年份、编号、音名等信息，有的甚至还记载了乐律理论和演奏曲目，简直是"青铜版音乐教科书"。

谢谢大家，期待我们在下一次的文化探索中再次相聚！

作者：刘夕宁

34 【辛亥革命】

各位亲爱的游客朋友们:

大家好!我是你们的导游,今天让我们把目光投向这场改变中国命运的伟大革命——辛亥革命。它发生在1911年,名字中的"辛亥"来源于中国传统干支纪年法。

辛亥革命的"主演"是孙中山先生,他可是中国近代史上响当当的人物,有"国父"之称。孙中山先生提出"驱除鞑虏,恢复中华,创立民国,平均地权",相当于为革命定制了一份明确的"作战纲领"。他领导的同盟会,就像是革命队伍的"特种部队",个个都是热血青年,怀着改变中国的梦想,誓要推翻清朝统治,建立共和政体。

说到"战斗",就不能不提武昌起义。1911年10月10日,湖北新军中的革命党人忍无可忍,打响了起义的第一枪。这枪声如同信号弹,点燃了全国革命的烽火。各地纷纷响应,清朝统治迅速土崩瓦解。这场"武昌起义",就像是历史舞台上的一次华丽转身,瞬间改变了中国的政治格局。

辛亥革命的成功,不仅结束了中国长达两千多年的封建帝制,建立了亚洲第一个民主共和国——中华民国,更开启了近代中国的进步潮流。当然,辛亥革命并非一帆风顺,革命果实一度遭到窃取,中国仍面临重重困难。但正如孙中山先生所说:"革命尚未成功,同志仍需努力。"辛亥革命播下的革命种子,已经深深植根于中国人民心中,为后来的新民主主义革命、社会主义革命奠定了基础。

总的来说,辛亥革命是中国历史上的重要里程碑,它不仅仅是一段历史,更是一种精神,一种追求民主、自由、进步的精神。让我们带着敬畏,继续前行在探索历史、理解现实的道路上。谢谢大家,期待我们在下一次的文化探索中再次相聚!

作者:刘夕宁

35 【红军长征精神】

亲爱的游客朋友们：

大家好！欢迎来到历史的长河，我是你们的导游，今天我们要一同踏上一段震撼心灵的红色之旅，探寻红军长征这段"地球上的红飘带"背后的伟大精神。

首先，让我们把目光投向人类历史上最伟大的战略转移——红军长征。长征，发生在1934年至1936年，是红军在极端艰难困苦的条件下，为保存和发展革命力量，被迫进行的战略大转移。这场历时两年、行程约两万五千里的"超级马拉松"，堪称"史上最硬核徒步行军"。红军战士们面对敌人的围追堵截、恶劣的自然环境，依然坚定信念，勇往直前，用双脚丈量出了一条通向胜利的道路。长征的"主演"是一群英勇无畏的红军战士，他们中有指挥若定的领袖，有舍生忘死的普通士兵。他们每一个人都是长征路上的英雄，用血肉之躯铸就了长征精神的丰碑。这就像一部英雄史诗，每个人物都有血有肉，有笑有泪，让人敬佩，让人感动。

长征并不是一场轻松愉快的旅行，它充满了艰难险阻，甚至是生死考验，在这种极端环境下，红军战士们展现出了惊人的毅力与智慧，创造了许多"长征奇迹"。比如"四渡赤水"，就像是红军在敌人的包围圈中跳起的"水上芭蕾"，让敌人晕头转向；"飞夺泸定桥"，则像是红军在危急关头上演的"极限挑战"，以超乎常人的勇气与速度，夺取了战略要地。这些"长征奇迹"，就像历史舞台上的精彩瞬间，让人拍案叫绝。

长征精神已经成为我们民族精神的重要组成部分，激励着一代又一代中国人在各自的"长征路"上奋勇前进。让我们带着这份敬意与思考，继续前行在探索历史、理解现实的道路上。

谢谢大家，期待我们在下一次的文化探索中再次相聚！

作者：刘夕宁

36 【"两弹一星"】

各位亲爱的游客朋友们：

大家好！我是你们的导游，今天我们要穿越时空，一起走进一段充满智慧与勇气、热血与荣耀的历史篇章——"两弹一星"工程。

首先，我们来聊聊这"两弹"。这里的"两弹"，指原子弹和氢弹，也就是大家耳熟能详的核武器。想象一下，它们就像两位脾气暴躁的大叔，一个叫"老原"，一个叫"氢哥"。老原性格直率，爆发力十足，一旦发威，方圆十里之内瞬间变"烤箱"；而氢哥呢，看似内敛，实则能量惊人，他的威力比老原还要大几百倍，一旦"开嗓"，那可是连太空都能听见的"惊天动地"。

然后，咱们再来看看这个"一星"。它可不是夜空中最亮的那颗星星，也不是星座占卜里的幸运星，而是咱们中国的卫星，这位低调又实力派的"太空使者"。在浩瀚无垠的宇宙中，它就像一位默默坚守岗位的信使，传递着地球与太空的"亲密对话"，为我们的通信、导航、气象预报等各项事业提供着不可或缺的服务。可以说，没有它，我们的生活可能就要回归"通信基本靠吼，导航基本靠狗"的原始状态了。

那么，"两弹一星"是如何诞生的呢？这就不得不提到一群被称为"国之脊梁"的科研英雄们。他们就像一支支"科学特战队"，在那个物资匮乏、技术封锁的年代，硬是凭借着一股"有条件要上，没条件创造条件也要上"的精神，成功研发出了这些大国重器。20世纪60年代，当世界还处在冷战的阴霾之下，中国却凭借"两弹一星"的成功研制，一举打破了超级大国的核垄断，不仅极大地提升了国家安全防御能力，更向全世界宣告：中国人民有志气、有能力独立自主地建设自己的科技强国！

好了，关于"两弹一星"的话题就聊到这儿，欢迎随时找我交流探讨，我会尽我所能，为大家答疑解惑，让我们的旅行更加丰富多彩。谢谢大家！

作者：刘夕宁

37 【红旗渠精神】

各位亲爱的游客朋友们:

大家好!我是你们的导游,今天我要带领大家领略一种独特的精神风貌,它既非山水间的自然奇观,也非古建筑中的历史遗韵,而是深深镌刻在中国人心灵深处的一种精神力量——红旗渠精神。

首先,让我来给各位描绘一下"红旗渠"这位主角。它并非一条普通的小溪或河流,而是咱们中国北方的一条"人工天河"。您可能会想:"人工天河?难不成是哪位神仙下凡,挥舞法杖,一夜之间造出来的?"哈哈,非也非也。这条"天河"可是实实在在由勤劳智慧的林县人民,历时近十年,一锤一钎、一土一石亲手凿出来的。想象一下,那是一幅怎样的壮丽画卷啊!崇山峻岭间,一条银色巨龙蜿蜒盘旋,从太行山巅引水入田,彻底改变了干旱缺水的面貌。而这背后的奇迹缔造者,就是我们今天要深入探讨的"红旗渠精神"。

那么,红旗渠精神究竟是什么呢?简单来说,它就是"自力更生、艰苦创业、团结协作、无私奉献"。这十六个字,每一个都沉甸甸的,蕴含着无数感人的故事和无尽的力量。

"自力更生",这是红旗渠精神的灵魂。面对极度缺水的生存困境,林县人民没有坐等天降甘霖,也没有怨天尤人,而是选择了"自己动手,丰衣足食",他们以大无畏的气概,挑战大自然,硬是在巍峨的太行山中开凿出一条"生命之渠"。"艰苦创业",这是红旗渠精神的脊梁。修建红旗渠的过程,堪称一部现代版的"愚公移山"。面对恶劣的自然环境、简陋的施工条件,林县人民以无可比拟的毅力和坚韧,顶风冒雪,风餐露宿,用血肉之躯与坚硬的岩石较量。"团结协作",这是红旗渠精神的纽带。修建红旗渠绝非一人之力可成,它凝聚了当地人民的心血。"无私奉献"是红旗渠精神的底色。在修建红旗渠的过程中,涌现出了许多舍小家为大家的先进人物。他们有的放弃了个人的安逸生活,有的甚至献出了宝贵的生命,只为让家乡摆脱干旱,让子孙后代过上好日子。

好了,关于红旗渠精神的话题就聊到这儿。谢谢大家!

作者:刘夕宁

38 【成昆铁路】

亲爱的游客朋友们：

大家好！欢迎各位来到这趟特殊的旅程，我们将一同探访一条被誉为"人类征服自然的奇迹"和"世界铁路建设史上的丰碑"的伟大工程——成昆铁路。

成昆铁路，这条全长近1100千米的铁路巨龙，从繁华的四川成都出发，一路向南，穿越千山万水，最终抵达美丽的云南昆明。这条铁路不仅是一条连接两地的交通要道，更是一段人类与自然和谐共生的传奇。

在这条铁路上，我们见证了人类智慧的伟大。它跨越了海拔高差近3000米的复杂地形，途经大渡河、金沙江、龙川江等多条大江大河，穿越了被誉为"地质博物馆"的横断山脉。在如此恶劣的自然环境下，建设者们用他们的汗水和智慧，硬是在这地壳运动最活跃、地质构造最复杂的地区，开辟出了一条连接云贵高原与四川盆地的"生命线"。

而成昆铁路的建成，离不开被称为"成昆精神"的力量支撑。这种精神，是"为有牺牲多壮志，敢教日月换新天"的豪情壮志，是"逢山开路，遇水架桥"的决心勇气，是"艰苦奋斗，无私奉献"的崇高品格。正是有了这种精神，建设者们才能在面对重重困难时，始终保持坚定的信念和不屈的斗志，最终完成了这一伟大的工程。

如今，我们站在成昆铁路的起点，回望那段艰难而又辉煌的历史，心中充满了敬意和感慨。这条铁路不仅是一条连接两地的交通线，更是一条承载着人类智慧和勇气的精神线。它告诉我们，只要有坚定的信念和不屈的斗志，人类就能够战胜一切困难，创造出更多的奇迹。

在未来的旅程中，让我们带着这份敬意和感动，继续前行，让我们沿着成昆铁路的轨迹，去感受那些曾经挥洒汗水、付出艰辛的建设者们留下的印记，去领略那些因铁路而焕发生机的城市和乡村的变迁，去体验那些因铁路而更加紧密的人与人之间的联系和交流。

谢谢大家！

作者：刘夕宁

39 【青藏铁路】

各位尊贵的游客朋友们:

欢迎踏上这趟"云端之旅"！今天,我将带您揭开青藏铁路——这条"世界屋脊上的钢铁巨龙"的神秘面纱。

青藏铁路,全长1956千米,从青海西宁一路向西,穿越巍峨的昆仑,跨过辽阔的可可西里,翻越世界屋脊唐古拉山,直至雪域圣地拉萨。它的最高海拔处达到了5072米,比珠峰大本营还要高。这不仅是一条铁路,更是中国人智慧和勇气的结晶,是地球上最严酷环境下创造的现实奇迹。

那么,青藏铁路是如何在"第三极"上"翩翩起舞"的呢？这就离不开那熠熠生辉的"青藏铁路精神"。

首先,是"生态环保,和谐共生"的精神。面对这片地球上最后的净土,建设者们秉持"绿色施工"的理念,如同对待生命般呵护着雪域高原。他们采取各种环保措施,确保铁路与生态环境和谐共存,让青藏铁路成为人与自然和谐相处的典范。

其次,是"科技创新,攻坚克难"的精神。青藏铁路建设面临的环境和技术难题堪称世界级,但我们的建设者们不畏艰难,发扬大无畏精神,研发出一系列创新技术,成功驯服了高原的"猛兽"。他们的智慧和勇气,让青藏铁路成为科技创新的典范。

最后,是"以人为本,生命至上"的精神。青藏铁路不仅是经济线、生态线,更是民生线、团结线。建设者们始终把工人们的生命安全放在首位,采取各种措施保障他们的健康。这种对生命的尊重和关怀,让青藏铁路成为人性光辉的典范。

朋友们,青藏铁路不仅是一条铁路线,更是一条精神线。它承载着"青藏铁路精神"的熠熠光辉,这种精神将永远激励我们前行。无论时代如何变迁,无论科技如何进步,我们都应铭记这份精神,让它成为我们心中的灯塔,照亮前行的道路。

在接下来的旅程中,让我们带着这份敬意和感动,继续探寻更多的人类文明奇迹,共同领略中华大地的雄浑壮美和人文魅力。谢谢大家！

作者:刘夕宁

40 【港珠澳大桥】

亲爱的旅行家们：

欢迎搭乘今日的"超级工程探索专列"，我是你们的导游！今天我们一起探秘的是一座连接三地、跨越伶仃洋的"海上飞虹"——港珠澳大桥。

港珠澳大桥是一座令人瞩目的工程奇迹，其建设中的多个数字不仅反映了工程的规模与难度，也凸显了我国在基础设施建设领域的卓越成就。

55千米是港珠澳大桥的总长度，这一数字足以让它在世界跨海大桥中傲视群雄。大桥由海中部分主体工程、两个口岸人工岛、三条连接线组成，其中海中部分主体工程总长约29.6千米，包括22.9千米长的桥梁段和6.7千米长的岛隧工程。这样的跨度不仅考验了建设者的技术和勇气，也体现了我国在桥梁建设领域的领先地位。

120年是港珠澳大桥的设计使用年限。这一数字显示了我国在桥梁设计和建造方面的前瞻性和高标准。大桥采用了先进的技术和材料，确保了其长期稳定性和安全性，为未来的交通发展奠定了坚实基础。

42万吨是港珠澳大桥主体工程的主梁钢板用量。这一数字相当于10座"鸟巢"体育场或60座埃菲尔铁塔的重量，这凸显了大桥的雄伟与坚固，同时，也反映了我国在钢铁产业和桥梁建设方面的强大实力。

此外，6.7千米是港珠澳大桥海底隧道的长度，这也是大桥难度最大的工程部分。这条海底隧道在几十米深的海底进行精准对接，展现了我国在深海工程领域的精湛技艺。

这些数字不仅是对港珠澳大桥的定量描述，更是对其技术难度、建设规模、设计理念的深刻解读。它们共同构成了这座世界级工程奇迹的独特魅力，展现了我国在基础设施建设领域的卓越成就和综合国力的不断提升。

未来，港珠澳大桥将继续发挥其重要作用，为粤港澳大湾区的经济社会发展注入新的活力，同时也将成为展示中国智慧和力量的重要窗口。接下来是实地体验环节，谢谢大家！

作者：刘夕宁

41 【北京四合院】

各位游客朋友们：

大家好！欢迎大家来到这千年古都，我是你们的导游，今天，我将带领大家走进饱含东方韵味、充满京味儿的建筑艺术瑰宝——北京四合院。这不是一次简单的游览，而是一场与历史的深度对话、一次与传统文化的亲密握手。

咱们先来聊聊四合院的起源吧！早在元代，北京的四合院就已经初具规模了。那时候的北京是元大都的所在地，来自全国各地的工匠们汇聚于此，他们带来了各地的建筑技艺和文化元素，逐渐形成了具有北京特色的四合院建筑。明清时期，四合院是北京城的主要住宅形式，无论是皇亲国戚还是平民百姓，都纷纷建造四合院。可以说，四合院见证了北京从元大都到明清古都的沧桑巨变。

走进四合院，您会发现这里不仅仅是一个居住的空间，更是一个充满故事的文化载体。每一座四合院都承载着家族的历史和记忆。比如，有的四合院曾经是某位名人的故居，他们在这里留下了许多珍贵的文化遗产；有的四合院则是家族几代人共同生活的场所，他们在这里度过了欢乐与悲伤交织的时光。这些故事让四合院变得生动起来，仿佛每一块砖、每一片瓦都在诉说着过往的岁月。

除了历史故事，四合院还蕴含着丰富的文化内涵。它体现了古代中国人对家庭、对社会的理解和追求。四合院的布局讲究阴阳平衡、天地人和，既体现了古代哲学思想，又反映了中国人对和谐生活的向往。同时，四合院还承载着传统伦理道德和家族观念，它教导人们要尊老爱幼、和睦相处，传承家族的优良传统和文化。

朋友们，北京四合院就像是一部浓缩的历史长卷，它讲述着老北京的故事，承载着中华文化的精髓。每一座四合院都是一部独特的历史故事集，它们交织在一起，构成了北京城丰富多彩的人文景观。希望通过今天的讲解，能让您对四合院有更深入的了解和喜爱。在未来的旅程中，我还会带您领略更多中国传统文化的魅力。谢谢大家，祝旅途愉快！

作者：刘明

42 【福建土楼】

各位游客朋友们:

大家好!欢迎来到美丽的福建,我是你们的专业导游,非常荣幸能够陪伴大家一同探索福建土楼的神秘魅力。福建土楼,是这片土地上的一颗璀璨明珠,以其独特的建筑风格和深厚的文化内涵,吸引着无数游客的目光。

土楼,作为福建特有的传统建筑形式,承载着丰富的历史和文化信息。它们以土为主要材料,经过精心设计和巧妙施工,形成了坚固耐用的建筑体系。这些土楼不仅具有防御功能,能够抵御外敌的侵袭,还兼具居住、生活、生产等多重功能,是福建人民智慧和勤劳的结晶。

走进土楼,仿佛穿越了时空,回到了古代社会。你可以看到院落中央的空地上,人们正在晾晒谷物,妇女们忙着做家务,孩子们在追逐嬉戏。土楼的内部结构也非常独特,一层层的房间紧密相连,形成了独特的生活空间。这里的居民相互关爱、和睦相处,共同营造了一个温馨和谐的家园。

除了建筑本身,土楼的文化内涵也十分丰富。每一座土楼都承载着家族的历史和荣耀,墙壁上雕刻着精美的图案,楹联和壁画则记录着家族的传统和价值观。这些元素共同构成了土楼独特的文化氛围,让人们感受到了福建人民深厚的文化底蕴。

在福建,还有一些著名的土楼景点值得我们去探索。比如,南靖的田螺坑土楼群,以其独特的造型和精美的装饰而闻名遐迩;永定的土楼王——承启楼,更是以其雄伟壮观的气势和丰富的文化内涵吸引着无数游客前来参观。

朋友们,福建土楼不仅是一处旅游景点,更是一段历史的见证,一种文化的传承。在这里,我们可以感受到福建人民对生活的热爱和对家园的守护。希望大家能够珍惜这次难得的机会,用心去感受土楼的魅力,去体验福建的风土人情。

最后,我想对大家说,土楼之旅不仅是一次视觉的盛宴,还是一次心灵的洗礼。希望大家在欣赏土楼美景的同时,也能够思考其背后的文化内涵和历史价值。谢谢大家!让我们携手共赴这场难忘的福建土楼之旅吧!

作者:刘明

43 【皖南古村落】

各位游客朋友们：

大家好！欢迎来到风景如画的皖南，我是你们的导游。今天，我们将一同探寻那些藏匿于青山绿水间的皖南古村落。

皖南古村落，宛如一幅幅展开的山水画卷，白墙黛瓦、马头墙、石板路，每一处都透露出古朴典雅的气息。这些古民居错落有致，庭院深深，仿佛每一座房子都藏着一个古老的故事。精致的木雕、砖雕、石雕，无不展现着古代工匠的精湛技艺和无穷智慧。

漫步在古村落的街巷间，仿佛穿越了时空，回到了那个遥远的年代。你可以感受到这里的人们保持着传统的生活方式，日出而作，日落而息，过着宁静而充实的生活。清晨，当第一缕阳光洒落在村庄时，人们便开始了忙碌的一天；傍晚，当夕阳的余晖洒满大地时，人们便围坐在一起，享受着天伦之乐。

在皖南古村落，你还可以亲身体验到丰富的民俗活动。每逢佳节，村民们都会穿上盛装，载歌载舞，欢庆佳节，这些活动不仅丰富了游客的文化体验，还让人们更加深入地了解了皖南地区的传统文化。此外，这里的自然风光也是一大亮点，青山绿水、云雾缭绕，使人仿佛置身于一幅天然的水墨画中。

朋友们，皖南古村落以其独特的魅力吸引着无数游客前来探访。在这里，你可以感受到中国传统文化的深厚底蕴，也可以领略到自然风光的无限魅力。无论是摄影爱好者还是文化追寻者，都能在这里找到属于自己的乐趣和感动。

最后，我想说的是，皖南古村落不仅是一处旅游景点，还是一段历史的见证、一种文化的传承。希望大家在欣赏美景的同时，也能深入体验这里的文化和生活，让自己的心灵得到一次真正的洗礼和升华。

谢谢大家！期待与您共同度过一个难忘的皖南古村落之旅！

作者：刘明

44 【藏族碉楼】

各位游客朋友们：

大家好！欢迎来到神奇的雪域高原，我是你们的导游。今天，我们将一同探寻藏族碉楼的奥秘与魅力。

站在碉楼脚下，抬头仰望，您会被其雄伟壮观所震撼，这些碉楼，不仅是藏族人民智慧的结晶，更是他们与自然和谐共生的最好见证。它们屹立在高山之巅，历经风雨洗礼，依然坚固如初，诉说着古老而传奇的故事。

碉楼多为多层结构，内部空间布局灵活多变。走进碉楼内部，您会发现藏式家具古朴典雅，壁画精美绝伦，佛龛神圣庄严，每一处细节都透露出藏族人民对生活的热爱与对信仰的虔诚。除了欣赏碉楼的建筑之美，您还可以了解藏族碉楼背后的故事，古代藏族勇士曾凭借碉楼，成功击退了无数次来犯之敌，这些英勇事迹被世代传颂，成为藏族文化的重要组成部分。每当夕阳西下，碉楼的剪影映照在金色的草原上，仿佛在诉说着那些英勇无畏的传说。

此外，藏族碉楼还承载着丰富的精神内涵。它们不仅是藏族人民生存智慧的结晶，更是他们坚韧不屈精神的象征。面对严酷的自然环境，藏族人民不仅学会了与之和谐共处，还创造了如此雄伟的建筑，展现出强大的生命力与创造力。这些碉楼，就像是一部部活的历史，让我们能够更深入地了解藏族文化的内涵与精髓。

朋友们，藏族碉楼是雪域高原上一道独特的风景线。它们以其独特的建筑风格、深厚的历史底蕴和无畏的精神风貌，向世人展示着藏族文化的魅力与力量，无论您是建筑爱好者、历史迷还是文化探寻者，相信都能在碉楼之旅中找到属于自己的震撼与感动。

最后，我想说的是，藏族碉楼不仅是一处旅游景点，更是一段历史的见证、一种文化的传承。希望大家在欣赏美景的同时，也能深入体验这里的文化和生活，让自己的心灵得到一次真正的洗礼和升华。

扎西德勒！祝大家在藏族碉楼之旅中收获满满，旅途愉快！

作者：刘明

45 【苏州园林】

各位游客朋友们：

大家好！欢迎来到人间天堂——苏州，我是你们的导游。今天，我们将一同领略闻名遐迩的苏州园林的迷人魅力。这些园林不仅是休闲娱乐之地，更是中国传统文化的瑰宝，是江南水乡最温婉的诗篇。

苏州园林遍布古城内外，各有千秋。它们犹如散落在姑苏大地上的珍珠，每一颗都闪耀着独特的光芒。走进园林，你会被那细腻入微的艺术匠心所折服，每一处景观都经过精心设计和布局，移步换景，让人流连忘返。那曲折的回廊，仿佛在诉说着古老的故事；那灵动的池塘，倒映着天光云影，宛如一幅流动的画卷，而那些雅致的亭台楼阁，让人心驰神往，它们或翼然于水上，或隐于花木之间，既是观景的佳处，也是休息的好地方。

苏州园林背后还蕴藏着丰富的历史文化内涵。这些园林多为明清时期士大夫的私家宅院，他们追求自然与人的和谐统一，将山水之美融入日常生活中。在园林中漫步，你可以感受到那份崇尚自然、追求和谐的生活哲学。同时，这些园林也是古代文人墨客修身养性、寄情山水的场所，他们在这里吟诗作画，留下了许多珍贵的文化遗产。

此外，苏州园林还蕴含着深厚的精神内涵。它们不仅是艺术的结晶，更是古代人们理想生活方式的体现。这些园林以山水为骨架，以花木为肌肤，以亭台楼阁为点缀，构成了一个个完美的空间。在这里，你可以感受到那份宁静与安详，仿佛置身于一个世外桃源。

朋友们，苏州园林是中国传统文化的瑰宝，它们以其精致的造园艺术、深厚的文化底蕴和独特的审美情趣，向世人展示了中国传统文人的生活美学与哲学思考。无论你是园林艺术爱好者、历史文化探寻者，还是寻求心灵宁静的旅行者，相信都能在苏州园林中有所收获。

最后，我衷心祝愿大家在苏州园林之旅中玩得开心，游得尽兴，收获满满的东方美学体验。谢谢大家！

作者：刘明

46 【北京颐和园】

各位游客朋友们：

大家好！欢迎来到北京颐和园，这座集皇家园林艺术之大成的瑰宝。我是您的导游，接下来将由我为大家讲解颐和园的历史渊源、文化内涵和建筑特色。

颐和园，位于北京西郊，占地面积约3.009平方千米，是清代皇家园林的代表作。它始建于乾隆年间，原名为清漪园，后经战火损毁，又在慈禧太后的主持下得以重建，并更名为颐和园，这一名称寓意着皇家的颐养天年和对天下太平的美好祈愿。

我们首先来到的是东宫门，这座宏伟的牌楼见证了颐和园的历史变迁。穿过牌楼，一条长廊展现在我们眼前，长达728米的长廊不仅连接了昆明湖的两岸，更是世界上较长的画廊。长廊两侧梁枋上绘有上万幅彩画，内容丰富多彩，既展现了中国的山水花鸟之美，又反映了历史典故和民间生活，是中华文化的瑰宝。

接下来，我们将乘船游览昆明湖。湖面辽阔，碧波荡漾，远处的万寿山和近处的十七孔桥构成了美丽的画卷。这十七孔桥之所以设计成十七个孔，正是因为在中国传统文化中，"九"是最大的阳数，"九"寓意着皇家的至高无上，十七孔桥其正中的大孔从桥两端数来正好是第九个孔，这种对数字的讲究，体现了皇家园林设计的独特之处。

颐和园不仅是一座美丽的皇家园林，更是一部厚重的历史长卷。它见证了中华民族的荣辱兴衰，承载着丰富的历史文化信息。从乾隆盛世的皇家消夏胜地，到近代遭受列强洗劫的悲惨历史，再到新中国成立后精心修复开放的辉煌重生，颐和园的历史变迁反映了中华民族的坚韧与复兴。

各位游客朋友们，颐和园是一座集自然美景、人文景观和历史文化于一体的皇家园林。希望大家在游览过程中，能够充分领略到它的独特魅力，感受到中国传统文化的博大精深。同时，也请大家爱护这里的一草一木，共同保护这份宝贵的历史文化遗产。谢谢大家！

作者：刘明

47 【承德避暑山庄】

"清风拂山岗,明月照大江。"各位游客朋友们,大家好!欢迎来到承德避暑山庄,这里不仅是清风明月的绝佳去处,更是清朝皇家避暑消夏的秘密花园。我是你们的导游,今天,就请跟随我一起,穿越时空的隧道,共同领略这座皇家园林的无限魅力吧!

承德避暑山庄,名字听起来就让人心生向往。想象一下,在古代的炎炎夏日,皇帝与后妃们离开闷热的紫禁城,来到这里享受清凉,是不是有种"逃离尘世,追寻清凉"的感觉!

走进山庄,你会被这里的布局所震撼。宫殿区、湖泊区、平原区、山峦区,四大区域各具特色,又相互呼应,仿佛是大自然与人类智慧的完美结合。特别是那湖泊区,碧波荡漾,荷花盛开,仿佛江南水乡的美景重现眼前。想象一下,当年的皇帝与后妃们泛舟湖上,欣赏着湖光山色,享受着清凉的夏风,那景色简直美不胜收!

此外,承德避暑山庄还展现了多民族文化融合。这里不仅有汉族文化的烙印,还融入了蒙、藏等少数民族的文化元素。承德避暑山庄是一座集自然风光、人文景观、历史文化于一体的皇家园林,在这里,你不仅可以欣赏到美丽的景色,还可以感受到深厚的文化底蕴。希望大家在游览的过程中,能够用心去感受这座园林的独特魅力,同时也能够尊重和保护这里的一草一木,让后人也能继续欣赏到这份美丽。

最后,我想说,承德避暑山庄不仅是一座园林,更是一部历史长卷,它见证了清朝的兴衰,也承载了无数的故事和传说。希望大家在游览的过程中,能够用心去聆听这些故事,感受这座园林的历史和文化底蕴。好了,话不多说,让我们继续探索这座美丽的皇家园林吧!

作者:刘明

48 【京剧】

各位游客朋友们：

大家好！欢迎来到京剧的世界，这里是一个色彩斑斓、魅力四溢的艺术殿堂。我是你们的导游，今天将带领大家一同领略京剧这门集唱、念、做、打于一体的综合性表演艺术的独特魅力。

京剧，作为中国国粹，已有两百多年的辉煌历史。它起源于清代中叶，融合了徽剧、汉剧等地方戏曲的精华，在北京这片文化沃土上绽放出璀璨的光彩。京剧不仅是中国的文化名片，更是世界戏剧舞台上的一颗璀璨明珠。

走进京剧的世界，首先映入眼帘的便是那一张张鲜活生动的脸谱。红脸关公、黑脸包拯、白脸曹操……红色脸谱，通常象征忠勇正直；黑色脸谱，则多象征刚正不阿、铁面无私；白色脸谱，往往象征着阴险狡诈。除了这些常见的脸谱色彩，京剧还有绿色、蓝色、紫色等多种颜色的脸谱，每一种颜色都对应着不同的性格特征和人物类型。通过色彩和图案的巧妙组合，脸谱将人物的性格和情感刻画得鲜明生动，让观众在欣赏表演的同时，也能深刻感受到角色的内心世界。

京剧的行当划分也十分精细，包括生、旦、净、丑四大类。生角英俊潇洒，旦角柔美多姿，净角威武雄壮，丑角诙谐幽默。这些行当在舞台上相互映衬，共同演绎出一个个精彩纷呈的故事。

京剧的表演艺术更是达到了炉火纯青的境地。唱、念、做、打，每一项都需要演员们付出辛勤的努力和汗水。那高亢激昂的唱腔、抑扬顿挫的念白、优美娴熟的身段表演，以及惊心动魄的武打场面，都让人为之倾倒。

朋友们，京剧是一门博大精深的艺术，它承载着中华民族的文化精髓和历史记忆。通过欣赏京剧，我们不仅可以感受到中华文化的独特魅力，还可以了解到中国历史的沧桑变迁。希望大家在今天的京剧之旅中，能够深深感受到这门艺术的魅力，并希望大家能够将这份对京剧的热爱带回家，与家人朋友分享这份美好的艺术体验。谢谢大家！

作者：刘明

49 【川剧变脸】

各位游客朋友们：

大家好！欢迎来到巴山蜀水之间，领略川剧变脸的独特魅力。我是你们的导游，今天将带大家一同走进这门集艺术、技巧、神秘于一身的表演形式。

川剧变脸，作为川剧艺术的瑰宝，以其瞬间的情绪切换和神秘莫测的面谱变换而著称。它不仅是川剧表演中的一大亮点，更是中国传统文化中的一颗璀璨明珠。

变脸的面谱，是川剧变脸的核心所在。每一张面谱都经过精心绘制，色彩鲜艳、图案独特。红色面谱代表忠勇正直，黑色面谱寓意刚正不阿，白色面谱则象征阴险狡诈。演员们通过巧妙的手法，将这些面谱瞬间变换，展示出人物性格的多样性和情感的变化。

而变脸的技巧，更是令人叹为观止。演员们借助特制的服装和道具，通过扯、抹、吹、运等多种方式，实现面谱的快速更换。尤其是那"扯脸"的技巧，更是让人瞠目结舌，演员们似乎拥有魔法般的手法，在瞬间扯下一张面谱，又换上另一张，令人惊叹不已。

除了面谱和技巧，川剧变脸的音乐、唱腔、灯光等元素也相得益彰。激昂的音乐、高亢的唱腔，为变脸表演增添了浓厚的艺术氛围，而炫目的灯光和华丽的服装，则将表演推向了高潮。

在欣赏川剧变脸的同时，我们也能够感受到中国传统文化的博大精深。它让我们了解到，在戏曲艺术的舞台上，演员们通过精湛的表演技巧和独特的艺术形式，将人物内心的复杂情感展现得淋漓尽致。

希望大家在今天的旅程中，能够真正感受到川剧变脸的魅力，并将这份美好的记忆带回家，与亲朋好友分享。让我们共同欣赏接下来的精彩的川剧变脸表演吧！

作者：刘明

50 【二十四节气】

　　春雨惊春清谷天,夏满芒夏暑相连。秋处露秋寒霜降,冬雪雪冬小大寒。每月两节不变更,最多相差一两天。上半年来六廿一,下半年是八廿三。

　　亲爱的游客们,欢迎踏上这场领略中华农业智慧与自然韵律的旅程!我是你们的导游,今天,让我们共同探寻二十四节气这部饱含古人智慧的"农业百科全书"。

　　二十四节气,是中国古代农耕文明的瑰宝,它依据地球在黄道上的位置变化,精细划分了春夏秋冬四季的转换,以及每个季节中气候、物候的微妙变化。这不仅仅是一部历法,更是我们祖先与自然和谐相处的智慧结晶。

　　春天,从立春开始,大地回暖,万物复苏。雨水时节,春雨绵绵,滋润着每一寸土地,为春耕播种带来了希望。惊蛰一到,万物复苏,春雷唤醒了沉睡的生灵,田野间充满了生机与活力。春分时节,昼夜平分,春意正浓,人们踏青赏花,享受着春天的美好。

　　夏天,立夏标志着季节的转换,万物进入生长的旺季。小满时节,麦穗初黄,丰收在望。芒种到来,农人们忙着抢收抢种,田野里一片繁忙景象。夏至时节,白天最长,阳光最为炽热,人们通过各种方式消暑纳凉,期待着秋天的到来。

　　秋天,立秋虽至,暑气未消,但早晚已感凉意。处暑之后,秋风送爽,硕果累累,人们开始收获一年的辛勤劳动。白露时节,露珠晶莹,象征着天气转凉,秋天真正来临。秋分时节,昼夜再次平分,金风送爽,人们沉浸在丰收的喜悦之中。

　　冬天,立冬拉开冬季的序幕,北风呼啸,大地开始进入休眠期。小雪、大雪时节,雪花纷飞,银装素裹,大地披上了一层厚厚的冬装。冬至时节,白昼最短,黑夜最长,人们围炉取暖,品尝着热腾腾的饺子或汤圆,感受着家的温暖。小寒、大寒时节,天寒地冻,但人们依然怀揣着对春天的期盼,等待着新一轮生命的循环。

　　二十四节气不仅指导着我们的农业生产,更蕴含着深厚的文化内涵和民俗风情。它让我们更加敬畏自然、顺应自然、保护自然,实现人与自然的和谐共生。希望通过今天的旅行,您能更加深入地了解二十四节气的魅力所在,感受到中华文化的博大精深。谢谢大家!

作者:刘明

第五部分　英语口语测试

作者:刘明、刘夕宁

题干	参考英文对话
Dialogue 1 Perform as a local guide. The tour group has lunch in a restaurant. One of the tourists complains the food is too cold and the service is so poor. Your dialogue will include the following points: (1) Apologize. (2) Give a reason for the problem. (3) Promise to take action. (4) Answer questions if there are any.	**Local Guide:** Good afternoon, everyone. I hope you're all enjoying your lunch. I'm here to ensure your dining experience is as pleasant as possible. **Tourist:** Not really. My meal is quite cold, and the service has been rather slow. **Local Guide:** I'm really sorry for the inconvenience you've experienced. I apologize, T1. **Tourist:** What's the reason for this? **Local Guide:** The kitchen is a bit understaffed today due to unforeseen circumstances, which has affected both the food preparation time and the overall service. I understand it's not up to our usual standards. **Tourist:** I see. So, what are you going to do about it? **Local Guide:** I promise to take action immediately. I'll speak with the manager and have your meal heated up. Additionally, we'll ensure the staff are aware of the situation to prevent any further delays. **Tourist:** Can we get a discount for this? **Local Guide:** Of course, I'll discuss that with the manager as well. We value your satisfaction and will do our best to make it up to you. **Tourist:** Alright, thank you for addressing the issue. **Local Guide:** You're welcome. If you have any more questions or concerns, please feel free to ask. Your feedback is important to us. **Tourist:** No, that should be all for now. Thank you. **Local Guide:** Not a problem at all. Enjoy the rest of your meal, and I hope the rest of your day is more enjoyable. **Tourist:** Thanks, I appreciate it. **Local Guide:** My pleasure. Have a great afternoon.

Key Vocabulary and Phrases

apologize 道歉

understaffed 人手不足的

unforeseen 意料之外的情况

take action 采取行动

value your satisfaction 重视你的满意

feedback 反馈

题干	参考英文对话
Dialogue 2 Perform as a local guide in a Beijing city bus tour. The tourists ask you a lot of questions. Your dialogue will include the following points: (1) Introduce the sculpture on your left. (2) Introduce the places of interest in the area. (3) Give a brief introduction of the next stop. (4) Answer questions if there are any.	**Local Guide:** Good morning, everyone! Welcome to Beijing, the ancient capital of China. My name is Tom, and just like the famous cat from the classic cartoon "Tom and Jerry", I'm here to guide you through our wonderful city. As we start our journey, let's take a look to your left. There stands the Monument to the People's Heroes, a grand tribute to the heroes who sacrificed for the country. It is a symbol of the arduous course of the Chinese people's bloody struggle since the Opium War. **Tourist 1:** What places of interest are we going to see? **Local Guide:** We have a fantastic itinerary planned for you. We'll be passing by the Forbidden City, which was the imperial palace for the Ming and Qing dynasties. We'll also visit the Temple of Heaven, where emperors prayed for good harvests. And of course, we can't miss the iconic Great Wall at Badaling. **Tourist 2:** How long will it take to get to the next stop? **Local Guide:** Our next stop is the Summer Palace, and it's about a 30-minute ride from here. It was a royal garden for the emperors and their families to escape the summer heat. **Tourist 3:** Can we take a boat ride on the lake there? **Local Guide:** Absolutely! The Summer Palace is known for its beautiful Kunming Lake. You'll have the opportunity to take a leisurely boat ride and enjoy the scenery. **Tourist 4:** What about food? Are there any local delicacies we should try? **Local Guide:** Beijing is famous for its culinary delights. You must try Peking Duck, which is a world-renowned dish. There are also street foods like Jianbing and Zhajiangmian that are not to be missed. If you have any more questions, feel free to ask. Enjoy your tour, and let's explore the wonders of Beijing together!

Key Vocabulary and Phrases

Monument to the People's Heroes 人民英雄纪念碑
itinerary 行程
the Forbidden City 紫禁城
the Temple of Heaven 天坛
iconic 象征性的
royal 皇家的
leisurely 悠闲的

题干	参考英文对话
Dialogue 3 Perform as a local guide. After the tour group checks in, you make a brief introduction. Your dialogue will include the following points: (1) Give a brief introduction of the hotel. (2) Room service, valet service and children's facilities. (3) Inform the dinner time and place. (4) Answer questions if there are any.	**Local Guide**: Good afternoon, everyone! I'd like to extend a warm welcome to all of you on behalf of our travel agency. My name is Sarah, and I'll be your local guide for the next few days. Let's start by getting to know the hotel where you'll be staying. The hotel you're in is the Grand Plaza Hotel, known for its elegant design and top-notch service. It's conveniently located near the city center, and it offers a stunning view of the skyline. In terms of services, we have 24-hour room service for your convenience. If you need any assistance with your luggage, our valet service is at your disposal. For our younger guests, there's a children's play area with a variety of toys and games. Now, regarding dinner, it will be served tonight at 19:00 in the hotel's main dining hall. The hall is located on the second floor, and you'll find a diverse menu featuring both local and international cuisines. If you have any questions or need further information, please feel free to ask. It's my pleasure to assist you and ensure your stay is as comfortable as possible. **Tourist**: What's included in the room service? **Local Guide**: Room service includes a wide range of dishes from the hotel's restaurant as well as a selection of snacks and beverages. You can order at any time using the menu in your room. **Local Guide**: If there are no more questions, I wish you a pleasant rest of the day. Remember, if you need anything, don't hesitate to reach out.

Key Vocabulary and Phrases

elegant 优雅的

top-notch 高质量的

stunning 令人震惊的

valet service 代客泊车服务

at your disposal 可用的

diverse 多样的

beverage 饮料

题干	参考英文对话
Dialogue 4 Perform as a local guide. You are helping the tour group check in at the reception of the Hilton Hotel. Your dialogue will include the following points: (1) Greetings. (2) Request the tourists' passports. (3) Gives the room number and directions. (4) Advises them about the time for lunch.	Welcome, esteemed members of the "Explore the City" tour group! My name is Tom, and I'll be your local guide for your stay at the Hilton Hotel. Let's make your check-in process as smooth as possible, shall we? 　　Firstly, I'd like to extend a warm welcome to the Hilton Hotel. It's a pleasure to have you here. To proceed with the check-in, I'll collect your passports from each member of the group. If you could gather them together, that would be a great help. While you're doing that, please feel free to make use of our comfortable lobby area. We have a variety of beverages and light refreshments available for you to enjoy while you wait. Once I have your passports, I'll quickly process the check-in and provide you with your room keys. Your rooms are located on the fifth floor, with numbers ranging from 501 to 510. You'll find the elevator just a short walk down the hall to your left, which will take you directly to your floor. For your convenience, our bellboys are here to assist with your luggage. They'll ensure that your belongings are safely transported to your rooms. Now, let's talk about lunch. Our on-site restaurant is open from 12:30 to 14:30. To make the most of your dining experience and avoid any potential wait times, I suggest you arrive at the restaurant around 12:45 PM. 　　Enjoy your stay, and don't hesitate to reach out if you need any assistance!

Key Vocabulary and Phrases

esteemed 尊敬的
passport 护照
bellboy 行李员
luggage 行李

题干	参考英文对话
Dialogue 5 Perform as a local guide. You are picking up the tour group at the railway station platform. Your dialogue will include the following points: (1) Greetings. (2) Ask about the trip. (3) Check the luggage. (4) Answer questions if there are any.	Good morning, everyone! Welcome to our beautiful city. I'm Tom, your guide for the next few days, and I'm looking forward to showing you around. How was your journey? I hope it wasn't too tiring. Did you have a comfortable ride? Now, let's check your luggage. Please make sure all your belongings are with you and nothing is left behind. We'll need to make sure everything is accounted for before we head to the hotel. Should you have any more questions or need assistance at any point during your stay? Please don't hesitate to reach out. My goal is to make your experience as enjoyable and hassle-free as possible. Let's get your luggage loaded and embark on the adventure that awaits! I'm looking forward to showing you the best our city has to offer. Let's make some wonderful memories together!

Key Vocabulary and Phrases

railway station 火车站
belonging 物品
account for 对……负责,解释

题干	参考英文对话
Dialogue 6 Act as a local guide. You are taking a tour group in Shandong province during the Spring Festival. The tourists are interested in Chinese cultures such as Wushu, the Spring Festival. Your dialogue will include the following points: (1) Give a brief introduction to Wushu, such as Taijiquan. (2) Give a brief introduction to the customs of the Spring Festival. (3) Answer some questions asked by the tourists.	As your local guide in Shandong province, I'm thrilled to be accompanying you during this festive Spring Festival. Firstly, let's talk about Wushu, a crucial aspect of Chinese culture. Wushu is a traditional Chinese martial art that combines physical skills, self-defense techniques, and mental discipline. Among its various forms, Taijiquan is particularly renowned. Taijiquan emphasizes slow, flowing movements and breath control, promoting both physical health and inner peace. It's not just a fighting technique; it's also a way of life, teaching us to harmonize with nature and ourselves. Now, turning to the spring festival, also known as the Chinese New Year. It's a time of reunion and celebration, marked by a series of customs and traditions. Families gather together to enjoy a reunion dinner, often featuring dishes that symbolize prosperity and good luck. There's also the custom of giving red envelopes containing money as a gesture of good fortune and blessing. The festival is also known for its vibrant dragon and lion dances, fireworks, and colorful lanterns, all adding to the festive atmosphere. Now, I'd be happy to answer any questions you have about Wushu, the spring festival, or anything else related to Chinese culture. What would you like to know?

Key Vocabulary and Phrases

reunion dinner 团圆饭
red envelope 红包
dragon and lion dance 舞龙舞狮
firework 烟花
lantern 灯笼

题干	参考英文对话
Dialogue 7 Perform as a local guide. You are on the way to the hotel after picking up the tourists from the railway station. Your dialogue will include the following points: (1) Greetings. (2) Introduce the bus driver. (3) Introduce the places of interest in the city. (4) Introduce the hotel. (5) Give best wishes. (6) Answer questions if there are any.	Hello everyone! As your local guide, I'm delighted to welcome you to our city. It's a pleasure to have you here. I hope your journey was smooth. Now, let me introduce our bus driver, Mr. Zhang. He's an experienced driver and will ensure we get to our destinations safely. During our stay, you'll have the opportunity to visit some of the city's most remarkable places of interest. From ancient temples to modern landmarks, our city is a perfect blend of history and culture. You'll definitely enjoy the scenic views and fascinating stories behind each attraction. And speaking of accommodation, we're heading to a comfortable hotel where you'll be staying. The hotel offers excellent facilities and services, ensuring a pleasant stay for you. The rooms are spacious and well-appointed, and the restaurant serves delicious local cuisine. Before we arrive at the hotel, I'd like to extend my best wishes to all of you. I hope your stay in our city will be memorable and enjoyable. Now, if there are any questions or concerns you may have, please feel free to ask. I'm here to help and ensure your satisfaction.

Key Vocabulary and Phrases

destination 目的地

place of interest 名胜古迹

accommodation 住宿

facility 设施

spacious 宽敞的

well-appointed 设备齐全的

题干	参考英文对话
Dialogue 8 Perform as a tour guide taking a group to the seashore. Make sightseeing precautions before they begin the tour. Your dialogue will include the following points: (1) Remind the tourists of things to take with them. (2) Give advice about how to relax and enjoy themselves on the seashore. (3) Forbid any swimming without permission. (4) Tell the group the time of gathering.	Good day, everyone! As your tour guide for today's seashore adventure, I'm excited to share this beautiful coastline with you. Before we begin our tour, there are a few important things I'd like to remind you of. Firstly, please make sure you've brought all the essentials. Sunscreen is a must to protect your skin from harsh sunrays. A hat and sunglasses will also help keep you cool and comfortable. Don't forget your water bottle to stay hydrated throughout the day. While at the seashore, remember to relax and enjoy the moment. Take a stroll along the shore, feeling the soft sand between your toes. Listen to the waves crashing on the shore and let the sea breeze blow away your worries. However, safety is our utmost priority. I must emphasize that swimming without permission is strictly forbidden. The sea can be unpredictable, so please stick to the designated swimming areas and follow the instructions of the lifeguards. Lastly, please be punctual for our group gatherings. We will meet at the designated spot at 16:00 sharp to head back. If you need to take a break or explore somewhere, please inform me first. Let's embark on this journey together and create lasting memories!

Key Vocabulary and Phrases

sunscreen 防晒霜
designated swimming area 指定游泳区
lifeguard 救生员
punctual 守时的
embark on 开始

题干	参考英文对话
Dialogue 9 Perform as a local guide. You are discussing the two-day tour in Nanjing with the tour leader. Your dialogue will include the following points: (1) Explain the departure time. (2) Confirm the scenic spots on the first day. (3) Confirm the shopping on the second day. (4) Answer questions if there are any.	Good morning, tour leader! As your local guide for the two-day tour in Nanjing, I'm excited to share with you the highlights of our itinerary. We will kick off the tour at 8:00 sharp tomorrow from the hotel lobby. Please ensure everyone is ready on time. On the first day, we'll visit the Ming Tombs, a historical site where the Ming Dynasty emperors were buried. Its magnificent tombs and surrounding scenery are truly breathtaking. After that, we'll proceed to the Confucius Temple Complex, a culture hub famous for its ancient buildings and bustling marketplace. On the second day, we'll dedicate the morning to exploring the Old Town of Nanjing, where you'll find plenty of traditional handicrafts and souvenirs to take home. In the afternoon, we'll visit the Nanjing Museum, a repository of the city's rich historical and cultural heritage. Do you have any questions or concerns about the tour? I'm here to answer any questions you may have. I'm looking forward to a memorable tour with you and your group. Let's make the most of our time in Nanjing!

Key Vocabulary and Phrases

magnificent 宏伟的
breathtaking 惊人的
culture hub 文化中心
bustling 熙熙攘攘的
handicraft 手工艺品
souvenir 纪念品
heritage 遗产

题干	参考英文对话
Dialogue 10 Perform as a local guide. You are having the cruise tour on the West Lake with the tour group. Your dialogue will include the following points: (1) Talk about the boat. (2) Introduce the buildings on the islet. (3) Introduce Su Causeway and other famous scenic spots. (4) Answer questions if there are any.	Good morning, everyone! Welcome to the cruise tour on the West Lake. As your local guide, I'm thrilled to share with you the beauty and charm of this renowned lake. Firstly, let's talk about the boat we're sailing in. This traditional Chinese wooden boat offers a comfortable and scenic ride. You'll find the seats spacious and the views breathtaking. As we cruise along, you'll notice some charming buildings on the islet ahead. That's the Three Pools Mirroring the Moon, a pavilion with elegant architecture and a prime viewing spot for the lake's beauty. Moving on, we'll soon reach Su Causeway, a famous scenic spot named after the Song Dynasty poet Su Dongpo. This scenic path not only showcases Su Dongpo's governance talent, but also a beautiful walkway lined with willow trees and offering stunning views of the lake. And of course, there are many other scenic spots worth visiting, such as the Leifeng Pagoda and the Six Harmonies Pagoda. Each spot has its own unique charm and historical significance. Now, do you have any questions about the tour or the lake? I'd be happy to answer them. Enjoy the cruise and immerse yourself in the beauty of the West Lake!

Key Vocabulary and Phrases

cruise tour 游船观光

islet 小岛

pavilion 亭子

stunning 惊人的

Six Harmonies Pagoda 六和塔

题干	参考英文对话
Dialogue 11 Perform as a local guide. You are leading your tour group on the way to a shadow puppetry performance. Your dialogue will include the following points: (1) Introduce the history of Chinese shadow puppetry. (2) Introduce the main features of Chinese shadow puppetry. (3) Answer questions if there are any.	Good afternoon, everyone! I'm your local guide, and I'm delighted to lead you to a fascinating performance of Chinese shadow puppetry. Firstly, let me introduce you to the rich history of this art form. Chinese shadow puppetry, known as "皮影戏"(/pí yǐng xì/, shadow puppet play), has a long tradition in China, dating back to the Han Dynasty. It has evolved over the centuries, combining various elements of folklore, music, and visual arts, reflecting the wisdom and creativity of our ancestors. Now, let's talk about the main features of Chinese shadow puppetry. One distinctive aspect is the use of translucent leather puppets, which are manipulated by skilled puppeteers to create lifelike movements and expressions. The puppets are projected onto a screen, creating a magical and enchanting effect. The stories told through shadow puppetry are often traditional tales of heroes, villains, and romantic legends, captivating audiences with their vivid narratives and emotional depth. Before we arrive at the performance, do you have any questions about shadow puppetry? I'd be happy to answer them. Well, that's all for now. I hope you're as excited as I am about this upcoming performance. Let's enjoy the show and immerse ourselves in the world of Chinese shadow puppetry!

Key Vocabulary and Phrases

  Chinese shadow puppetry 皮影戏
  translucent leather puppet 透光皮革木偶
  manipulate 操纵
  lifelike movement and expression 栩栩如生的动作和表情
  captivate 使着迷
  vivid narrative 生动的叙述

题干	参考英文对话
Dialogue 12 Perform as a local guide. You are touring Du Fu's Thatched Cottage in Chengdu. Your dialogue will include the following points: (1) Introduce the itinerary in the afternoon. (2) Introduce Du Fu's Thatched Cottage. (3) Talk about Du Fu. (4) Answer questions if there are any.	**Guide:** Hello, everyone! I'm your guide for today. Afternoon's plan is to visit the famous Du Fu's Thatched Cottage and enjoy a local lunch. Any questions? **Tourist 1:** Could you tell us more about the cottage? **Guide:** Of course! It was home to Du Fu, a great poet. His work is full of life's ups and downs, showing us the past. **Tourist 2:** What makes Du Fu special? **Guide:** Du Fu captured people's joys and sorrows in his poems. His words still touch our hearts. **Tourist 1:** Is there anything unique we should see there? **Guide:** Definitely. The cottage itself is a piece of traditional architecture. And the garden offers a peaceful setting for reflection. **Tourist 2:** Can we buy some local crafts as souvenirs? **Guide:** Of course. There's a market with various crafts. It's a great way to remember your visit. **Tourist 1:** That sounds lovely. Thanks for the info. **Guide:** My pleasure! If you have more questions, just ask. Let's make this an unforgettable journey!

Key Vocabulary and Phrases

itinerary 行程
thatched cottage 茅草屋
poet 诗人
ups and downs 起起落落
joys and sorrows 欢乐与悲伤
architecture 建筑
peaceful 平静的
unforgettable 难忘的

题干	参考英文对话
Dialogue 13 Perform as a local guide. You are touring Yan'an. Your dialogue will include the following points: (1) Greetings. (2) Introduce the scenic spot in Yan'an. (3) Talk about the history of Yan'an. (4) Answer questions if there are any.	Good day, everyone! Welcome to Yan'an, a city steeped in rich history and culture. I'm your local guide, and I'm thrilled to show you around this beautiful place. Firstly, let me introduce some of the must-see scenic spots in Yan'an. We have revolutionary sites like the Yan'an Revolutionary Memorial Hall, which preserves the relics and stories of the Chinese revolution. There's also the Tower of the Yellow River, a symbol of Yan'an's close connection with the mighty river. These places offer a glimpse into the city's past and present. Now, let's talk about the history of Yan'an. This city played a pivotal role in China's modern history. During the War of Resistance Against Japan, Yan'an served as the base for the Communist Party of China, attracting many revolutionaries and intellectuals. It was here that many crucial decisions were made, shaping the course of China's future. Yan'an is also known for its rich revolutionary culture and spirit, which continues to inspire people today. Do you have any questions about Yan'an or its history? I'd be happy to answer them. Well, that's a brief introduction to Yan'an. I hope you'll enjoy your stay here and discover more of its hidden gems. Let's proceed to our first scenic spot and begin our journey through Yan'an's rich history and culture.

Key Vocabulary and Phrases

steeped in 充满
must-see 必看的
relic 遗迹
pivotal role 关键角色
War of Resistance Against Japan 抗日战争
Communist Party of China 中国共产党
revolutionary culture and spirit 革命文化和精神

题干	参考英文对话
Dialogue 14 Perform as a guide. You are confirming the meal reservation with a waitress. Your dialogue will include the following points: (1) Introduce yourself. (2) Check the reservation list. (3) Confirm the time. (4) Prepare dishes for a vegetarian. (5) Confirm the type of payment.	**Waitress**: Good evening. How may I assist you? **Guide**: Good evening. I'm the guide for the group, and we have a reservation under the name "Green Travel Tours". **Waitress**: Let me check the reservation list, please. **Guide**: Certainly. We're expecting to dine at 19:30. **Waitress**: Yes, I see the reservation here. You're scheduled for 19:30. Is there any dietary restriction we should be aware of? **Guide**: Yes, one of our guests prefers a vegetarian meal. Could you accommodate that? **Waitress**: Absolutely, we have several vegetarian options available. **Guide**: That's great. Lastly, could you confirm the type of payment we can use? **Waitress**: We accept both credit cards and mobile payments. **Guide**: Perfect, thank you for confirming everything. We appreciate your assistance. **Waitress**: It's my pleasure. We look forward to serving your group.

Key Vocabulary and Phrases

dine 进餐

dietary restriction 饮食限制

vegetarian 素食者

accommodate 安排

option 选择

payment 支付方式

credit card 信用卡

mobile payment 移动支付

题干	参考英文对话
Dialogue 15 Perform as a local guide. You are talking about Chinese cuisine with tourists. Your dialogue will include the following points: (1) Introduce three major cuisines in the world. (2) Talk about the four famous cuisines in China. (3) Introduce the cutting skills. (4) Answer questions if there are any.	**Local Guide**: Hello, everyone! As your local guide, I'd like to talk about the fascinating world of Chinese cuisine. When we think about the major cuisines in the world, we often mention Italian, French, and Chinese. China is known for its four great traditions in cooking: Sichuan, Cantonese, Shandong, and Jiangsu cuisines. Each has its own unique flavors and techniques. **Tourist 1**: I've heard that Chinese chefs are masters of cutting. Can you tell us more about that? **Local Guide**: Absolutely. Chinese chefs are renowned for their cutting skills. The precision and the variety of cuts are essential to bring out the best in each dish. **Tourist 2**: How do the different cuts affect the taste? **Local Guide**: The way ingredients are cut can alter their texture and how they cook, which in turn affect the taste. For instance, thinly sliced onions release more flavor when stir-fried. **Tourist 2**: That's quite an art. Do you have any questions for us? **Local Guide**: Not at the moment, but feel free to ask if something comes up. I'm here to provide you with all the insights into the culinary world of China. **Tourist 1**: Thank you for the informative talk. We're looking forward to trying the food! **Local Guide**: My pleasure! I'm sure you'll enjoy the culinary delicacies of China.

Key Vocabulary and Phrases

cuisine 菜肴
renowned 著名的
precision 精确度
essential 必要的
alter 改变
texture 质地
thinly sliced 薄片
informative 信息丰富的
delicacy 美味佳肴

题干	参考英文对话
Dialogue 16 Perform as a local guide. You are talking about the chopsticks with tourists. Your dialogue will include the following points: (1) Introduce the history of chopsticks. (2) Talk about the table manners. (3) Introduce how to use the chopsticks. (4) Answer questions if there are any.	**Local Guide**: Hello, everyone! As your local guide, I'm excited to share with you a bit about the traditional Chinese eating utensils—chopsticks, which have been a part of our culture for thousands of years. **Tourist 1**: They look so delicate. How do we use them properly? **Local Guide**: Great question. To use chopsticks, you hold one stick still with your thumb and index, and then manipulate the other stick with your middle and ring fingers to pick up food. **Tourist 2**: Are there any rules we should follow when eating with chopsticks? **Local Guide**: Definitely. For example, it's considered rude to point with your chopsticks at people. Also, you should never stick them vertically into your bowl of rice as it resembles a ritualistic act. **Tourist 1**: What if we want to pass food to someone else? **Local Guide**: If you need to pass food, it's best to use a serving spoon or plate. Passing food directly with chopsticks is not customary. If you drop one, simply place the remaining chopstick on the table, and a waiter will provide you with a new pair. It's seen as a sign that you need a replacement. **Tourist 1**: That's very considerate. Thank you for the insight. **Local Guide**: My pleasure! Enjoy your dining experience, and remember, practice makes perfect.

Key Vocabulary and Phrases

chopstick 筷子
index 食指
manipulate 操作
resemble 类似
customary 习惯的
considerate 考虑周到的

题干	参考英文对话
Dialogue 17 Perform as a local guide. The tour group is in the tea store. Your dialogue will include the following points: (1) Introduce green tea. (2) Introduce the black tea. (3) Give advice. (4) Answer questions if there are any.	**Local Guide:** Greetings, everyone! As we step into our local tea store, let me share some insights into the world of tea. We'll start with green tea, which is known for its healthful properties. Green tea, typically has a lighter flavor and is less processed than other types. It's rich in antioxidants that are beneficial for one's health. **Tourist 1:** What about black tea? I'm quite fond of it. **Local Guide:** Black tea undergoes a full fermentation process, which gives it a stronger taste and color. It's a popular choice for those who prefer a bolder flavor. When selecting tea, it's important to consider the aroma, the color, and the shape of the leaves. High-quality green tea leaves are often more vibrant and have a fresh, grassy scent. **Tourist 2:** How should we store the tea to maintain its freshness? **Local Guide:** To preserve the quality, store your tea in an airtight container, away from direct sunlight, heat, and moisture. Brewing is an art. For green tea, use water that's just below boiling point, and don't over-steep, or you may end up with a bitter taste. **Tourist 1:** I've heard that tea can be quite expensive. What determines the price? **Local Guide:** The price can be influenced by several factors, including the grade of the tea leaves, the region it's from, and the harvesting time. Generally, the younger the leaves, the higher the quality and price. If you have any more questions, feel free to ask. Now, let's enjoy the tea-tasting session and discover your favorite flavors!

Key Vocabulary and Phrases

health benefits 健康益处

oxidation 氧化

antioxidants 抗氧化剂

impurities 杂质

crucial 关键的

malt 麦芽

题干	参考英文对话
Dialogue 18 Perform as a local guide. The tour group is in the silk shop. Your dialogue will include the following points: (1) Introduce Chinese silk. (2) Introduce this store. (3) Give advice for family gifts. (4) Try on the blue one.	**Local Guide**: Welcome to our renowned silk shop, esteemed visitors. Chinese silk, known as for its luxurious texture and shine, has a history that dates back over five thousand years. This store specializes in traditional silk products, from elegant scarves to exquisite dresses. Each piece is crafted with meticulous care. For family gifts, I recommend our silk pillowcases. They're not only a symbol of comfort and luxury but also believed to reduce wrinkles and keep hair smooth. **Tourist 1**: That sounds like a wonderful idea. What about clothing? **Local Guide**: Clothing made from silk is both comfortable and stylish. Why don't you try on the blue one? It's one of our bestsellers and the color **complements** many skin tones. **Tourist 2**: I've heard that silk can be quite delicate. How should we take care of it? **Local Guide**: That's a great question. Silk should be hand-washed gently in cold water and air-dried. Avoid using harsh detergents as they can damage the fibers. **Tourist 1**: Thank you for the advice. This is a beautiful shop with a rich selection. **Local Guide**: My pleasure. If you have any more questions, feel free to ask. Enjoy your shopping experience!

Key Vocabulary and Phrases

luxurious 奢华的
meticulous 细致的
recommend 推荐
complement 补充
air-dried 自然晾干
detergent 洗涤剂

题干	参考英文对话
Dialogue 19 Act as a local guide to explain laundry service for your tour group. Your dialogue will include the following points: (1) Tell the tourists the hotel has laundry service. (2) Tell the tourists how to get this service. (3) Tell the tourists they should pay laundry service by themselves.	**Local Guide**: Good morning, everyone! I hope you all had a restful night. I'd like to inform you about the laundry service available here at the hotel. If you need to get your clothes cleaned, the hotel offers a convenient laundry service. You can simply fill out a laundry form, which you can find in your room, and place it along with your clothes in the designated laundry bag. You can leave the bag outside your room door before 9:00, and our staff will collect it. The laundry will be returned to you by the next evening, neatly folded or on hangers as needed. **Tourist 1**: Is there an extra charge for this service? **Local Guide**: Yes, there is. The cost of the laundry service is not included in your room rate. You'll need to settle the bill directly with the hotel upon receipt of the service. Please be aware that express service is available at an additional fee if you need your items back sooner. **Tourist 1**: That sounds very efficient. Thank you for the information. **Local Guide**: You're welcome! If you have any further questions or need assistance, don't hesitate to contact the front desk. Enjoy the rest of your stay!

Key Vocabulary and Phrases

laundry service 洗衣服务
designated 指定的
neatly 整洁地
settle 结算
express 快速的
additional 额外的

题干	参考英文对话
Dialogue 20 Perform as a local guide. A tourist wants you to accompany him to buy some gifts. Your dialogue will include the following points: (1) Introduce the gift shops. (2) Agree to accompany. (3) Set the meeting place and time. (4) Take a taxi with the app.	**Local Guide**: Hello there! I've heard you're looking for some local gift shops to find presents for your loved ones. There are several charming shops around that offer a variety of traditional and modern gifts. **Tourist**: That sounds perfect. Could you accompany me to help pick out some gifts? **Local Guide**: I'd be delighted to join you. Let's make the most out of your shopping experience. **Tourist**: Thank you. Where and when should we meet? **Local Guide**: How about we meet at the hotel lobby at 10 a.m. tomorrow? It's a convenient starting point, and from there, we can take a taxi to the shopping district. **Tourist**: That works for me. How do we get a taxi around here? **Local Guide**: It's quite simple. You can use a taxi app on your smartphone to book a taxi. It's a quick and efficient way to get around the city. **Tourist**: Great, I'll download the app. I appreciate your help. Looking forward to our shopping trip tomorrow. **Local Guide**: My pleasure! I'll make sure to bring a list of the best places to visit. See you at 10:00 sharp!

Key Vocabulary and Phrases

charming 迷人的
delight 高兴
lobby 大厅
convenient 方便的
smartphone 智能手机
efficient 高效的

题干	参考英文对话
Dialogue 21 Perform as a local guide. A tourist doesn't feel well on the way to the scenic spot. Your dialogue will include the following points: (1) Soothe the tourist. (2) Tell the driver to the nearest hospital. (3) Take care of the tourist. (4) Take the other tourists as scheduled.	**Local Guide**: I'm sorry to hear that you're not feeling well. Let's try to get you some comfort first. Please, sit down and relax. Is it alright if I get you a glass of water? **Tourist**: Thank you. I think I might be getting a migraine. **Local Guide**: I understand, migraines can be quite debilitating. I'm going to inform the driver to take us to the nearest hospital right away, so we can get you checked out. **Local Guide**: (To the driver) Could you please change our route and head to the nearest hospital? One of our tourists is feeling unwell. **Driver**: Of course, I'll get us there as quickly as possible. **Local Guide**: (To the tourist) In the meantime, I'll stay with you and make sure you're as comfortable as possible. We have a first aid kit on hand if you need any over-the-counter medication. **Tourist**: That's very kind of you. I appreciate your help. **Local Guide**: Of course, your well-being is our priority. To the rest of the group, we'll continue to the scenic spot as scheduled, but I'll arrange for alternative transportation for those who prefer to stay with our friend here. **Tourist**: Please don't disrupt the plans for everyone. I'll be alright. **Local Guide**: We appreciate your understanding, but our main concern is your health. We'll keep the group updated and ensure everyone has a smooth experience today.

Key Vocabulary and Phrases

soothe 偏头痛

debilitating 使人虚弱的

route 路线

first aid kit 急救包

over-the-counter 非处方的

题干	参考英文对话
Dialogue 22 Perform as a local guide. A tourist complains the bus is too messy. Your dialogue will include the following points: (1) Apologize. (2) Give a reason for the problem. (3) Promise to take action. (4) Answer questions if there are any.	**Local Guide**: I'm truly sorry to hear about the condition of the bus. We strive to provide a clean and comfortable travel experience for all our guests. **Tourist**: It's quite disappointing. I expected better maintenance. **Local Guide**: I understand your concern, and I apologize for the inconvenience. The mess is due to an unexpected increase in passengers on the previous route, which left us with less time than usual for cleaning. I assure you that I'll inform the company immediately, and the bus will be thoroughly cleaned at the next stop. We value your comfort and feedback, and we're committed to addressing this issue. **Tourist**: Thank you for the explanation. I appreciate you taking action. **Local Guide**: You're welcome. We're here to ensure your trip is as pleasant as possible. If you have any further concerns or questions, please feel free to let me know. **Tourist**: Will there be a problem with our schedule? **Local Guide**: The cleaning will be done swiftly, and we've allowed some buffer time in our schedule to accommodate such unforeseen circumstances. Your satisfaction is our top priority, and we'll do our best to minimize any impact on our itinerary.

Key Vocabulary and Phrases

maintenance 维护
inconvenience 不便
unexpected 意外的
thoroughly 彻底地
feedback 反馈
committed to 承诺
address 解决
buffer 缓冲

题干	参考英文对话
Dialogue 23 Perform as a local guide. The tour group is going to leave for the USA tomorrow. You are confirming the itinerary for the next day with the tour leader. Your dialogue will include the following points: (1) Confirm flight tickets. (2) Departure time. (3) Check out procedure. (4) Remind of the documents.	Local Guide: Good afternoon, I'd like to go over our itinerary for tomorrow with you to ensure everything is in order for your departure to the USA. Tour Leader: That sounds good. Let's go through it. Local Guide: I've confirmed our flight tickets. We'll be taking Flight UA078 departing from Terminal 3 at 8:15. Tour Leader: And what's the procedure for checking out of the hotel? Local Guide: Check-out is at 6:00 sharp. Our luggage will be picked up by the hotel staff and transported directly to the airport. You'll need to have your room keys returned to the front desk by then. Tour Leader: That's quite early. What about breakfast? Local Guide: The hotel will provide a boxed breakfast that you can take with you. It's included in your stay, and it's designed to accommodate our early departure. Tour Leader: I see. What about the documents? Passports and visas? Local Guide: Please ensure that each traveler has their passport and visa with them. It's advisable to keep these documents in your hand luggage for easy access at the airport. Also, don't forget to complete the customs declaration forms, which I'll distribute tonight. Tour Leader: Alright, that should cover everything. Thank you for the reminder. Local Guide: You're welcome. If you have any more questions or need further assistance, please let me know. I wish you a pleasant journey.

Key Vocabulary and Phrases

itinerary 行程
departure 出发
procedure 程序
customs declaration 海关申报

题干	参考英文对话
Dialogue 24 Suppose you are a tour leader. Some tourists would like to watch the performance of Impressions of the West Lake in the evening. Your dialogue will include the following points: (1) Tell these tourists that they should pay for the performance themselves. (2) Suggest that they should go there by taxi. It is about half an hour to drive from the hotel to the West Lake. (3) After the performance, they could use the Didi Car-hailing app to rent a car and go back to the hotel.	Tour Leader: Good evening, everyone. I understand that some of you are interested in watching the Impressions of the West Lake performance tonight. It's a wonderful cultural experience, but please be aware that the cost of the tickets is not included in the tour package, so you will need to cover the expense yourselves. Tourist 1: That's fine. How do we get to the West Lake from here? Tour Leader: The most convenient way to get there is by taxi. It's approximately a 30-minute drive from our hotel to the venue at West Lake. I recommend using a reliable taxi service to ensure a safe and comfortable journey. Tourist 2: What about returning to the hotel after the show? Tour Leader: After the performance, you can use the Didi Car-hailing app to rent a car. It's a popular and efficient way to get transportation back to the hotel. The app is user-friendly and widely used here in China. Tourist 1: Thank you for the information. We appreciate your help. Tour Leader: You're welcome. Remember to check the performance schedule and make sure you leave with enough time to catch the show. If you have any other questions or need further assistance, feel free to ask. Tourist 2: We will. We're looking forward to the performance.

Key Vocabulary and Phrases

car-hailing 叫车服务
expense 费用
venue 场地
reliable 可靠的
user-friendly 用户友好的

题干	参考英文对话
Dialogue 25 The tour group is on the way to the theater. A tourist asks the guide a lot of questions. Your dialogue will include the following points: (1) Introduce the history of Peking Opera. (2) Explain the make-up. (3) Introduce the famous artist Mei Lanfang. (4) Answer questions if there are any.	**Tour Guide:** As we make our way to the theater, I'd like to share some insights about the Peking Opera, which is a quintessential part of Chinese culture with a history that spans over two centuries. **Tourist:** That's fascinating. What's the significance of the makeup the performers wear? **Tour Guide:** The makeup, or facial painting, is quite expressive and symbolic. Each color and pattern represents a character's personality, social status, and role in the story. It's an art form. Speaking of which, we must mention Mei Lanfang, one of the most famous Peking Opera artists of all time. Mei was renowned for his portrayal of female roles, despite being male, and his performances were known for their elegance and grace. **Tourist:** How has Peking Opera evolved over time? **Tour Guide:** While the core elements have been preserved, Peking Opera has indeed evolved. Modern productions sometimes incorporate new technologies and creative storytelling to engage contemporary audiences while staying true to the traditional art form. **Tourist:** I'm looking forward to the performance. Do you have any tips for a first-timer? **Tour Guide:** Just enjoy the experience. Listen to the music, watch the performers' movements, and try to understand the story. You might find it helpful to read the synopsis in the program. And don't hesitate to ask if you have more questions. **Tourist:** Thank you for the information. I appreciate it.

Key Vocabulary and Phrases

expressive 富有表现力的
symbolic 象征的
personality 个性
portrayal 扮演
grace 高雅
evolve 演变
contemporary 当代的
audience 观众
synopsis 概要

题干	参考英文对话
Dialogue 26 Perform as a tour leader. You are taking your tour group to Mount Wuyi. Your dialogue will include the following points: (1) Introduce the scenic spots in Mount Wuyi. (2) Introduce the cultural sites in Mount Wuyi. (3) Introduce the local tea in the area. (4) Answer questions if there are any.	**Tour Leader:** Good morning, everyone! We're on our way to Mount Wuyi, a UNESCO World Heritage site renowned for its breathtaking natural beauty and rich cultural significance. As we journey through the scenic spots, you'll witness the picturesque Nine Bend River and the majestic Heavenly Tour Peak. In addition to the natural wonders, Mount Wuyi is also home to several cultural sites, including ancient temples and rock inscriptions that date back over a thousand years. **Tourist:** What about the local products? I've heard that the tea from this region is quite famous. **Tour Leader:** You're absolutely right. The area is particularly known for its Wuyi Rock Tea, which is celebrated for its distinct flavor and aroma. We'll have a chance to visit a local tea plantation where you can sample and learn about the traditional processing methods. After our exploration of the mountain, we'll stop by a tea house where you can enjoy a cup of freshly brewed tea and perhaps pick up some local tea as a souvenir. **Tourist:** Can we also try some traditional local cuisine? **Tour Leader:** Certainly! We have a local meal planned for you at a restaurant that specializes in traditional Wuyi dishes. You'll get to taste some authentic flavors of the region. If you have any more questions or need any assistance during our visit, please don't hesitate to ask. Our goal is to make your trip as enjoyable and informative as possible.

Key Vocabulary and Phrases

scenic spot 景点
cultural site 文化遗址
distinct flavor 独特的风味
aroma 香气
tea plantation 茶园
authentic 正宗的

题干	参考英文对话
Dialogue 27 Perform as a local guide. A tourist is very angry because the bathroom is in terrible condition. Your dialogue will include the following points: (1) Apologize. (2) Give a reason for the problem. (3) Promise to take action. (4) Answer questions if there are any.	**Local Guide:** I'm deeply sorry to hear about the unsatisfactory condition of the bathroom. We strive to maintain a high standard of cleanliness and comfort for all our visitors. **Tourist:** It's completely unacceptable. I expected much better. **Local Guide:** I understand your frustration, and I apologize for any inconvenience this has caused. The issue is due to an unexpected surge in visitors earlier, which has affected the regular cleaning schedule. I assure you that I'll notify our cleaning team immediately to address the situation. We'll have the bathroom thoroughly cleaned and checked to ensure it meets our usual standards. **Tourist:** What can we do in the meantime? We can't use it like this. **Local Guide:** I understand your concern. There's an alternative bathroom located nearby that you can use. I can guide you there right now. Again, I apologize for this issue and appreciate your understanding. **Tourist:** Thank you. I hope this will be resolved soon. **Local Guide:** It certainly will. If you have any further questions or need additional assistance, please feel free to reach out to me. Your satisfaction is our top priority.

Key Vocabulary and Phrases

unsatisfactory 不满意的
frustration 挫折
surge 激增
regular 定期的
alternative 可供选择的

题干	参考英文对话
Dialogue 28 Perform as a local guide. A tourist is very angry because some of his valuables were stolen. Your dialogue will include the following points: (1) Apologize. (2) Get the details. (3) Promise to take action. (4) Answer questions if there are any.	**Local Guide:** I am truly sorry to hear about the theft of your valuables. This is certainly not the experience we want our visitors to have. **Tourist:** I'm very upset. I had important items with me, and now they're gone. **Local Guide:** I understand how distressing this must be for you. Could you please provide me with more details? When did you notice the items were missing, and what were they? **Tourist:** I noticed just a few minutes ago. A camera and a wallet with some cash were taken. **Local Guide:** I'll report this incident to our security team immediately and we will start a search. We also have a protocol in place for such situations and will involve the local authorities if necessary. **Tourist:** What can I do in the meantime? I need to cancel my credit cards. **Local Guide:** You're right to take action on your personal accounts. While you're doing that, I will ensure our team is doing everything possible to locate your belongings. If you think of any additional information that could help, please let me know. **Tourist:** Thank you for your help. I hope this can be resolved quickly. **Local Guide:** I will do my utmost to assist you. Your safety and satisfaction are our main concerns. If you have any more questions or need further assistance, don't hesitate to reach out.

Key Vocabulary and Phrases

theft 盗窃
distressing 令人痛苦的
security team 保安团队
protocol 协议
authority 当局
utmost 最大的
satisfaction 满意

题干	参考英文对话
Dialogue 29 Perform as a tour guide. You get a last minute notice of "change of plan" which requires you to rush to the high speed railway station to meet a tour group. The tourists have been waiting for a long time when you get there and they are full of grumbles. Your dialogue will include the following points: (1) Make an apology. (2) Explain the reasons for being late. (3) Propose some solutions. (4) Ask tourists to follow you to the parking lot. (5) Answer questions if there are any.	Tour Guide: I'd like to start by offering a sincere apology for the delay in our meeting. I understand you've been waiting, and I apologize for any inconvenience this has caused. Tourist 1: What happened? We were expecting you much earlier. Tour Guide: There was an unexpected traffic situation due to an accident on the main road, which caused a significant delay in my arrival. I appreciate your patience and understanding in this matter. To make up for the lost time, I propose we quickly proceed to the high-speed train that's waiting for us. We'll make the most of the remaining time and ensure you have a memorable visit. Tourist 2: How long do we have before the train departs? Tour Guide: We have approximately 30 minutes until the train departs. I will personally assist you with your luggage and guide you through the process to expedite things. Now, if you would all please follow me to the parking lot where our transportation to the station is ready. We'll get you on your way as swiftly as possible. Tourist 1: Are we going to miss our train? Tour Guide: I've been in contact with the railway staff, and they're aware of our situation. The train will wait for us, but we should hurry to avoid any further delays. If you have any questions or concerns, please feel free to ask as we make our way to the station. Your satisfaction is my priority, and I'm here to assist you.

Key Vocabulary and Phrases

inconvenience 不便
traffic situation 交通情况
memorable 难忘的
depart 离开
expedite 加快
priority 优先事项

题干	参考英文对话
Dialogue 30 Perform as a local guide. Now, you are taking Tom, an individual tourist, from Beijing Daxing International Airport to the Beijing Hotel. You are talking with him. Your dialogue will include the following points: (1) Introduce yourself, your travel agency and the driver. (2) Give a brief introduction to the city and the hotel. (3) Answer some questions asked by the tourist.	**Local Guide**: Hello, Tom! Welcome to Beijing. My name is Li Hua, and I'll be your local guide today. This is our driver, Wang Fei. We're both here representing the Beijing Travel Agency. **Tom**: Nice to meet you both. This is my first time in Beijing. I've heard a lot about it. **Local Guide**: It's a pleasure to have you, Tom. Beijing is a city rich in history and culture. As we drive to your hotel, you'll get to see some of the iconic landmarks like the Great Wall and the Forbidden City. The Beijing Hotel, where you'll be staying, is located near the city center and is known for its excellent service and proximity to many attractions. **Tom**: That sounds great. What's the best way to get around the city? **Local Guide**: Beijing has a comprehensive public transport system. The subway is fast and efficient, and it's a great way to explore the city. Taxis are also widely available. For sightseeing, we recommend using our agency's tour services for a more informative experience. **Tom**: How about local cuisine? Where should I try it? **Local Guide**: Beijing has a diverse culinary scene. For traditional dishes, you can visit hutongs, where you'll find many local restaurants serving dishes like Peking Duck and Zhajiangmian. Our agency also offers food tours if you're interested in a guided culinary adventure. **Tom**: That's very helpful. Thank you. I'm looking forward to the trip. **Local Guide**: You're welcome, Tom. We aim to make your stay as enjoyable as possible. If you have any more questions or need assistance during your stay, please don't hesitate to contact us.

Key Vocabulary and Phrases

travel agency 旅行社
iconic 标志性的
landmark 地标
comprehensive 全面的

题干	参考英文对话
Dialogue 31 Perform as a local guide. The tour leader demands to change the hotel to a better one nearby. Your dialogue will include the following points: (1) Ask the tour leader the reasons for changing. (2) Confirm with the tour leader that the extra payment above stipulated price and the fees for canceling reservation should be covered by the tourists. (3) Report the case to your travel agency. (4) Tell the tour leader the instruction of the travel agency. (5) Answer questions if there are any.	**Local Guide:** Good afternoon, I understand you've requested a change of hotel. May I ask what has prompted this request? **Tour Leader:** The current hotel doesn't meet our expectations. We require a better facility nearby. **Local Guide:** I see. Please be aware that changing to a higher-rated hotel would result in an additional cost, which would be above the stipulated price. Additionally, there may be cancellation fees for the current reservation. These costs would need to be covered by the tourists in your group. **Tour Leader:** I understand the financial implications. We're willing to cover the extra payment and any cancellation fees. **Local Guide:** In that case, I will report this situation to our travel agency and seek their guidance on how to proceed. **Local Guide:** (After contacting the agency) The travel agency has agreed to assist with the hotel change, subject to availability. They've also reminded us to confirm the additional costs with the tourists before proceeding. **Tour Leader:** Thank you for your help. I will discuss with the group and get back to you. **Local Guide:** Please take your time. We want to ensure everyone is comfortable with the decision. If you have any further questions or need more information, feel free to ask.

Key Vocabulary and Phrases

stipulated 规定的
facility 设施
higher-rated 评级较高的
cancellation fee 取消费用
availability 可用性
proceed 进行

题干	参考英文对话
Dialogue 32 Perform as a tour leader. The driver is parking the coach in the parking lot of the Intercontinental Hotel. You and your group are still on the coach. Your dialogue will include the following points: (1) Ask the tourists to stay in the coach. (2) Ask the tourists for their passports. (3) Ask the driver to keep the coach closed. (4) Answer questions if there are any.	**Tour Leader:** Everyone, please remain seated in the coach for a moment while the driver parks our vehicle in the parking lot of the Intercontinental Hotel. **Tourist 1:** How long will it take to check in? **Tour Leader:** We'll start the check-in process as soon as the coach is properly parked and secured. Now, I'll need everyone to hand me your passports so I can take them to the hotel reception for registration. **Tourist 2:** What about our luggage? **Tour Leader:** Don't worry about your luggage for now. The hotel bellboys will assist with that once we've completed the check-in. In the meantime, I'll ask the driver to keep the coach closed to ensure our belongings are safe. **Driver:** Sure, I'll keep it locked until you give the all-clear. **Tour Leader:** Thank you, and once I return from the reception with the room keys, we can all head in and start settling into our rooms. If you have any questions or concerns, please feel free to ask before we begin the process. **Tourist 1:** How about the schedule for tomorrow? **Tour Leader:** We'll go over the itinerary for tomorrow during dinner tonight. It includes a city tour and a visit to a local museum, so make sure to get a good rest.

Key Vocabulary and Phrases

coach 大巴车
registration 注册
itinerary 行程

题干	参考英文对话
Dialogue 33 Perform as a local guide. After identifying your group, you find that a guest lost one piece of luggage and looks very anxious. You try to help him get the luggage back. Your dialogue will include the following points: (1) Soothe the guest. (2) Ask the guest details about the luggage: size, color, material, etc. (3) Contact the concerned department of the airport. (4) Tell the guest you will keep in contact with the department concerned when the guest is in your city. (5) Answer questions if there are any.	**Local Guide**: I understand you're concerned about your missing luggage. Let's try to address this issue step by step. First, take a deep breath and let's gather some information that can help us locate it. **Tourist**: Thank you. I'm just worried because I had important items in that bag. **Local Guide**: I can imagine how distressing this must be for you. Can you please describe the luggage for me? Any details such as its size, color, and material would be helpful. **Tourist**: It's a medium-sized black suitcase, made of hard plastic. It has a red stripe on the side. **Local Guide**: Excellent. I'll contact the airport's lost and found department right away with this description. They're very efficient and will likely have it returned to you soon. **Local Guide**: (After making the call) I've informed the airport's concerned department, and they've started a search. I'll make sure to keep in contact with them while you're in the city. As soon as we have any updates, I'll let you know. **Tourist**: I appreciate your help. What should I do in the meantime? **Local Guide**: While we're waiting for news, let's continue with the tour. I can arrange for some essentials to be delivered to your hotel if needed. If you have any other questions or need further assistance, please don't hesitate to ask.

Key Vocabulary and Phrases

distressing 令人痛苦的

describe 描述

department 部门

update 最新消息

essential 必需品

题干	参考英文对话
Dialogue 34 Perform as a local guide. Mr. Black, one guest in your tour group, wants to celebrate his mother's birthday in the hotel the day after tomorrow. Your dialogue will include the following points: (1) Tell Mr. Black that the hotel can make the arrangements for the party. (2) Confirm the time and place of the party. (3) Remind Mr. Black that he should pay the expenses of the party. (4) Answer questions if there are any.	**Local Guide:** Good afternoon, Mr. Black. I've been informed that you're interested in organizing a birthday celebration for your mother at the hotel. The hotel is fully equipped to make all the arrangements for the party. **Mr. Black:** Yes, that's correct. I'd like to make it a memorable occasion. Can the hotel help with the decorations and catering as well? **Local Guide:** Absolutely, they offer a comprehensive package that includes both decorations and catering services. We just need to confirm the time and place you have in mind for the celebration. **Mr. Black:** I was thinking of having it in the hotel's private dining room, around 19:00 the day after tomorrow. **Local Guide:** That sounds like a wonderful plan. I'll coordinate with the hotel to ensure everything is prepared for that time. Just a gentle reminder that you'll be responsible for the expenses of the party, which will be based on the hotel's standard rates and the services you choose. **Mr. Black:** I understand. Can I see a menu for the catering and perhaps some photos of previous decorations? **Local Guide:** Certainly, I can provide you with a menu and examples of their work. I'll also be happy to assist you with any other details or answer any questions you may have.

Key Vocabulary and Phrases

arrangement 安排
comprehensive 全面的
decoration 装饰
catering 餐饮服务
responsible 有责任的
expense 费用
standard rate 标准费率

题干	参考英文对话
Dialogue 35 Perform as a local guide. You verify the itinerary with Mr. Smith, the tour leader. You find that there is one more tourist attraction in his tour plan. Mr. Smith insists that the trip should be arranged according to his plan. Your dialogue will include the following points: (1) Make a phone call to your travel agency to know the reason for the difference. (2) Apologize to Mr. Smith for the mistake made by your agency. (3) Confirm the new itinerary with the tour leader. (4) Answer questions if there are any.	Ladies and gentlemen, good morning! I hope you all had a restful night. My name is Li Hua, and I'll be your local guide for today's excursion. Let's go through the itinerary to ensure we have a smooth and enjoyable journey. First, we'll be visiting the ancient temple, followed by a scenic boat ride on the river. After that, we'll enjoy a traditional lunch before heading to the museum and concluding our day at the botanical garden. However, I've noticed there's an additional attraction listed in your plan, the city's art gallery, which wasn't mentioned in our original schedule. To clarify this discrepancy, I will make a phone call to our travel agency to understand the reason for this difference. [Li Hua makes a phone call] I apologize for this confusion, Mr. Smith. It seems there's been a miscommunication. Our agency is committed to providing you with the best experience, and we value your preferences. Let's confirm the new itinerary together. Would you like to include the art gallery in our plans, or shall we stick to the original schedule? Thank you for your understanding, Mr. Smith. We're now confirmed to proceed with the inclusion of the art gallery. It's a wonderful place to appreciate local art and culture. If you have any questions or need assistance during our tour, please feel free to ask. Now, let's embark on this exciting day ahead and make some beautiful memories!

Key Vocabulary and Phrases

excursion 远足,短途旅行
botanical 植物学的
gallery 画廊,美术馆
discrepancy 差异,矛盾
miscommunication 误会,信息传递错误

题干	参考英文对话
Dialogue 36 Perform as a local guide. You are on the way to the Great Wall. The tourists want to know more about it. Make a dialogue with them. Your dialogue will include the following points: (1) Introduce the significance of the Great Wall. (2) Introduce the main scenic spots in the Great Wall. (3) Give precautions. (4) Answer relevant questions.	**Local Guide**: Ladies and gentlemen, as we journey towards the Great Wall, I'd like to share some fascinating insights about this magnificent structure. The Great Wall is not just a defensive fortification; it's a symbol of China's rich history and architectural ingenuity. It stretches over 21196 miles and is truly a wonder of the world. One of the main scenic spots we'll be visiting is the Badaling section, which is the most visited and restored part of the wall. Here, you'll see the wall's impressive watchtowers and enjoy a panoramic view of the surrounding mountains. Another highlight is the Jinshanling area, known for its well-preserved architecture and natural beauty. As we explore, I'd like to remind you to stay on the designated paths to protect the historical structure. Also, the steps can be steep and uneven, so please watch your step and stay hydrated. Now, if you have any questions or need assistance, feel free to ask. I'm here to ensure you have a safe and memorable experience. **Tourist**: How old is the Great Wall? **Local Guide**: The construction of the Great Wall dates back to 7th century BC, but the sections we'll see today were built during the Ming Dynasty, roughly between the 14th and 17th centuries. **Tourist**: What's the best time to visit the Great Wall? **Local Guide**: The best time to visit is in the spring or autumn when the weather is mild. Avoiding the peak summer and winter months will also mean fewer crowds and a more enjoyable visit.

Key Vocabulary and Phrases

defensive fortification 防御性堡垒
architectural ingenuity 建筑独创性
panoramic view 全景
designated paths 指定路径
steep 陡峭的
uneven 不平坦的
hydrate 水分, 补水

题干	参考英文对话
Dialogue 37 Perform as a local guide. A tourist complains that there are too many sites of cultural heritage in the itinerary and asks to change for natural scenery. Make a dialogue with the tourist. Your dialogue will include the following points: (1) Listen and repeat the tourist's request. (2) Explain the reasons. (3) Report to your travel agency. (4) Offer solutions.	**Local Guide:** Ladies and gentlemen, I hope you're enjoying your trip so far. I understand that our itinerary is packed with visits to various sites of cultural heritage, such as ancient temples and museums. However, I've received feedback from one of you who would prefer to experience more of the natural scenery that our region has to offer. **Tourist:** Could we possibly adjust the schedule to include more natural attractions? **Local Guide:** I've taken note of your request, and I appreciate your enthusiasm for exploring the outdoors. Our region is indeed blessed with breathtaking landscapes and diverse ecosystems. The cultural heritage sites on our itinerary were selected to provide you with a comprehensive understanding of our history and traditions, but I understand that everyone has different interests. I will promptly relay your feedback to our travel agency and explore options to accommodate your preferences without compromising the overall group experience. We aim to make your trip as enjoyable and personalized as possible. In the meantime, I can suggest a few alternatives. We could potentially swap one of the cultural visits for a trip to a nearby national park or a scenic hike in the mountains. Alternatively, we could extend our stay at one of the natural spots already on the itinerary to allow for more exploration time. Your satisfaction is our priority, and we'll do our best to find a solution that works for everyone. Thank you for your understanding and feedback.

Key Vocabulary and Phrases

compromise 妥协,折中

personalized 个性化的

题干	参考英文对话
Dialogue 38 Perform as a tour leader. You are calling the Hilton Hotel for the first time to reserve meal for your tour group. Your dialogue with the receptionist will include the following points: (1) Tell the receptionist who you are. (2) Give detailed information of your tour group. (3) Ask for special food arrangement for some tourists allergic to seafood and some local special dishes for the other guests. (4) Answer questions if there are any.	**Tour Leader:** Hello, the Hilton Hotel reception. This is Mark, tour leader for the EcoTrek Adventure Tours. I am arranging a group dining reservation for our upcoming stay. We'll be arriving with a group of 25 tourists on the 15th of next month. Our travelers come from various backgrounds, and we have four individuals who are allergic to seafood. We would greatly appreciate it if you could accommodate their special dietary needs. Additionally, we're interested in introducing our group to your local cuisine. Could you provide some options that highlight the flavors of your region? I'd also like to inquire about the possibility of a group discount, as we'll be dining in for all meals during our three-day stay. Lastly, what time would you recommend for our group to have dinner to avoid any peak hours? **Receptionist:** Thank you for the details, Mr. Mark. We can certainly cater to your group's dietary needs and preferences. Let's aim for a 18:30 dinner reservation to ensure a more peaceful dining experience. **Tour Leader:** That sounds perfect. Thank you for accommodating our request.

Key Vocabulary and Phrases

upcoming 即将到来的
allergic 过敏的
dietary 饮食的
discount 折扣
peak hour 高峰时间

题干	参考英文对话
Dialogue 39 Perform as a tour guide. One of the tourists wants to know something about Shandong cuisine. Your dialogue with the tourist will include the following points: (1) Briefly introduce Shandong cuisine, including three regional cuisines. (2) Introduce the local cuisine including some local special dishes. (3) Recommend some restaurants. (4) Answer questions if there are any.	**Tour Guide:** Good morning! As we explore the rich tapestry of China's culinary landscape, I'd like to shed some light on Shandong cuisine, which is one of the Eight Great Traditions of Chinese cooking. Shandong cuisine, also known as Lu cuisine, is renowned for its diverse flavors and sophisticated cooking techniques. It encompasses three regional styles: Jiaodong, Jinan, and Kongfu, each with its own array of distinctive dishes. Locally, we take pride in dishes such as "sweet and sour Yellow River carp", "Dezhou braised chicken", and "sea cucumber braised with scallion", which are not only delicious but also steeped in history. These dishes offer a perfect blend of flavors, from the sweetness of the carp to the savory depth of the braised chicken. If you're eager to sample these delicacies, I'd recommend visiting some of the well-regarded restaurants in the city. Jvfengde and Yanxitang are particularly famous for their authentic Shandong dishes and have received accolades for their culinary excellence. Should you have any dietary restrictions or preferences, please feel free to let me know, and I'll be glad to assist you with personalized recommendations. **Tourist:** That sounds fascinating. Are there any vegetarian options within Shandong cuisine? **Tour Guide:** Absolutely! Shandong cuisine also offers a variety of vegetarian dishes that are just as flavorful. For instance, Braised Chinese cabbage with vinegar and Jinan Stewed Bean Curd are excellent choices for those seeking a meat-free dining experience.

Key Vocabulary and Phrases

culinary 烹饪的
sophisticated 复杂的,精致的
accolade 称赞,奖励
vegetarian 素食的

题干	参考英文对话
Dialogue 40 Perform as a local guide. You are leading your tour group on the way to Xidi and Hongcun, the ancient villages in southern Anhui province. Your dialogue will include the following points: (1) Introduce the history of the two ancient villages. (2) Introduce the main features of the architecture. (3) Introduce the local dishes or snacks. (4) Answer questions if there are any.	**Local Guide:** Greetings, everyone! As we journey towards the picturesque Xidi and Hongcun villages in southern Anhui province, allow me to share some insights into these historical gems. Xidi and Hongcun are both UNESCO World Heritage Sites, with a history that dates back over 900 years. These villages are not just ancient; they're a testament to the traditional Hui-style architecture, characterized by their intricate wood carvings, elegant stone archways, and curved tile roofs. The buildings here are more than just residences; they're a showcase of the region's cultural heritage. You'll notice the attention to detail in every wooden beam and the harmonious blend of nature and structure in the village layout. Speaking of local flavor, the cuisine here is as rich as the history. Traditional dishes include the "braised pork with soy sauce" and "stinky tofu", which might sound intimidating but is a delicacy that many locals swear by. For a lighter bite, you can try the "savory rice cakes" or "fried sesame balls", which are popular snacks among the villagers. If you have any questions about the villages, the architecture, or the culinary delights, please don't hesitate to ask. I'm here to ensure your visit is both informative and enjoyable. **Tourist:** How has the village managed to preserve its ancient architecture so well? **Local Guide:** That's a great question! The villages have been carefully maintained by the local community and supported by preservation efforts to keep the traditional style intact for future generations to appreciate.

Key Vocabulary and Phrases

historical gem 历史珍宝
UNESCO World Heritage Site 联合国教科文组织世界遗产地
Hui-style architecture 徽派建筑
intricate 复杂的, 精细的
braised pork with soy sauce 红烧猪肉配酱油
stinky tofu 臭豆腐
savory rice cake 咸味年糕
fried sesame ball 芝麻球

题干	参考英文对话
Dialogue 41 Perform as a local guide. A member of an inbound group asks to cancel his journey due to a serious illness. Your dialogue will include the following points: (1) Ask for the reasons for cancellation. (2) Soothe the tourist. (3) Tell him he can talk to his travel agency about travel insurance claims and the possibility of a refund on any unused portions. (4) Tell him the agency may offer help and all expenses incurred are to be covered by himself. (5) Answer questions if there are any.	**Local Guide**: I'm sorry to hear that you're not feeling well. Could you please tell me what's brought this on? Your health and comfort are our top priorities. **Tourist**: I've been feeling quite unwell, and my doctor has advised me against continuing the journey. **Local Guide**: I'm truly sorry to hear that. It's important to prioritize your health. In cases like these, you should definitely reach out to your travel agency. They can guide you through the process of filing a claim with your travel insurance, which may cover some of your expenses and potentially provide a refund for any unused services. Please remember that while our agency is here to assist you in any way we can, the expenses incurred due to illness are typically the responsibility of the traveler. However, I'll make sure to put you in touch with the right people who can help you navigate this situation. If you have any questions or need further assistance, feel free to ask. We're here to make this process as smooth as possible for you. **Tourist**: Thank you for your understanding. I appreciate the guidance on how to proceed with the insurance claim. **Local Guide**: You're welcome. I hope you have a swift recovery, and we're here to assist you with any further questions or concerns you may have.

Key Vocabulary and Phrases

priority 优先事项
reach out 联系
file a claim 提交索赔
potentially 可能地
unused 未使用的
incur 招致,引发
navigate 导航;找到正确方法

题干	参考英文对话
Dialogue 42 Perform as a tour guide. A tourist in room 400 is very annoyed about the loud music and noises from room 401. Make a dialogue with the tourist. Your dialogue will include the following points: (1) Apologize. (2) Give explanations. (3) Offer solutions. (4) Answer questions if there are any.	Tour Guide: Good evening, I'm the tour guide on duty. I understand that you're in room 400 and have been experiencing some disturbances due to the noise from the adjacent room. I want to sincerely apologize for the inconvenience you've been facing. Tourist: It's been quite disruptive. I was hoping for a peaceful night after our long day of touring. Tour Guide: I can only imagine how that might affect your rest. We have a strict noise policy, and I'll make sure to address this issue with the guests in room 401 immediately. In the meantime, we can arrange for you to be moved to another room further away from the disturbance, if that would be more comfortable for you. Additionally, we can provide you with earplugs to help block out any remaining noise. We value your comfort and will do our best to ensure the rest of your stay is undisturbed. Tourist: Thank you. That sounds like a good solution. I appreciate your prompt response. Tour Guide: You're welcome. If you have any further concerns or questions, please don't hesitate to reach out to us at any time. Your satisfaction is our top priority.

Key Vocabulary and Phrases

inconvenience 不便
disturbance 干扰
earplug 耳塞
prompt 迅速的,及时的

题干	参考英文对话
Dialogue 43 Perform as a local guide. Some foreign tourists are interested in Chinese Dragon Dance. They want to know more about it. Your dialogue will include the following points: (1) Briefly introduce Chinese Dragon Dance. (2) Tell them they may have a close look at Dragon Dance on the square near the hotel from 18:00 to 20:00. (3) Answer questions if there are any.	**Local Guide:** Greetings, everyone! I've noticed your curiosity about the Chinese Dragon Dance, a traditional performance that's rich in cultural significance. The dance is a representation of power, strength, and good fortune in Chinese culture. It's typically performed during festivals and important celebrations, such as the Chinese New Year and the Dragon Boat Festival. The dance involves a long, flexible dragon figure, which is manipulated by a team of skilled dancers underneath. Accompanied by lively music and the rhythmic beating of drums, the dragon comes to life, weaving and undulating through the streets. I'm pleased to inform you that there's an opportunity for you to witness this captivating spectacle firsthand. On the square near our hotel, a Dragon Dance performance is scheduled from 18:00 to 20:00. It's a wonderful chance to experience this ancient art form up close. **Tourist:** That sounds fascinating! What should we expect during the performance? **Local Guide:** You can expect a vibrant and dynamic display. The dragon, often adorned with colorful lights, will perform a series of choreographed movements. It's a sight that beautifully blends athleticism and artistry. If you have any more questions or need further details about the event, feel free to ask. Enjoy the performance tonight!

Key Vocabulary and Phrases

Dragon Dance 舞龙
Chinese New Year 春节
Dragon Boat Festival 端午节
manipulate 操纵
drum 鼓
adorn 装饰
choreograph 编舞
athleticism 运动员身份,竞技性

题干	参考英文对话
Dialogue 44 Perform as a local guide. A tourist from Australia wants to buy a souvenir. He is asking for your advice. Your dialogue will include the following points: (1) Inquire details of the souvenir. (2) Tell him he can bargain with the shopkeeper and give some tips on bargaining. (3) Tell him to buy things that he will not regret. (4) Answer questions if there are any.	**Local Guide**: Hello, I understand you're looking for a souvenir to remember your visit. Could you please share more details about what type of souvenir you're interested in? We have a wide array of options, from traditional handicrafts to modern trinkets. **Tourist**: I'm quite interested in local art pieces. But I'm not sure about the prices. **Local Guide**: That's a great choice! Local art pieces can be a wonderful representation of our culture. You'll find that many shops in the market are open to bargaining, which is a common practice here. It's important to start with a lower offer than what you're willing to pay, and be polite in your negotiations. Remember to take your time, enjoy the process, and don't be afraid to walk away if the price isn't right. Also, consider the quality and uniqueness of the item. It's always wise to purchase something you truly love and won't regret later. If you have any more questions or need assistance, feel free to ask. I'm here to help ensure you have a satisfying shopping experience. **Tourist**: Thank you for the advice. I'll keep those bargaining tips in mind. **Local Guide**: You're welcome! Enjoy your shopping, and if you need any more guidance, don't hesitate to reach out.

Key Vocabulary and Phrases

trinket 小饰品
bargaining 讨价还价
negotiation 谈判
uniqueness 独特性

题干	参考英文对话
Dialogue 45 Perform as a local guide. Before the tour starts, with everyone on board, you talk to the tourists over a loudspeaker. Your dialogue will include the following points: (1) Give a brief introduction to today's tour. (2) Tell them there will be a short stopover in a shopping center in the afternoon. (3) Answer questions if there are any.	**Local Guide**: Good morning, everyone! I hope you're all settled in and ready for a day full of exploration. My name is Li, and I'll be your local guide for today's tour. We have a fantastic itinerary planned that includes a visit to the ancient city walls, a stroll through the picturesque old town, and a boat ride on the river that winds through the heart of our city. In the afternoon, we'll be making a short stopover at the Central Shopping Center. This will give you an opportunity to pick up some local specialties or perhaps do a bit of shopping for souvenirs. The stopover will last for about an hour, providing you with ample time to explore the shops at your leisure. Throughout the day, I'll be sharing interesting facts and stories about the places we visit. If you have any questions along the way, please don't hesitate to ask. Your comfort and enjoyment are my top priorities. So, sit back, relax, and get ready to discover the charm of our beautiful city. **Tourist**: Thank you for the overview. Could you tell us more about the river boat ride? **Local Guide**: Absolutely! The river boat ride is a highlight of the tour. It offers a unique perspective of the city's skyline and allows you to see landmarks from a different vantage point. We'll have a guided commentary on board that will provide insights into the history and significance of each site you see along the river. If there are any more questions, feel free to chime in. Let's make today a day to remember!

Key Vocabulary and Phrases

stroll 漫步
picturesque 如画的,美丽的
stopover 短暂停留
specialty 特色菜,特产
river boat ride 游船
skyline 天际线
vantage point 视角
guided commentary 导游解说

题干	参考英文对话
Dialogue 46 Perform as a local guide. You are checking out for ten double rooms of the tour group in the front office, but the cashier makes a mistake. Your dialogue will include the following points: (1) Tell the cashier who you are. (2) Check out for the group. (3) Tell the cashier that the group has stayed in the hotel for 4 days in all, but he has miscalculated the number of days. (4) Answer questions if there are any.	Local Guide: Good afternoon, I'm here to check out for the tour group that's been staying at your hotel. We have a total of ten double rooms booked under the name "Global Explorer Tours". Cashier: Hello, one moment while I process your bill. Local Guide: Thank you. I'd like to verify a few details. We've stayed for a total of four days, but it seems there might be a mistake in the calculation of the days on the bill. Cashier: Oh, let me double-check that for you. Local Guide: Certainly, I appreciate your attention to this. We arrived last Monday and today is Friday, so it's four nights in total. Cashier: I apologize for the oversight. Yes, you're correct, it's four days. Let me correct that immediately. Local Guide: Thank you. If there are any further questions or if there's anything else you need from me, I'm here to assist. Cashier: No, that should be all set now. Thank you for bringing that to my attention. Local Guide: You're welcome. It was a pleasure staying at your hotel and working with your team.

Key Vocabulary and Phrases

  miscalculate 计算错误
  calculation 计算
  oversight 疏忽
  assist 帮助

题干	参考英文对话
Dialogue 47 Perform as a tour guide to see a couple off at the airport. The couple has stayed in China for five days. Your dialogue will include the following points: (1) Make sure everything is in the luggage. (2) Show your regret and ask for their impressions of China. (3) Best wishes to the tourists.	**Tour Guide:** As we approach the airport, I just want to double-check with you both to ensure that you've got everything packed in your luggage. It's always a good idea to go through your belongings one last time. **Couple:** Thank you for the reminder. We've just finished packing, and we believe we have everything. **Tour Guide:** It's been a pleasure hosting you during your five-day stay in China. I'm a bit sad to see you go. Could you share with me what your impressions of China have been like? **Couple:** Oh, it's been an incredible experience. The history, the culture, the food—everything has been so fascinating. We've taken so many photos and made memories that we'll cherish forever. **Tour Guide:** I'm delighted to hear that you've enjoyed your trip. It's always heartwarming for us to know that our visitors leave with such wonderful impressions. We hope to see you again in the future, and we wish you a safe and comfortable journey back home. **Couple:** Thank you so much for everything. Your guidance has made our trip truly memorable. **Tour Guide:** You're welcome. It was my honor to be your guide. Safe travels, and please keep the memories of China close to your hearts.

Key Vocabulary and Phrases

luggage 行李
belonging 个人物品
impression 印象
cherish 珍惜
heartwarming 温暖人心的
safe travels 一路平安

题干	参考英文对话
Dialogue 48 Perform as a local guide. The tour group arrives at the airport and gets off the coach. They will take the flight HJ355 to Hangzhou. Your dialogue will include the following points: (1) Get some carts for their luggage. (2) Get the boarding passes and luggage claim cards for the tourists. (3) Remind the tourists to get their boarding passes ready for security check. (4) Say goodbye to the tour group.	**Tour Guide**: As we approach the airport, I just want to double-check with you both to ensure that you've got everything packed in your luggage. It's always a good idea to go through your belongings one last time. **Couple**: Thank you for the reminder. We've just finished packing, and we believe we have everything. **Tour Guide**: It's been a pleasure hosting you during your five-day stay in China. I'm a bit sad to see you go. Could you share with me what your impressions of China have been like? **Couple**: Oh, it's been an incredible experience. The history, the culture, the food—everything has been so fascinating. We've taken so many photos and made memories that we'll cherish forever. **Tour Guide**: I'm delighted to hear that you've enjoyed your trip. It's always heartwarming for us to know that our visitors leave with such wonderful impressions. We hope to see you again in the future, and we wish you a safe and comfortable journey back home. **Couple**: Thank you so much for everything. Your guidance has made our trip truly memorable. **Tour Guide**: You're welcome. It was my honor to be your guide. Safe travels, and please keep the memories of China close to your hearts.

Key Vocabulary and Phrases

luggage 行李
belonging 个人物品
impression 印象
cherish 珍惜
heartwarming 温暖人心的
safe travels 一路平安

题干	参考英文对话
Dialogue 49 Perform as a local guide. You accompany your guest to the hospital. You tell the doctor the symptoms of the guest. Your dialogue will include the following points: (1) Describe the symptoms. (2) Ask if the guest can continue the following sightseeing activities. (3) Inquire details concerned.	**Local Guide:** Good afternoon, Doctor. I'm here with a guest who's been feeling unwell during our tour. The primary symptoms he's been experiencing include a headache, fatigue, and a mild fever. **Doctor:** I see. How long has he been feeling this way? **Local Guide:** These symptoms started about two days ago. He also mentioned a slight cough and body aches. **Doctor:** Thank you for the information. Let's get a quick examination done. **Local Guide:** Before we proceed, may I ask if he's fit enough to continue with the sightseeing activities scheduled for the next few days? **Doctor:** It depends on the examination results. I'll be able to give you a better idea once I've assessed his condition. **Local Guide:** Thank you, Doctor. I also need to inquire about any dietary or activity restrictions he might need to follow. **Doctor:** Once we have a clearer picture of what he's dealing with, I'll provide you with all the necessary details and recommendations. **Local Guide:** I appreciate your guidance. We'll ensure he gets the necessary rest and care. **Doctor:** That's very responsible of you. We'll take good care of him here.

Key Vocabulary and Phrases

symptom 症状
fatigue 疲劳
fever 发烧
examination 检查
assess 评估
dietary 饮食的
restriction 限制

题干	参考英文对话
Dialogue 50 Perform as a local guide. Your guests complain that the dishes are too salty and there is no seafood or meat dishes. Your dialogue will include the following points: (1) Apologize first. (2) Make explanations. (3) Offer solutions.	**Local Guide**: I'm truly sorry to hear that the dishes served did not meet your expectations. We strive to provide a satisfying dining experience for all our guests. **Guests**: We were expecting more variety, especially in terms of seafood and meat options. The dishes are also quite salty. **Local Guide**: I apologize for any misunderstanding. Our menu is designed to reflect the local flavors, which can sometimes be a bit salty for those not accustomed to it. I'll ensure your feedback is passed on to the chef so they can make adjustments for the remaining meals. As for the lack of seafood and meat dishes, I'll speak with the restaurant manager immediately to see if we can add some options to your meal plan. We want to make sure you have a diverse and enjoyable dining experience. In the meantime, is there anything else I can assist you with? Perhaps some alternative dishes or a different restaurant that might better suit your preferences? **Guests**: Thank you for understanding. We appreciate your help in resolving this issue. **Local Guide**: You're welcome. It's important to me that your trip is a pleasant one. I'll take care of it right away and keep you updated on the changes.

Key Vocabulary and Phrases

expectation 期望

variety 多样性

adjustment 调整

diverse 多样的

dining experience 用餐体验

alternative 可供选择的

题干	参考英文对话
Dialogue 51 Perform as a local guide. The tour leader tells you that some guests vomit severely. Deal with it by making a dialogue with the tour leader. Your dialogue will include the following points: (1) Inquire the details. (2) Suggest that they may be suffering from food poisoning. (3) Ask the guests to drink plenty of water. (4) Call the ambulance if necessary.	**Local Guide**: Hello, I've just been informed that some of the guests are unwell. Could you please provide me with more details about their condition? **Tour Leader**: Yes, a few of our guests have been vomiting quite severely. It started a couple of hours ago after our lunch at the local restaurant. **Local Guide**: I see. It sounds like they might be suffering from food poisoning. It's important that they drink plenty of water to stay hydrated. Has anyone already done that? **Tour Leader**: We've given them water, but the vomiting hasn't stopped. **Local Guide**: In that case, we should consider calling an ambulance to ensure they receive proper medical attention. I'll make the call right away. **Tour Leader**: That would be best, thank you. We want to make sure everyone is safe and taken care of." **Local Guide**: Absolutely. I'll also inform our travel agency about the situation so they can assist with any further arrangements. Let's prioritize the health and safety of our guests. **Tour Leader**: Thank you for your prompt action. I'll stay with the guests and make sure they're as comfortable as possible until the ambulance arrives.

Key Vocabulary and Phrases

vomit 呕吐
severely 严重地
food poisoning 食物中毒
hydrated 保持水分的
ambulance 救护车
medical attention 医疗照顾
prioritize 优先处理

题干	参考英文对话
Dialogue 52 Perform as a local guide. After a day's visit, one of your guests wants to go out by himself. Your dialogue will include the following points: (1) Satisfy the requirement if it does not affect the whole plan of the group. (2) Remind the guest to take the name card of the hotel and not to stay out too late. (3) Ask the guest to be careful.	**Local Guide:** Certainly, if you'd like to explore a bit on your own after our day's visit, that can be arranged. It won't affect our group's plan as long as you're back by the agreed time for tomorrow's activities. **Guest:** Thank you. I just want to experience the local nightlife a bit. Do you have any recommendations? **Local Guide:** Of course. Here's the name card of the hotel with its address and phone number. Please make sure to take it with you, so you can find your way back easily. And as a reminder, it's advisable not to stay out too late, especially if you're unfamiliar with the area. **Guest:** I appreciate the advice. I'll keep that in mind. **Local Guide:** Excellent. Please be careful while you're out. Stay in well-lit, populated areas, and keep your personal belongings secure. If you need any assistance or have any questions, don't hesitate to call the hotel or reach out to me. **Guest:** Thank you for your concern. I'll be cautious and make sure to be back by the agreed time. **Local Guide:** That's great to hear. Enjoy your evening, and we'll see you tomorrow for our next set of adventures.

Key Vocabulary and Phrases

arranged 安排好的
name card 名片
nightlife 夜生活
advisable 明智的,适当的
well-lit 照明良好的

题干	参考英文对话
Dialogue 53 Perform as a local guide. Half an hour before lunch, the tourists of the group require that the western meal arranged for them be changed to a Chinese one. Your dialogue will include the following points: (1) Explain to the tourists that such requests should be made 3 hours in advance. (2) If the guests insist, tell them that they should cover the expense themselves. (3) Answer questions if there are any.	**Local Guide**: Ladies and gentlemen, I understand that you've requested a change in your lunch arrangements from a western meal to a Chinese one. While we're always happy to accommodate your preferences, I must explain that such requests are typically made at least three hours in advance. This allows us and the restaurant enough time to prepare and make the necessary changes to the menu. **Tourists**: We didn't realize that. But we really prefer to have Chinese food today. What are our options? **Local Guide**: If you insist on changing the meal to a Chinese one at this late notice, I'm afraid you would need to cover the expense yourselves. The restaurant will have to make special arrangements, which may incur additional costs. **Tourists**: We're willing to cover the costs. Can you help us with the arrangements? **Local Guide**: Of course, I'll do my best to assist you. I'll speak with the restaurant immediately and see what can be done. If you have any further questions or concerns, please feel free to ask. **Tourists**: Thank you for your help. We appreciate your understanding. **Local Guide**: You're welcome. It's my pleasure to ensure your trip is as enjoyable as possible. I'll keep you updated on the arrangements.

Key Vocabulary and Phrases

preferences 偏好

insist 坚持

expense 费用

incur 招致,引发

题干	参考英文对话
Dialogue 54 Perform as a local guide. You find one of your foreign tourists is bargaining at a roadside stand over some "antiques". You go forward and have a conversation with the guest. Your dialogue will include the following points: (1) Persuade the guest not to buy antiques at the roadside stand. (2) Offer some shops for authentic antiques with an invoice. (3) Introduce the customs rules regarding the antiques.	**Local Guide:** Good afternoon! I noticed you're looking at some interesting items here at the roadside stand. While it's great to see you engaged with our local culture, I would like to advise against purchasing antiques from here. **Tourist:** Oh, really? I thought I might have found a good deal on some beautiful pieces. **Local Guide:** I understand the appeal, but the authenticity of antiques can be difficult to verify without proper expertise. Instead, I can recommend some reputable shops that specialize in antiques and provide an invoice, which is essential for customs clearance. **Tourist:** That sounds like a much safer option. Could you tell me more about the customs rules for antiques? **Local Guide:** Absolutely. When it comes to antiques, customs regulations are quite strict. You'll need an invoice to prove the legality of the purchase and the item's value. Additionally, some items may be subject to export restrictions, so it's important to be aware of these rules to avoid any issues when you leave the country. **Tourist:** Thank you for the advice. I appreciate your guidance and will definitely check out the shops you mentioned. **Local Guide:** You're welcome. It's my pleasure to help ensure your shopping experience is both enjoyable and compliant with the law. If you have any more questions or need further assistance, feel free to ask. **Tourist:** I will. Thanks again for looking out for me.

Key Vocabulary and Phrases

  antique 古董
  roadside stand 路边摊
  invoice 发票
  custom clearance 海关清关
  regulations 规则,规章制度
  export restriction 出口限制
  compliance 遵守,遵从

题干	参考英文对话
Dialogue 55 A tourist from the UK in Mr. Zhang's group wants to buy a jade carving in a designated store, but he notices a flaw in the carving and it is the only one left in the store. The tourist then leaves some money with Mr. Zhang and asks him to buy one for him when it's available and have it shipped to the UK. Act as Mr. Zhang to make a dialogue with the guest. Your dialogue will include the following points: (1) Refuse first. (2) If it is hard to refuse, report to the superior for instructions. (3) Get enough money from the tourist for purchasing and shipping.	**Mr. Zhang:** I understand your interest in the jade carving, but I must respectfully decline your request to purchase and ship the item on your behalf. It's our policy to encourage guests to handle their own transactions for security and personal satisfaction. **Tourist:** I really appreciate your honesty, Mr. Zhang. However, since there's only one left and it's flawed, I trust you to get a perfect one for me once it's available. I'm willing to leave the money required with you." **Mr. Zhang:** "I appreciate your trust, and I'll consult with my supervisor to see if there's a way we can assist you with this. One moment, please. [After consulting with the supervisor] **Mr. Zhang:** I've spoken with my supervisor, and we've agreed to help you with your request. However, we'll need a deposit from you to cover the cost of the jade carving and the shipping fees to the UK. We'll provide you with a receipt and keep you updated on the process. **Tourist:** Thank you, Mr. Zhang. I'm grateful for your assistance. Here's the money for the deposit, and I look forward to receiving the jade carving. **Mr. Zhang:** You're welcome. We'll ensure the transaction is handled with the utmost care. If you have any more questions or need further assistance, please don't hesitate to ask. **Tourist:** Thank you once again. I'm confident in your service.

Key Vocabulary and Phrases

jade carving 玉雕
flaw 瑕疵
designated 指定的
superior 上级
instruction 指示
receipt 收据

题干	参考英文对话
Dialogue 56 As a local guide, you are on the way to visit Suzhou Gardens. The tourists seem to be quite interested in them. Your dialogue will include the following points: (1) Introduce the characteristics of Suzhou Gardens. (2) Introduce some representative gardens in Suzhou. (3) Answer any questions asked by the tourists.	**Local Guide**: As we head to the Suzhou Gardens, let me highlight their unique characteristics. These gardens are masterpieces of Chinese landscape art, with a perfect blend of architecture and nature. They feature tranquil ponds, rockeries, and pavilions, offering a peaceful retreat. Notable gardens include the Humble Administrator's Garden, known for its water features, and the Master of the Nets Garden, famous for its compact design. Each garden is a haven of serenity and a testament to traditional Chinese garden design. If you have any questions about these cultural gems or need more information, please ask. I'm here to ensure you get the most out of your visit. **Tourist**: Thank you. Could you tell us more about the Lingering Garden? **Local Guide**: Certainly. The Lingering Garden is celebrated for its diverse landscapes and architectural styles. It's a place where you can appreciate the artistry in every detail, from the stone bridges to the lush gardens. It's a perfect spot to linger and enjoy the beauty of Suzhou's gardens. Take your time to explore and let the tranquility of these gardens inspire you. If you need any further assistance, I'm at your service.

Key Vocabulary and Phrases

masterpiece 杰作
landscape art 风景艺术
tranquil 安静的
haven 避风港,安全地方
serenity 平静
artistry 艺术技巧

题干	参考英文对话
Dialogue 57 Perform as a local guide. Tomorrow is the birthday of a tourist. You call the housekeeping department of the Hilton Hotel to make the arrangements. Your dialogue will include the following points: (1) Tell the housekeeping who you are. (2) You would like turn-down service for Ms. Li in Room 808 because tomorrow is her birthday. (3) A small cake and some roses will be sent to the hotel while the tour group is out. You would like to have the cake put on the table of Room 808 and the flowers put in a vase.	**Local Guide:** Good afternoon, Hilton Hotel housekeeping. This is Li Ming, the local guide for the "Explore China" tour group. I'm calling to arrange a special turn-down service for one of our guests, Ms. Li, who is staying in Room 808. Her birthday is tomorrow, and we'd like to do something a bit extra to make her day special. **Housekeeping:** Hello, Mr. Li. We'd be happy to help make Ms. Li's birthday memorable. What did you have in mind for the turn-down service? **Local Guide:** Thank you. I've arranged for a small cake and some roses to be sent to the hotel while our group is out on tour. Could you please ensure that the cake is placed on the table in Room 808, and the roses are arranged nicely in a vase? **Housekeeping:** Absolutely, Mr. Li. We'll take care of it. Is there a specific time you'd like us to prepare the room? **Local Guide:** Yes, if it could be done around 5 PM, that would be perfect. Our group usually returns by then, and it would be a lovely surprise for Ms. Li. **Housekeeping:** Noted, and we'll make sure everything is in place by the time you all return. Is there anything else you need assistance with? **Local Guide:** That will be all for now. Thank you very much for your help. I appreciate the excellent service. **Housekeeping:** It's our pleasure. We look forward to making Ms. Li's birthday celebration a delightful one. Have a great day, Mr. Li.

Key Vocabulary and Phrases

housekeeping 客房服务
turn-down service 夜床服务
memorable 难忘的
surprise 惊喜

题干	参考英文对话
Dialogue 58 Perform as a tour guide. The tour group is going to travel by plane, but one of the tourists lost his passport and he is very anxious. Your dialogue will include the following points: (1) Listen carefully for his requirement. (2) Soothe the tourist. (3) Offer solutions.	Tour Guide: Please, sir, let's find a quiet place to sit down so we can discuss your situation. I understand this is a very stressful time for you, but we'll do our best to find a solution. Tourist: I can't believe I've lost my passport! What am I going to do? I can't travel without it. Tour Guide: Firstly, let's not panic. We'll start by retracing your steps to see if we can locate your passport. If that doesn't work, the next step would be to contact your embassy for a replacement. I'll assist you with that process. Tourist: Thank you. I appreciate your help. I'm just worried about the time it might take. Tour Guide: I understand your concern. While we're working on that, let's also inform the airline about the situation. They may have procedures in place for such situations. It's important that we explore all possible solutions. Tourist: That sounds like a good plan. I hope we can resolve this quickly. Tour Guide: We'll do everything we can to ensure your travel plans are not significantly disrupted. In the meantime, try to stay calm. These things can often be resolved more smoothly when we approach them with a clear mind.

Key Vocabulary and Phrases

stressful 有压力的
solution 解决方案
retrace 追溯
embassy 大使馆
replacement 替换
disrupted 被打乱的

题干	参考英文对话
Dialogue 59 Perform as a tour guide. Due to the shortage of the tickets in the peak season, the tour group has to take another flight to the next destination, which is two hours later than the schedule. The tourists grumble. Your dialogue will include the following points: (1) Apologize to the tourists for the inconvenience. (2) Clarify the cause. (3) Tell the tourists the arrangements in the next two hours.	**Tour Guide**: Ladies and gentlemen, I'd like to address the change in our travel plans. I must apologize for the inconvenience caused by the ticket shortage during this peak season. We've had to adjust our itinerary, and our group will be taking a flight that departs two hours later than originally scheduled. **Tourist**: This is very inconvenient. What are we supposed to do for those two extra hours? **Tour Guide**: I understand your frustration, and we're doing our best to make the most of the situation. The airline has provided us with a comfortable waiting area near the gate where we can relax. Additionally, there's a food court nearby with a variety of dining options for those who wish to grab a bite. In the meantime, we can also explore the airport's shopping area, which offers a range of souvenirs and local products. I'll be available to assist with any queries or needs you may have during this time. **Tourist**: Thank you for the information. We appreciate your efforts to manage this unexpected change. **Tour Guide**: You're welcome. We value your comfort and experience with us. If you have any further questions or require additional assistance, please don't hesitate to reach out to me.

Key Vocabulary and Phrases

depart 出发
frustration 挫折
waiting area 等候区
food court 美食广场
query 查询

题干	参考英文对话
Dialogue 60 Perform as a tour guide. You are leading your tour group on the way to the airport to catch the flight when a guest tells you that he left his watch in the hotel room and he is very anxious. Your dialogue will include the following points: (1) Soothe the guest. (2) Ask the guest to double check whether he left the watch in the hotel. (3) Offer solutions.	Tour Guide: Please don't worry, Mr. Smith. Let's take a moment to see if we can locate your watch. Sometimes, items can be misplaced in the rush of packing. Guest: I'm quite certain I left it on the nightstand, but I'll double-check my bags just in case. Tour Guide: That's a good idea. While you do that, I'll contact the hotel and inform them of the situation. They can check the room for you. If the watch is found, we can arrange for it to be securely shipped to your home. Guest: Thank you. I appreciate your help. What if the watch isn't in the room anymore? Tour Guide: If the watch is not in the room, I'll assist you in filing a lost property report with the hotel. They have procedures in place for such situations, and we can follow up from there. In the meantime, let's continue to the airport as scheduled. We don't want to miss your flight. We'll keep you updated on the status of your watch. Guest: That sounds like a plan. I'm relieved to have your support in this matter. Tour Guide: It's my pleasure, Mr. Smith. We're here to ensure your trip goes as smoothly as possible, even in unexpected situations.

Key Vocabulary and Phrases

misplaced 放错地方
double-check 再次检查
ship 运输
filing 归档
lost property 失物
scheduled 预定的

题干	参考英文对话
Dialogue 61 Perform as a local guide in Jinan. Your guests want to taste some local snacks and ask for your advice. Make a dialogue with them. Your dialogue will include the following points: (1) Introduce some representative local snacks. (2) Recommend the guests where to have the genuine snacks in Jinan. (3) Tell the guests to pay attention to food hygiene.	**Local Guide**: Welcome to Jinan, the city of springs! If you're looking to sample some local flavors, we have a variety of snacks that are not to be missed. One of the most representative is the Jinan Roujiamo, a type of Chinese sandwich with braised meat that's truly delicious. **Tourists**: That sounds interesting. Where can we find these authentic snacks in Jinan? **Local Guide**: For the most genuine experience, I recommend heading over to the Furong food street. It's a bustling area with a wide array of food stalls and restaurants that offer local delicacies. **Tourists**: That's great. Are there any food safety concerns we should be aware of? **Local Guide**: While Jinan is known for its food hygiene, it's always a good idea to be cautious. Make sure to look for places with good ventilation and clean facilities. Also, it's best to consume food that's freshly prepared and served hot to ensure it's safe to eat. **Tourists**: Thank you for the advice. We're excited to try these local snacks. **Local Guide**: You're welcome. Enjoy your culinary adventure, and if you have any more questions or need further recommendations, feel free to ask.

Key Vocabulary and Phrases

representative 有代表性的
braised 炖煮
delicacies 美食
bustling 熙熙攘攘的
ventilation 通风
culinary 烹饪的
adventurous 爱冒险的

题干	参考英文对话
Dialogue 62 A tour guide is showing a group of foreign tourist around the Ancient Culture Street. The tourists show special interest in some souvenirs. Your dialogue will include the following points: (1) Brief introduction to Chinese calligraphy and China's Four Treasures of Study. (2) Brief introduction to the Chinese fans. (3) Answer questions if there are any.	**Local Guide**: Ladies and gentlemen, as we stroll through the Ancient Culture Street, you'll find a treasure trove of souvenirs that embody the essence of Chinese culture. One of the most revered items is the Chinese calligraphy, an art form that's not just about writing but also about the beauty of the characters themselves. Essential to this art are China's Four Treasures of Study, which include the brush, ink, paper, and inkstone. **Tourists**: These calligraphy tools look fascinating. How are they used in calligraphy? **Local Guide**: The brush is used to apply ink to the paper, which is specially made to absorb the ink and allow it to spread in unique ways. The ink is made from soot and animal glue, and the inkstone is used to grind the ink to the desired consistency. Together, they allow the calligrapher to create works that are both functional and aesthetically pleasing. Another popular souvenir is the Chinese fan. These fans are not only functional for providing a cooling breeze but are also intricately designed with paintings and calligraphy, making them a piece of art you can hold in your hand. **Tourists**: Can you tell us more about the history of the Chinese fan? **Local Guide**: Certainly. The Chinese fan has a history that dates back over 3,000 years. It was originally used as a royal symbol of authority and later became a popular item in daily life. The fan has also been a significant part of Chinese opera and dance, often used as a prop to enhance the performance. If you have any more questions or if there's anything else that catches your eye, feel free to ask. I'm here to help you understand and appreciate these cultural artifacts.

Key Vocabulary and Phrases

calligraphy 书法
treasure trove 宝库
revered 受尊敬的
character 字符
inkstone 砚台
consistency 一致性,浓度
intrinsically 本质地
prop 道具

题干	参考英文对话
Dialogue 63 Perform as a local guide. Two foreign tourists tell you that they get in touch with their long-lost friends and want to invite them to take part in the activities of the group. Your dialogue will include the following points: (1) Know the identities of the guests' friends. (2) Tell them that you will have to get the permission of the tour leader and other tourists first. (3) Tell them to get their friends' ID cards and travel fee ready.	Local Guide: That's wonderful news! It's always a pleasure to hear about reunions. However, before we can arrange for your friends to join our group activities, we need to establish their identities for safety and organizational purposes. Tourists: Of course, we understand. What do we need to do? Local Guide: I'll need to consult with our tour leader and also seek the consent of the other tourists in the group. It's important that everyone is comfortable with the addition to our activities. Tourists: That sounds reasonable. What happens once we have the permission? Local Guide: Once we have the green light, your friends will need to provide their ID cards for our records. This is a standard procedure for all participants in the tour. Additionally, there will be a travel fee that they'll need to cover to join the group. Tourists: Thank you for the information. We'll get in touch with our friends and let them know about the requirements. Local Guide: You're welcome. Please let me know as soon as possible so we can proceed with the arrangements. I'm here to assist you throughout the process. Tourists: We appreciate your help and will keep you updated.

Key Vocabulary and Phrases

identity 身份
reunion 重聚
organizational 组织的
consent 同意
procedure 程序
participant 参与者
travel fee 旅游费

题干	参考英文对话
Dialogue 64 Perform as a local guide. You are heading for Qingzhou Ancient Town with the tour group. However, you find that two members are not present when you do the nose count. Some tourists tell you that the two tourists would rather stay at the hotel. You have a conversation with the tour escort, Mr. Smith. Your dialogue will include the following points: (1) Ask him if he has already known it. (2) Reach an agreement with him about how to deal with the two tourists. (3) Make good arrangements for the two guests.	**Local Guide:** Good morning, Mr. Smith. I've just completed our headcount, and it appears that two of our group members are not present. I believe they've chosen to remain at the hotel. **Mr. Smith:** Yes, I'm aware of their decision. They informed me earlier that they'd prefer to relax rather than join the tour today. **Local Guide:** I see. It's important that we respect their choice. However, we should also ensure they have a safe and enjoyable stay at the hotel. Could we agree on a plan to assist them with their day? **Mr. Smith:** Absolutely. We can arrange for them to have access to the hotel's facilities and perhaps recommend some local attractions that are nearby for them to explore on their own. **Local Guide:** That sounds like a good arrangement. I'll also make sure to inform the hotel staff to expect them and to provide any assistance they may need. **Mr. Smith:** Thank you for your attention to their well-being. I'll stay in contact with them throughout the day to ensure they're comfortable. **Local Guide:** Excellent. We'll proceed with the tour and keep an open line of communication with you regarding the two guests. If there are any changes or they decide to join us later, we'll be ready to accommodate them. **Mr. Smith:** I appreciate your cooperation and thoroughness. Let's keep each other updated.

Key Vocabulary and Phrases

headcount 人数统计
facility 设施
local attraction 当地景点
well-being 福气,安康
thoroughness 彻底

题干	参考英文对话
Dialogue 65 Perform as a local guide. It is the meal time. When ten dishes with a soup as stipulated in the contract are served, five tourists tell you that they are Buddhist and ask you to arrange vegetarian meals for them. They say they mentioned this when they signed up for the tour. Make a dialogue with them. Your dialogue will include the following points: （1）Tell the tourists that you will confirm it with the travel agency. （2）Apologize for the mistake. （3）Offer solutions.	**Local Guide:** I'm so sorry for the oversight. I'll need to confirm with the travel agency about your dietary requirements as soon as possible. Please give me a moment. **Tourists:** We did specify that we are Buddhist and require vegetarian meals when we signed up for the tour." **Local Guide:** I apologize for the confusion and any inconvenience this may have caused. It seems there has been a miscommunication. Let me speak with the restaurant staff to see if we can arrange vegetarian meals for you right away. **Tourists:** Thank you. We appreciate your help in resolving this issue. **Local Guide:** Of course. In the meantime, I'll also contact our agency to ensure this detail is properly noted for the remainder of your stay. We want to make sure your dietary needs are met with every meal. I'll return shortly with an update on the vegetarian options available. Thank you for your understanding and patience. **Tourists:** We understand these things can happen. We're grateful for your prompt attention to this matter. **Local Guide:** Thank you for your kind words. I'll make sure to provide you with the best possible solution.

Key Vocabulary and Phrases

miscommunication 误解

resolve 解决

note 注意,记录

remainder 剩余部分

prompt 迅速的

题干	参考英文对话
Dialogue 66 As a local tour guide, you are on the way to Confucius Temple. The guests are very interested in it. Make a dialogue with him. Your dialogue will include the following points: (1) Introduce the importance of Confucius in Chinese history. (2) Give a brief introduction to Confucius Temple. (3) Answer some relevant questions.	**Local Guide**: As we make our way to the Confucius Temple, I'd like to share a bit about its significance. Confucius, who lived from 551 to 479 BC, is a pivotal figure in Chinese history. His philosophy, which centers around morality, ethics, and social harmony, has deeply influenced Chinese culture and is still relevant today. **Guests**: That's fascinating. How old is the Confucius Temple? **Local Guide**: The temple was originally built in 478 BC, just after Confucius's death, to commemorate him. It has been restored and expanded over the centuries, and now it's one of the largest and best-preserved Confucian temples in China. **Guests**: What can we expect to see there? **Local Guide**: You'll find a serene complex of buildings, including the Qian Ding Gate, the Hall of the Great Achievements, and the Kong Family Mansion. Each part of the temple has a unique story to tell about Confucius's life and teachings. We'll have the chance to explore these areas and learn more about his enduring legacy. **Guests**: It sounds like a place of great cultural importance. We're looking forward to it. **Local Guide**: Absolutely, it is. If you have any more questions or need further insights into the history and culture of the temple, feel free to ask. I'm here to enhance your understanding and appreciation of this remarkable site."

Key Vocabulary and Phrases

pivotal 关键的
philosophy 哲学
morality 道德
ethic 伦理学
social harmony 社会和谐
restored 修复的
serene 安详的
legacy 遗产

题干	参考英文对话
Dialogue 67 A member of an inbound group asks to cancel his journey for an emergency at home. Act as the local guide to make a dialogue with him. Your dialogue will include the following points: (1) Ask for the reasons for cancellation. B.Soothe the tourist. (2) Tell him how to deal with relevant fees. (3) Offer help for his leaving.	Local Guide: I'm here to assist you with any concerns you might have. I understand you've mentioned wanting to cancel your journey. Could you please share with me the reasons for this decision? Tourist: Yes, I'm afraid I have an emergency back home that requires my immediate attention. Local Guide: I'm truly sorry to hear that. Please know that we're here to support you during this challenging time. In terms of the cancellation, I'll need to inform our travel agency so they can guide you on the necessary steps and any relevant fees according to our policy. Tourist: Thank you. I appreciate your understanding and assistance. How should I go about this? Local Guide: Firstly, we'll need to formalize the cancellation process. I'll assist you with the paperwork and ensure that our agency is aware of the situation. As for your departure, we can arrange for a taxi to take you to the airport or help you with any necessary travel arrangements. Tourist: That would be very helpful. I'm a bit overwhelmed by the sudden change of plans. Local Guide: I completely understand, and we're here to make this process as smooth as possible for you. If you have any further questions or need additional support, please don't hesitate to reach out. Tourist: Thank you once again for your help. I'll start gathering my belongings and prepare to leave. Local Guide: You're welcome. We wish you the best and hope that everything at home is resolved swiftly.

Key Vocabulary and Phrases

departure 离开
paperwork 文档工作
overwhelmed 不知所措的
swiftly 迅速地

题干	参考英文对话
Dialogue 68 Perform as a local guide. You are leading your tour group to their rooms. But one of the tour group members is not satisfied with his room because the window cannot be opened. Your dialogue will include the following points: (1) Apologize for the inconvenience. (2) Ask the guest for the reasons of dissatisfaction. (3) Promise to talk with the hotel manager and change the room if possible.	**Local Guide:** Everyone, please follow me as I show you to your rooms. If you have any issues or special requests, feel free to let me know. **Tourist:** Excuse me, I've just checked my room, and there seems to be a problem. The window is not opening, and I was hoping for some fresh air. **Local Guide:** I apologize for the inconvenience. Can you please show me the issue? I'll assess the situation and see what can be done. **Tourist:** It's stuck. I've tried several times, but it won't budge. **Local Guide:** I see. I'm sorry for this dissatisfaction. Let me take some notes, and I promise to discuss this with the hotel manager immediately. We'll do our best to find you another room where the window can be opened, if that's possible. **Tourist:** Thank you for your understanding. I appreciate your prompt attention to this matter. **Local Guide:** You're welcome. We strive to ensure your stay is as comfortable as possible. I'll get back to you shortly with an update on the room change. **Tourist:** That's very kind of you. I look forward to hearing from you.

Key Vocabulary and Phrases

dissatisfaction 不满
assess 评估
stuck 卡住的

题干	参考英文对话
Dialogue 69 Perform as a tour leader. You turn to front desk and ask whether the WIFI service is available in the hotel. Your dialogue with the front desk staff will include the following points: (1) Make sure if the WIFI service is offered free to hotel guests around the clock. (2) Reconfirm the Internet access is available in the lobby and the rooms of the guests as well. (3) Ask how to use the device to surf the internet.	**Tour Leader**: Good morning, I'm the tour leader for the group that just checked in. I'd like to confirm if the hotel offers complimentary Wi-Fi service to its guests, and if it's available 24 hours a day. **Front Desk Staff**: Good morning! Yes, we do provide free Wi-Fi to all our guests, and it's accessible around the clock. **Tour Leader**: That's great to hear. Could you also confirm if the Internet access is available in both the lobby and the guest rooms? **Front Desk Staff**: Absolutely, our Wi-Fi coverage extends to all guest rooms as well as the lobby area for your convenience. **Tour Leader**: Excellent. How do our guests go about using the Wi-Fi to surf the internet? Is there a login process or any special instructions? **Front Desk Staff**: It's quite straightforward. Upon connecting to our Wi-Fi network, they'll be directed to a login page where they can enter a unique code sent to their registered mobile device. **Tour Leader**: Thank you for the information. I'll pass this on to the group. If there are any issues, we'll reach out to you. **Front Desk Staff**: Please do. We're here to ensure your group has a seamless online experience. If you need any further assistance, just let us know.

Key Vocabulary and Phrases

complimentary 免费的
around the clock 全天候
lobby 大厅
coverage 覆盖范围
straightforward 简单的
login 登录
seamless 无缝的,平滑的

题干	参考英文对话
Dialogue 70 Perform as a local guide. You are on the way to the Giant Panda National Park. The tourists want to know more about it. Make a dialogue with them. Your dialogue will include the following points: (1) Introduce the significance of the Giant Panda National Park. (2) Introduce the main scenic spots in the Giant Panda National Park. (3) Give precautions. (4) Answer relevant questions.	**Local Guide**: Ladies and gentlemen, as we journey to the Giant Panda National Park, let me share its significance. This park is a sanctuary for the giant panda, an endangered species and a national treasure of China. It's also a biodiversity hotspot, home to a variety of flora and fauna. **Tourists**: How large is the park and what can we expect to see there? **Local Guide**: The park spans a vast area and includes several scenic spots. The main attractions are the panda enclosures, where you can observe these cute creatures in a natural setting. There are also lush bamboo forests, which are the primary diet of the pandas, and serene mountain trails for hiking. Do remember to stay on the designated paths to minimize your impact on the environment. Also, keep a safe distance from the wildlife to avoid disturbing them or putting yourself at risk. **Tourists**: Are there any specific rules we should be aware of? **Local Guide**: Yes, photography is allowed, but please refrain from using flash, especially around the pandas. Also, do not litter; help us keep the park clean and pristine. If you have any questions or need assistance, feel free to ask. **Tourists**: Thank you for the tips. We're excited about the visit and will keep these precautions in mind. **Local Guide**: You're welcome. I'm here to ensure you have a safe and enjoyable experience. Let's proceed with our adventure to the Giant Panda National Park.

Key Vocabulary and Phrases

sanctuary 避难所
endangered 濒危的
biodiversity 生物多样性
enclosure 围栏
refrain 避免
pristine 原始的,未受破坏的

题干	参考英文对话
Dialogue 71 Perform as a local guide. As scheduled, the group will visit the Mount Huangshan this morning. But it rains heavily and it's very dangerous for the guests. You want to cancel the arrangement and go to consult with the tour leader. Your dialogue will include the following points: (1) Analyze the danger of going on the tour in such heavy rain. (2) Apologize. (3) Give explanations. (4) Offer solutions.	**Local Guide:** Good morning, everyone. I have to discuss a matter of concern with you. Given the current heavy rainfall, I've assessed the situation and concluded that proceeding with our trip to Mount Huangshan could pose significant safety risks. The trails can be slippery, and there's a heightened risk of landslides. **Tour Leader:** You're right to prioritize safety. What do you propose we do instead? **Local Guide:** I apologize for this unforeseen change in our plans. The weather is beyond our control, and our primary concern is the well-being of our guests. I suggest we remain in the hotel for the time being and perhaps engage in some indoor activities. We could also reschedule the visit to Mount Huangshan for tomorrow, weather permitting. **Tour Leader:** That sounds like a reasonable approach. Let's inform the group of the new arrangements and ensure everyone is comfortable with the changes. **Local Guide:** Absolutely. I'll also coordinate with the hotel to arrange for alternative activities. If anyone has any questions or concerns, I'll be more than happy to address them. **Tour Leader:** Thank you for your diligence. Let's work together to make sure the group's experience remains positive despite the weather.

Key Vocabulary and Phrases

assess 评估
safety risk 安全风险
slippery 滑的
landslide 山体滑坡
well-being 福气,安康
unforeseen 未预见的
diligence 勤奋

题干	参考英文对话
Dialogue 72 Several outbound tourists request that they stay behind to prolong their tour while the group has finished its scheduled itinerary and is going to leave China. Perform as the tour guide to make a dialogue with the tourists. Your dialogue will include the following points: (1) Make sure that the tourists' visas are valid after the intended tour. (2) Help them with their flight and hotel. (3) Ask the tourists to pay for the extra expenses by themselves.	**Tour Guide**: Ladies and gentlemen, I understand that some of you are interested in extending your stay in China. Before we proceed, we need to ensure that your visas are valid for the additional days you plan to stay. **Tourists**: Yes, we'd like to explore more of China. Could you help us with that? **Tour Guide**: Of course, I'd be happy to assist. However, please be aware that you will be responsible for any extra expenses incurred, such as accommodations and flights for the extended period. **Tourists**: That's understandable. Could you recommend a reliable travel agency to help us with the arrangements? **Tour Guide**: Certainly. I can connect you with a reputable agency that can help you with booking flights and hotels for your extended stay. They will also be able to provide you with any necessary travel advice and ensure your visas are properly extended. **Tourists**: Thank you for your help. We appreciate the guidance. **Tour Guide**: You're welcome. It's been a pleasure hosting you, and I hope you continue to have a wonderful time in China. If you have any more questions or need further assistance, don't hesitate to ask. **Tourists**: We will. Thanks again for making our trip so enjoyable.

Key Vocabulary and Phrases

valid 有效的

reputable 有名的, 声誉好的

guidance 指导

题干	参考英文对话
Dialogue73 Perform as a local guide. A coach suddenly stops on the way to the scenic spot, and the driver tells you that there is a mechanic error. After getting to know what happened, you have a conversation with Mr. Smith, the tour leader. Your dialogue will include the following points: (1) Apologize to him for the inconvenience. (2) Tell him that it's a minor problem and can be fixed in about half an hour. (3) Organize some games or activities when the group are waiting.	**Local Guide:** Good afternoon, Mr. Smith. I regret to inform you that we've encountered a slight setback. Our coach has experienced a mechanical issue, but the driver assures us it's a minor problem. **Mr. Smith:** I see. How long do you expect it will take to resolve?" **Local Guide:** The driver estimates that it can be fixed in approximately half an hour. In the meantime, I propose we organize some games or activities to keep our group entertained while we wait. **Mr. Smith:** That sounds like a good plan. What kind of activities do you have in mind? **Local Guide:** We could start with a trivia quiz related to the places we've visited. It's not only fun but also educational. Additionally, we have some portable musical instruments, and we could have a mini sing-along. I believe it would help to pass the time enjoyably. **Mr. Smith:** I think the guests will appreciate the effort to keep their spirits up. Let's go ahead and set up the activities. **Local Guide:** Thank you for your understanding and cooperation. I'll start organizing the games right away and will keep everyone informed about the coach's status. **Mr. Smith:** Please do. I'll assist you in any way I can to ensure our guests remain comfortable during this delay.

Key Vocabulary and Phrases

mechanical issue 机械故障
fixed 修复的
trivia quiz 趣味问答
portable 便携的
sing-along 合唱

题干	参考英文对话
Dialogue 74 Perform as a local guide. After check in at Holiday Inn, one of the tourists asks you how to use the Safe. Your dialogue will include the following points: (1) Introduce the open procedure. (2) Show how to change the password. (3) Answer some questions asked by the tourist.	**Local Guide**: Good evening and welcome to Holiday Inn. If you're looking to use the in-room safe, it's quite straightforward. First, you'll need to open the safe using the default password provided in the hotel's welcome booklet. **Tourist**: I see. How do I change the password to something personal? **Local Guide**: After the safe is open, press the small button inside, usually labeled "Set" or "Prog". Then enter your desired password, which is typically a combination of numbers. Once you've done that, press the button again to confirm and set the new password. **Tourist**: What if I forget my password? Is there a way to reset it? **Local Guide**: If you forget your password, you'll need to contact the hotel's front desk for assistance. They have a master code that can open the safe, but for security reasons, they'll need to verify your identity first. **Tourist**: That makes sense. What about the battery? How do I know when it needs to be replaced? **Local Guide**: The safe is usually powered by a long-lasting battery. If you notice that the safe is taking longer than usual to respond or the display is dim, it might be a sign that the battery needs replacing. However, this is quite rare, and you can always ask the hotel staff to check if you're unsure. **Tourist**: Thank you for the information. I feel more confident using the safe now. **Local Guide**: You're welcome. If you have any more questions or need further assistance, don't hesitate to reach out. We're here to ensure your stay is both comfortable and secure.

Key Vocabulary and Phrases

default password 默认密码
welcome booklet 欢迎手册
combination 组合
identity 身份
dim 暗淡的

题干	参考英文对话
Dialogue 75 A couple of senior tourists in an inbound tour group demand that their breakfast be served in their hotel room. Act as the tour guide to make a dialogue including the following points: (1) Ask the hotel whether they offer the room service. (2) After making sure the possibility, tell them that they should pay for the room service. (3) Answer questions if there are any.	**Local Guide:** Good morning, I understand you're interested in having breakfast served in your hotel room. Let me first check with the hotel to confirm if they provide room service for meals. **Senior Tourists:** Thank you. We're not very mobile, and it would be a great convenience for us. **Local Guide:** I've confirmed that room service is available at the hotel. However, I must inform you that there will be an additional charge for this service. The hotel has a menu with various breakfast options, and the cost will depend on what you choose to order. **Senior Tourists:** That's understandable. Are there any special instructions we need to know about when ordering? **Local Guide:** Yes, you can place your order by phone or through the hotel's app. Please specify any dietary restrictions or preferences when you order, and the staff will accommodate your needs as best as they can. **Senior Tourists:** Thank you for the information. We appreciate your assistance. **Local Guide:** You're welcome. If you have any more questions or need further assistance, please don't hesitate to contact me. I'm here to ensure your stay is as comfortable as possible.

Key Vocabulary and Phrases

additional charge 额外费用
specify 指定

题干	参考英文对话
Dialogue 76 Perform as a local guide. You are leading your tour group on the way to the Splendid China in Shenzhen. Your dialogue will include the following points: （1）Introduce Guangdong-Hong Kong-Macao Greater Bay Area. （2）Introduce the scenery on the way. （3）Give a brief introduction of the Splendid China. （4）Answer relevant questions.	**Local Guide:** Ladies and gentlemen, as we travel towards the Splendid China in Shenzhen, let me take this opportunity to introduce you to the Guangdong-Hong Kong-Macao Greater Bay Area. This region is a dynamic economic hub, encompassing major cities like Shenzhen, Guangzhou, Hong Kong, and Macao, and is known for its innovation and vibrant culture. **Tourists:** What can we expect to see along the way? **Local Guide:** On our journey, you'll be treated to scenic views of the city's modern skyline, lush green parks, and the bustling activity that characterizes this area. Keep an eye out for the iconic Shenzhen Bay Bridge, which is a marvel of engineering. Our destination, the Splendid China, is a renowned theme park that offers a miniature presentation of China's most famous cultural sites. You'll have the chance to see scaled-down versions of the Great Wall, the Terracotta Army, and the Potala Palace, among others, all in one place. **Tourists:** How large is the park and how long do we need to see everything? Splendid China is quite expansive, covering a significant area. To truly appreciate all the exhibits, I'd recommend allowing at least half a day. There are also various performances throughout the day that depict different ethnic customs and historical events. **Tourists:** That sounds fascinating. Are there any special exhibits we shouldn't miss? **Local Guide:** Absolutely. In addition to the architectural wonders, there are special exhibits like the "Folk Culture Village", which showcases the diversity of China's ethnic groups. And don't miss the live performances of traditional music and dance. They're a wonderful way to immerse yourself in Chinese culture.

Key Vocabulary and Phrases

Guangdong-Hong Kong-Macao Greater Bay Area 粤港澳大湾区
dynamic 充满活力的
hub 中心
miniature 缩小的
immerse 沉浸

题干	参考英文对话
Dialogue 77 Perform as a local guide. The tour group is on the way to the Yucun Village in Anji County Zhejiang Province. Make a dialogue with them. Your dialogue will include the following points: （1）Introduce the agritourism in China. （2）Introduce the development of Yucun Village. （3）Introduce the ecotourism in China. （4）Answer relevant questions.	**Local Guide**: Good morning, everyone! As we head towards the Yucun Village in Anji County, I'd like to tell you about the growing trend of agritourism in China. Agritourism involves traveling to rural areas to enjoy local farm produce and the natural scenery, which is becoming increasingly popular among urban dwellers seeking a closer connection with nature. **Tourists**: That sounds interesting. How has Yucun Village developed in this regard? **Local Guide**: Yucun Village is a prime example of successful agritourism development. Once a remote and impoverished area, it has transformed itself into a model eco-village. They've focused on sustainable practices, promoting local tea plantations, and offering visitors a chance to engage in farming activities and enjoy the tranquil rural life. **Tourists**: What about ecotourism? Is it related to agritourism? **Local Guide**: Absolutely. Ecotourism is the responsible travel to natural areas that conserves the environment and improves the well-being of local people. In China, this often involves visiting places like Yucun Village, where you can learn about the local ecology, contribute to conservation efforts, and experience the traditional culture. **Tourists**: Are there any specific activities we can participate in at Yucun Village? **Local Guide**: Certainly! You can take part in tea-picking sessions, try your hand at bamboo craft making, and even join a cooking class to learn how to prepare local dishes. There are also hiking trails where you can explore the beautiful surroundings. **Tourists**: It all sounds very engaging. We're looking forward to it. **Local Guide**: I'm glad to hear that. If you have any more questions or need more information about the activities, feel free to ask. We want to make sure your visit to Yucun Village is both enjoyable and informative.

Key Vocabulary and Phrases

agritourism 农业旅游
ecotourism 生态旅游
urban dweller 城市居民
sustainable practice 可持续的做法
tea plantation 茶园
tranquil 安静的
ecology 生态学
conservation effort 保护工作

题干	参考英文对话
Dialogue 78 Perform as a local guide. The tour group is on the way to a massage spa in Sanya. Make a dialogue with them. Your dialogue will include the following points: (1) Introduce health tourism in China. (2) Introduce the traditional Chinese medicine therapy. (3) Answer relevant questions.	**Local Guide:** Good afternoon, everyone! As we make our way to the massage spa here in Sanya, I'd like to take a moment to introduce you to the concept of health tourism, which is a growing trend in China. Health tourism involves traveling with the primary purpose of promoting one's well-being through various health and wellness services. **Tourists:** That sounds like a great idea. How does traditional Chinese medicine fit into this? **Local Guide:** Traditional Chinese medicine (TCM) plays a significant role in health tourism. It incorporates a variety of therapies, including acupuncture, herbal medicine, massage, and dietary therapy. The massage spa we're visiting offers several TCM-based treatments that can help with relaxation and rejuvenation. **Tourists:** Are there any specific benefits we can expect from these treatments? **Local Guide:** Absolutely. Many people find that TCM therapies can help alleviate stress, improve sleep, and boost overall health. The specific benefits can vary depending on the treatment and the individual's health condition. **Tourists:** What if we have dietary restrictions? Are the treatments customizable? **Local Guide:** Yes, TCM treatments are often personalized to suit each person's needs. When you arrive at the spa, you'll have the opportunity to discuss any dietary restrictions or health concerns with the practitioners. They will tailor the treatment to your specific requirements. **Tourists:** That's very considerate. We're looking forward to experiencing TCM for ourselves. **Local Guide:** I'm glad to hear that. If you have any more questions or need further information, please feel free to ask. We aim to make your spa experience as enjoyable and beneficial as possible.

Key Vocabulary and Phrases

traditional Chinese medicine 传统中医
health tourism 健康旅游
acupuncture 针灸
rejuvenation 恢复活力
practitioner 实践者,从业者

题干	参考英文对话
Dialogue 79 Perform as a local guide. An old couple in your tour group requests to stay out of the mountain-climbing program. Your dialogue will include the following points: (1) Get to know the reason and show your understanding. (2) If they can take care of themselves, give some precautions and grant their request. (3) Make clear the meeting place, time, the number of the tour bus, etc.	**Local Guide**: Mr. and Mrs. Smith, I noticed that you've expressed an interest in not participating in the mountain climbing program. May I ask for the reason? **Old Couple**: Well, we're concerned about the physical demands of the climb. We'd like to do something less strenuous. **Local Guide**: I completely understand your concerns. It's important that our activities are enjoyable and safe for everyone. If you feel up to it and wish to explore the area at your own pace, that's perfectly fine. Just be sure to take care and stay within the safe zones. **Old Couple**: Thank you for your understanding. We appreciate that. What are the important details we should remember for later? **Local Guide**: Certainly. The key details are as follows: The meeting place will be at the entrance of the park, and we'll reconvene at 15:00 sharp. Please make sure to be back at the tour bus, which is bus number 47, by 15:15 at the latest. We wouldn't want to leave without you. **Old Couple**: That's very clear. We'll make sure to be on time. Thank you. **Local Guide**: You're welcome. If you need any assistance or have any questions throughout the day, don't hesitate to reach out to me or any of the tour staff. Your comfort and safety are our top priorities.

Key Vocabulary and Phrases

strenuous 费力的

reconvene 重新集合

sharp 准时

题干	参考英文对话
Dialogue 80 While having dinner, one tourist is interested in the naming of the dish "fotiaoqiang" and asks you for the related cultural information. Your dialogue will include the following points: (1) Introduce the raw material, the cooking methods of the dish. (2) Describe the background of this dish. (3) Answer questions if there are any.	**Local Guide**: Good evening, everyone. I see there's curiosity about the dish "fotiaoqiang", which is one of the most famous dishes in Fujian cuisine. It's a complex dish made from a variety of high-quality ingredients, such as shark fin, abalone, sea cucumber, and fish maw, all simmered together in a rich broth. **Tourist**: That sounds very luxurious. What's the story behind the name? **Local Guide**: The name "fotiaoqiang" translates to "Buddha jumps over the wall". The story goes that the dish was so fragrant and delicious that even a Buddha, typically associated with asceticism, would be tempted to jump over a wall to taste it. It's a metaphor that speaks to the incredible aroma and taste of the dish. **Tourist**: How is it prepared? It must take a long time to make something so rich. **Local Guide**: Indeed, it does. The preparation requires a lot of time and skill. The ingredients are first soaked, then slowly cooked over low heat for many hours to allow the flavors to meld together. The cooking method is all about patience and the art of slow cooking. **Tourist**: It's fascinating to see how culture and cuisine are intertwined. Thank you for sharing this with us. **Local Guide**: You're welcome. I'm glad you find it interesting. If you have any more questions about the dish or any other cultural aspects of the cuisine, feel free to ask. Enjoy your meal!

Key Vocabulary and Phrases

ingredient 原料
simmer 煨煮
broth 肉汤
fragrant 芳香的
asceticism 禁欲主义
metaphor 隐喻
meld 融合